My Long Journey by Bus, Boat & Train.
A Backpackers Adventure in
India and Sri Lanka

Peter Morffew

**My Long Journey by Bus, Boat & Train.
A Backpackers Adventure in
India and Sri Lanka**

This book is also available in e book format
for the Kindle, Kobo, Nook and tablet.

Table of Contents

About Peter Morffew

Peter Morffew was born in Dulwich, London.
After leaving school he joined the British Army and
served abroad in Gibraltar and Belize; he also visited
Cyprus, Kenya, El Salvador, Denmark and Morocco.
After leaving the Army Peter had itchy feet and the urge
to travel was too hard to resist and decided to visit the
Seychelles. The intention was to stay for the winter but
had to return to the UK after a month. Once back Peter
felt compelled to travel abroad again, after three months
he flew out to India.
Staying for three months he travelled the length of this
marvellous exhilarating country, as well as crossing over
to Sri Lanka by ferry and experiencing the calm Buddhist
culture.
Since Peter's adventure in India and Sri Lanka he has
visited New Zealand twice, Australia and Malaya.

Preface

In January 1980 I decided to spend the rest of the winter somewhere warm. Choosing India I left the cold and wet British winter behind. My rucksack packed with everything I needed for the next few months, included my tent.

I had no planned itinerary, just advice from some Australians I worked with who had travelled around India and briefly loaned me their well-thumbed Lonely Planet guide.

In India and Sri Lanka I met many people who through their stories, experiences and advice helped me along my journey. Occasionally choosing somewhere from my map of India or Indian tourist guide maps made the trip that much more interesting, visiting places that were definitely off the beaten tourist trail.

This was a time when there was no internet, let alone Google or blogs to read about a town or city to find the best place to visit or stay; I went on the advice from fellow backpackers, Indians and Sinhalese; then took my chance.

This book is about my own personal adventure and experiences as I travelled to the far south of India, across to Sri Lanka via the ferry. Catching the ferry back to India to travel north, visiting many fantastic and exciting cities, towns and villages on my shoe string budget.

I experienced the different cultures dating back thousands

of years, and met many interesting people along the way. I hope you enjoy taking this adventure as much as I did visiting the many fantastic places the length of India and through Sri Lanka

My Long Journey by Bus, Boat & Train.

A Backpackers Adventure in India and Sri Lanka

Peter G. Morffew

Part One
A Culture Shock

Finding my way; with some help

The pilot announced that the plane was approaching Bombay airport and would be landing soon, "please fasten your seat belts". The flight had been overnight and restful but I was eager to get off the plane and stretch my legs. Looking out of the window in anticipation of what might be waiting, to my surprise a few hundred feet directly below were several hundred small flat roofed huts no bigger than a large garden shed, each separated by narrow alley ways.

In the allies children played and waved as women did their daily chores, directly under the airports flight path. Unable to believe how many huts there were so close to the end of the run way, a sense of trepidation came over me, unsure what was waiting for me in Bombay when I got off the plane.

Once landed the plane taxied towards a single story building then halted. Leaving the air conditioned interior of the plane I met a wall of tropical heat, a dramatic change from the cold wind and rain of Britain. I was directed along with the other passengers to a bus close by.

When full it travelled across the tarmac to the single storey building where we were ushered through a wide sliding door in to the stifling hot terminal.

Several very officious looking men in beige uniforms were strategically positioned. Joining a slow moving queue I waited to be checked in at the immigration desk. When it came to my turn the immigration officer looked at my passport photograph of me in a round neck jumper with a dark suntan, looked at me, looked at my passport again, paused briefly before theatrically stamping the visa page, handed my passport back and beckoned the next passenger.

As I turned to walk away with a sense of relief a man sitting on a high backless chair thrust out his hand gesturing for my passport. This was officialdom taken to extremes but felt obliged to comply with the non-verbal request and handed my passport over. The beige dressed official looked me up and down, looked at my passport and without any change of expression waved me on dismissively to the declaration channel.

The declaration desks were just a few yards away and looked very similar to the check out at a supermarket. Only one aisle was open where an Indian woman was being interrogated about a huge bottle of whisky she had declared. After a minute or so waiting I was beckoned through by a customs officer, surprisingly without any questions or checking of my luggage.

Making my way through the crowd I found myself in the terminal foyer with a marbled floor and huge revolving wooden doors Stepping outside I was instantly transfixed

3

by a busy roundabout with a carousel of taxis, rickshaws, buses and private cars either picking up or dropping people off. I just gawked in amazement as I tried to make head or tail of what to do next.

Out of the blue I heard a man's voice above the din of traffic,

"Hello have you just arrived?"

I looked in the direction of the voice and saw a slim, well dressed middle aged Indian gentleman who spoke with a public school English accent and a tall slim middle aged woman.

"Yes, I arrived this morning; it looks busy and chaotic", stating the obvious.

The man agreed and said "I am Doctor Singh and this is my wife Michelle. We are from London to visit my brother. He will be picking us up soon, would you like a lift? I am sure he will have room in his car".

Excitedly I replied "yes please".

Soon a silver Mercedes pulled up and Doctor Singh announced his brother had arrived. After talking to each other Doctor Singh's brother shook his head in a way that looked as if he did not agree or disagree.

Doctor Singh called out and surprisingly said "yes you can have a lift".

Not believing my luck put my rucksack into the boot and we drove away from the airport leaving the pandemonium behind.

"We will drop you off at a bus stop where you must catch the number 84 bus to the Commissariat, then make your way to the Waterfront".

4

It all sounded straight forward, what could go wrong? Getting out of the car at a bus stop and saying good bye I waited for a number 84 bus. Buses arrived every few minutes but the numbers on the front of them were in Hindi, smaller English numbers were towards the rear which I caught a quick glance of as they drove off before I had picked up my rucksack. It was going to be a challenge identifying a number 84 bus, and then some how get on before it drove off. Deciding I would have to be ready and as the bus pulled up, quickly check the number on the side then leap onto the bus platform at the rear and hang on to the handle bar for dear life.

By now I had attracted an audience, several people had gathered around me which made me apprehensive. A man spoke with the crowd and asked my name, then showed me a belt he was wearing which had a badge on the buckle," it is a police officer's belt" he proudly announced. Just at this moment Doctor Singh and his brother pulled up and instructed me to jump in to their car, much to my relief. Saying good bye to my audience I got in to the safety of the Mercedes.

"We will drop you off at a safer place not far from here, you must get on the bus quickly".

Easier said than done when you don't know any Hindi. We pulled up at a bus stop, said our good byes and again thanked Doctor Singh and his brother for the lift. I did not have to wait too long and managed to get on to a bus which looked like the right one. I asked conductor for the Commissariat and was given a ticket with out any comment except "two rupee!" Feeling this was a good sign I was on the right bus relaxed; as much as I dared. The bus made its way along the busy roads with my face almost pressed up against the window marvelling at the fleeting urban scenery. The bus occasional stopped briefly before taking off with an abrupt jerk.

After about half an hour the conductor shouted "Commissariat". Quickly picking up my rucksack I jumped off the platform just as the bus came to a sudden halt. As my feet touched the pavement the bus drove off . Looking around I saw several buildings, a very tall one had an archetypal Indian domed roof, another directly beside me disgorged streams of people on to the street through large door ways.

Starting to make my way along the crowded pavement and trying to remember the directions I was given when a boy asked "do you need somewhere to stay?"

I was taken aback by his forwardness, warily suspicious said "yes",

"I will take you to a good hotel follow me".

Thinking I had nothing to lose followed and told the boy I wanted to get to the Waterfront.

"yes! That is where I take you".

Whilst watching where the boy was going I also looked around at the amazing buildings as we weaved our way through the crowds. The pedestrian traffic on the pavement was compact and almost claustrophobic. The phrase jammed in like sardines was very apt and made the London rush hour look sedate in comparison. Crossing the road looked perilous, car drivers didn't seem to care or wait for pedestrians; even a red traffic light was no guarantee for your safety.

We arrived at a large round about, it looked absolutely manic as the raucous traffic whirled around it with wanton abandon. Some people were sitting by some railings holding out their hands with short stumpy fingers as if to beg; one person also had a disfigured nose, I naively asked the boy what was wrong with them. "They were bad in a previous life" he replied in a matter of fact way.

Crossing over each junction seemed to be a leap of blind faith and something no sensible person should attempt. Implicitly trusting my young guide I followed him across each junction and somehow survived the ordeal. Once across the roundabout I followed him between two tall buildings along a short stretch of road which led in to a large plaza where several yellow and black taxi cabs were parked and a tall structure with an extremely high arch stood; the people walking under it were tiny in comparison and could not help but stare in wonder.

My guide called and beckoned me to follow him as we walked past a tall white building about twenty storeys high, cars pulled up and men in uniforms opened the car doors for the passengers; this looked like a good place to stay even though it did appear to be very sumptuous.

I followed along an esplanade facing out to a bay, at the end were several five storey buildings. We entered one of them and instantly felt the cool air. We climbed up four flights of stairs to be confronted with a small office. My guide and the man in the office exchanged some words in Hindi and then I was instructed to sign in the visitor's

7

book.

"How long you want to stay.

" five nights", this seemed to be long enough to get my bearings before catching a train out of Bombay.

He talked to the gentleman behind the desk in Hindi again, "that is 120 Rupees".

This sounded a lot but after some mental arithmetic calculated it was about six pounds. Having paid the man gave me a key and showed me to a small cubicle that was meant to be a bedroom. At first I was surprised, but glad to be some where that was secure and could leave my rucksack and rest, even if it did look dingy.

The euphemistic bedroom had grubby walls and a bare mattress that had seen far better days a long time ago, possibly from the days of the Raj. There were communal showers and the toilets looked very strange, it consisted of a hole in the floor with a ceramic surround and two indents indicating where to put your feet. Going to the toilet did not look like a comfortable experience.

After booking in, having a cold shower and putting on a change of clothes I went out to explore the local area. I walked along the promenade on the Waterfront to have a closer look at this huge arch. The Waterfront was set on a bay where a number of ships were at anchor and some small white towers protruded out of the water.

Small boats were moored up by the tall arch, people walked along the Waterfront in all types of dress; men in flowing Arabic robes wearing white head scarves with bands holding it in place, Indian men in white shirts and trousers. Indian women in brightly coloured, flowing saris; Indian children in threadbare clothes begged asking for baksheesh or paisa and some westerners wearing a variety of styles.

I walked up to the arch and stood underneath it and was instantly cooled by the shade.

Carved above the arch was an inscription 'The Gate Way to India was erected in 1911 to commemorate the arrival of King George V and Queen Mary in India'. I could not help staring in awe at the magnificent structure. The boats moored by the arch were advertised on a bill board 'Boat trips to Elephanta Island'. This sounded interesting and promised myself a trip out to Elephanta Island where ever it may be.

Next to the gateway to India was a palmist and a man who was inserting some sort of prong in to a man's ear then extracting something. Close by was a street market with vendors selling a variety of goods such as string lampshades, soap stone ornaments, semi-precious stones, tea and post cards. One stall had a map of Bombay, it was detailed but the writing was small, but was better than nothing.

In front of the Gate Way to India was a small fenced off lawn with a statue of a man mounted on a horse. Parked on the road close by was a horse and carriage ready to take tourists around the sites. The large white building I saw earlier towering above the others around it had a sign above the entrance,"Taj Mahal Hotel". The front of the hotel had a constant stream of expensive vehicles dropping off and picking up passengers. It looked luxurious, beyond the limits of my shoe string budget.

9

Next to the Taj Mahal hotel was a long white building with a red roof and numerous windows, also several doors under a long porch. One of the doors had net curtains and looked like a small restaurant. Feeling hungry I decided it would be a good place to eat my first meal in Bombay. Inside the restaurant it was cool, an instant change from the afternoon heat outside. Several people sat at tables sedately eating. The restaurant was decorated in a typical quaint English fashion with white painted walls, white net curtains at the windows, white starched table clothes, stainless steel cutlery, serviettes and metal condiments on the table.

A smartly dressed waiter wearing a white shirt and trousers gave me a menu which was in English and had a selection of meals that you would expect to see on any British Menu. Omelettes, bacon and eggs, a variety of sandwiches, cakes which were on a cake trolley, tea or coffee. Opting for an omelette and a pot of tea I relaxed and waited.

Looking out of the window it struck me of the stark contrast between the restaurant with its calm, cool and peaceful English ambiance and the busy, hot lively Indian life that was going on outside. The restaurant felt like the ideal place where you could escape to if Indian street life became too much.

A large tea pot was brought out with a bone china cup and saucer along with a small china jug of milk. My first cup of tea in India tasted perfect; the omelette followed shortly which was cooked to perfection. I wanted to make the most of this meal and took my time befitting the

10

ambiance of the room, a perfect place to eat each day. I pawed over my map trying to get an idea of the size of Bombay and where prominent land marks were, such as the post office.

After my meal I left the restaurant and crossed the road to the promenade where the horse and open carriage was still waiting for customers. More people had arrived on the Waterfront including a street vendor with a large wicker basket strung over his shoulder full of peanuts with conical paper cups tucked in to the peanuts. A hand written label advertising the price of a cup of peanuts; at 25 paisa how could I refuse and bought one. I decided to browse the market stalls; each vendor did their best to sell me their merchandise but felt reluctant to buy anything on my first day in India except for a few post cards. Whilst I browsed the stalls several children followed me, some asked for paisa as the vendors shouted at them "jow!". From the stalls I walked to the busy roundabout to see if it might have calmed down, it looked even more manic. Pedestrians quickly crossed at the brief gaps between each vehicle which did not stop or slow down, at times just missing the pedestrian.

There were shops on the far side and what looked like a café with people sitting at tables out on the pavement. The people with disfigured hands were still there.

Along the pavement a huge bill board hung above a broad door way. The bill board had a double portrait of a young man and woman on a yellow back ground and large bold writing in Hindi, it looked like a poster for a film. Either side of the building were several small shops. Whilst

11

standing in amazement on the busy pavement several
people bumped in to me and wondered whether I should
try to cross over the roundabout, reluctant to risk life and
limb so soon after arriving. Deciding it was a fool hardy
idea I went back to the Waterfront.
Walking between the high buildings on the road leading
to the Waterfront a smiling boy asked if I wanted any post
cards and held up a selection for me to see.
"No I have some".
"Okay, you want some hashish",
Surprised by his inquisitive enquiry replied " no",
not to be put off said "it is good hashish".
Again saying "no" went to walk away, before I took
another step he asked if I wanted an Opium Den
Not saying anything I briskly walked away to make it
obvious I was definitely not interested.
The sun was getting low in the sky, it felt cooler at the
waters edge. The Waterfront was busier, the air was filled
with the sound of different languages making it feel very
exotic. As the sun started to set it lit up the sky with a
golden tropical glow which silhouetted the ships in
Bombay harbour; the yellow stone of the Gateway to
India reflected the sunlight and looked as if it was covered
in gold leaf.
As night fell the street lights came on, the vendors lit their
lanterns so the customers could see their wares and the
lights on the ships reflected across the bay.
The heat of the day gave way to a cool sea breeze and
more people thronged to the Waterfront.
Whilst looking out at the bay I suddenly heard a clicking

sound above the chatter and the water lapping against the promenade wall. I looked around and to my surprise was a guy sitting on a skate board pushing his self along the pavement. The clicking was the skate board wheels running over the uneven paving slabs. He stopped, looked at me and said "hello my names Bob", to my surprise he sounded American. Having told Bob my name it was then I noticed he didn't have any legs and the skate board was his way of getting around. Bob was slightly built, about 25 and had a dark skin which could have been a dark suntan or he was Indian.

He was wearing black trousers and a cheque shirt. Bob ask me what I was doing and explained I had just arrived today and was enjoying the cool evening breeze.

During our conversation Bob explain that I needed to be careful in Bombay and not get taken in by the professional beggars. "They will try all sorts of tricks to get your money, some parents had broken their sons or daughters arm so that people would feel sorry for them". This sounded extreme and unbelievable but replied I would keep this in mind.

Bob explained he was American and had lost everything. His Dad had sent him some money to get back home but he had spent it all and the American consulate would not help him. "Will you be travelling any where" asked Bob, "yes I plan to travel south but don't have definite plan". "What ever you do don't stand still for too long. Thieves will cut open your rucksack and take stuff out of it and you won't notice it is gone, keep moving what ever you do even if it's just from side to side. And what ever you

13

do don't walk around with your camera over your shoulder, people will think you are wealthy and try to steal it.

I thanked Bob for the advice then mentioned I was going to go back to my guest house.

"Where are you staying?" asked Bob,

"at the end of the promenade",

"I know the guest house, it's not very good, you need to stay at the Salvation Army Hostel in Mereweather road". Asking where that was?

"It's right behind the Taj Mahal Hotel" replied Bob. "You will have to be there early in the morning to be booked in".

Saying thanks again for the advice I walked back along the promenade listening to the sea lapping against the brick wall. Back at the building I climbed the four flights of steps to my guest house in the dark with barely enough light to see the stairs.

Letting myself in to my small room I laid down on the bed and decided to take Bobs advice and book in at the Salvation Army Hostel; then almost immediately fell straight to sleep.

Amazing and exciting Bombay

The next morning I was up early, had a cold shower and went down stairs in to the already hot morning sun. Across the narrow road was a man with a wheeled barrow selling what looked like meat. Unable to curb my curiosity had a closer look. There were various pieces of uncooked meat and what was obviously a brain from some animal, flies flitting about the uncovered meat made it look uninviting. Behind the barrow were some swastikas daubed on the wall which took me by surprise but remembered that this was a good luck sign in India, maybe the good luck was needed when you bought the meat on display. The vender gestured to me to buy some but I declined the opportunity to challenge my digestive system and set off to find Mereweather road and book in to the Salvation Army Hostel.

Following the directions Bob gave me the night before I found the road and saw a small queue outside a whitewashed building which I took to be the Salvation Army Hostel. Joining the queue saw the large red sign above the closed door with the familiar white writing. Some of those queuing were talking about their time in India and their exploits, I listened to the antidotes, some sounded a bit exaggerated and farfetched but who was I to judge that the individual stories were not exaggerated. Eventually the doors opened to reveal a stark white interior, we climbed the flight of stairs and waited at a

15

glass fronted kiosk. Each person was systematically booked in on the register. Producing my passport as proof of identity I booked in for three nights at 18 Rupee's (about £1) per night for a bed in a dormitory with a shower, three meals, afternoon tea and clean sheets. Having been told my dormitory I returned to the dingy guest house to collect my things.

Telling the owner I was booking out was difficult because of my lack of Hindi and the owner did not appear to understanding English, that was until I asked for a refund then the conversation became strained. After a lengthy discussion we came to an amicable agreement and got my money back. Collecting my things quickly I moved in to my new plush accommodation. The interior throughout the hostel was painted white and looked pristine clean, much better than my experience of the previous night with the grubby walls and not so hygienic mattress.

It was getting late and I needed something to eat. I left the calm of the Salvation Army Hostel and walked to the large roundabout. I was met with a sight of bustling, chaotic mayhem with vehicles of all shapes and sizes, wheeled carts loaded high with bales pulled and pushed by men, cars, scooters, bicycles, articulated buses and hundreds of pedestrians. My ears were bombarded by a cacophony of traffic noise and people shouting. A number of men were carrying long trays on their heads with metal pots in them, also some cyclists had similar trays with pots hanging from their bicycles, this looked so strange and could not help wonder what the metal pots were and why so many people were carrying several at a time.

Crossing a road at the roundabout looked precarious without my guide and envisaged I would end up with some sort of injury but throwing caution to the wind I stepped off the kerb and surprisingly made it to the other side, much to my relief. Just along the pavement were the people without their fingers begging and gave them some money. I now realised these poor people were lepers and were doing their best to scrape some money together to feed them selves and in some cases their family. It seemed so harsh that others thought their plight was caused by them being bad in a previous life.

The railing they sat by was part of the Prince of Wales Museum, a place that deserved a visit.

Further on past the metal railings were shops selling a wide variety of merchandise of all descriptions, food, camera's, antiques, hardware, jewellery and some didn't appear to be selling anything, the signs above the shop entrance was the only give away. Some of the shop owners tried to beckon me in by waving their hand but I declined the invitations with a smile and holding up the palm of my hand, I just wanted to see Bombay.

After crossing several more roads I felt more confident that I would make it to the other side. At a wide busy junction was an ornate fountain some twenty feet high in the middle of the road; squinting at my map this was the Floral Fountain. A large number of pedestrians were crossing this busy junction without coming to any grief which amazed me considering how reckless some of the drivers appeared to be.

Managing to cross the road I stood in the shade of a large

building that I discovered was The Commissariat and where the British Consulate had its office. It was about 11am and the pavement was jammed packed shoulder to shoulder with pedestrians. On the corner of the Commissariat was a portly man standing by a large flat topped wooden box with what looked like lottery tickets invited me to buy one. I shook my head and held up my camera and he posed for me.

A short distance just beyond the Commissariat was a cross roads, on one of the junction's corners were park benches under some trees by what looked like a water fountain; behind this was a large expanse of parched grass and further along the road was a tall building with a central domed tower, several smaller domed towers and verandas with white decoration, giving the appearance of icing sugar. It look grandiosely majestic and important. This was where I had been dropped off by the bus the previous day. The parched grass turned out to be a very long playing field, opposite was an identical playing field where a game of cricket was being played. It looked surreal watching a game of cricket with a back drop of Imperial style buildings and palm trees.

Walking past the two playing fields along the bustling pavement it struck me I was the only white person in the sea of Indians but nobody paid any attention to me as I struggled against the human tide going in the opposite direction. Most of the people were coming from the large domed towered building with arch windows and tops of the painted veranda.

A sign above its wide entrance said 'Churchgate Street

Station'. Going inside the cool air washed chilly over me. The foyer of the building was busy with people buying train tickets at a metal grill kiosk; the clattering mechanical noise echoed in the back ground, walking under an arch I found myself in the train station with what looked like thousands of commuters filing off the platforms towards the exit as if they were being marshalled en masse. There were no barriers and any one could walking on to the platforms which seemed strange coming from London where you could not get on a platform without a ticket.

I realised there also wasn't a tannoy announcing the arrival and departure of the trains Whilst looking at weathered iron architecture a girl and boy approached me and held out her hands. The girl had wild bedraggled hair and was wearing a long green cape and the young boy was in shorts, both looked grubby. Thinking about what I was told the night before about professional beggars I could not help feel these two were not professional beggars at all. Giving them five rupees (about 25p) the two put their hands together as if to pray. After getting them to pose for a photograph they vanished in to the crowd of passengers going off to their various destinations in Bombay.

Refreshing as the cool interior of the crowded station was it felt a bit claustrophobic.

Stepping out into the bright hot sun again I crossed a main road and found myself on a wide promenade that curved round a bay in a perfect U shape. My map read this was Back Bay. A low wall followed the promenade and at the head of the bay was a white strip which was over looked by a tree lined hill and high rise flats. Standing high above the tree tops was the silhouette of some sort of tower with smoke rising from it.

Making my way along the promenade I heard the clatter of trains, across the road was a railway line up above the road leading in to the distance. Getting closer to the white strip I realised it was a wide beach of bright white sand. There were a large number of people on the beach and two white Arab horses. At the edge of the beach was a kiosk serving food and close by was a sign, 'Chowpatty Beach'.

Looking up at the tree line I felt it would be a good place for a scenic view across Bombay, at the far end of the wide beach I discovered a steep narrow path leading up under the shade of the overhanging trees.

Eventually making it to the top I walked in to an open air restaurant under a low tree canopy. There was an extensive menu chalked up on a board and after some consideration I ordered a tea and opted for a Chicken Biriyani.

Sitting at a table next to a wooden fence I had a majestic view overlooking Bombay, high above the tallest buildings and the noise and felt disconnected from the Bombay below, it was so much more relaxing and calm. I had a perfect view of the almost perfect wide sweeping U shape of the bay with the tall building on the far side and the almost perfect white sand of Chowpatty Beach directly below.

The plate of Chicken Biryani was brought to the table

with a fork. The rice was a golden yellow along with two poppadum's. Breaking a poppadum in half I used it to scoop up some rice, the Chicken Biriyani had a wonderful ginger flavour to it, something I had not experienced before. Finishing my meal I made my way out from under the shade of the trees on to a perfectly manicured lawn with interspersed rose beds, it looked just like a garden in a large country estate. There was the faint murmuring of conversations in Hindi but other than that it was quiet and peaceful. On the far side of the gardens was a sheer drop of about 300 feet, opposite were two skyscrapers and could see in to the top floor windows.

This quiet corner of Bombay was so tranquil. After a few hours I made my way down the path under the over hanging branches and out in to the afternoon sun and the noise of the street. I walked back around the bay to Churchgate Street Station and joined the packed crowds. The pedestrian traffic felt even more congested, just like the packed trains of the London Underground in the rush hour, except here every body was moving along the wide pavement.

I was not getting anywhere fast and gave up struggling against the crowds and took a turning off the main road to wait for the pedestrian traffic to ease off. In the park a game of cricket was in full swing, an ideal position to photograph the cricketers with the Commissariat as a backdrop. As I was framing a photograph a brass band struck up, turning around I saw several musicians wearing pure white jackets, trousers and peaked hats playing outside a house. Soon, out of the building came a couple

21

wearing brightly coloured clothes, looking as if they dressed for a wedding, the bride was draped in a gold sari and jewellery. With the band playing the couple got in to a waiting car and drove off in to the busy traffic.

Once they were gone the crowd that had gathered outside the house dispersed in various directions.

After admiring the view and watching the cricket match for some time I slowly made my way back towards the Salvation Army Hostel. Just before the busy roundabout I came across a small stall selling cigarettes, heaven, just what I needed. Whilst perusing the various brands a woman stopped and spoke to the stall holder The man picked up a bright green leaf, placed some sort of nut on it then scooped some white paste from a jar and placed a dollop next to the nut then rolled the leaf up tightly and gave it to the woman; she placed this small green package in her mouth and started to chew it, dumbfounded I stared and wondered what it tasted like, also what was the white paste?

Having bought my cigarettes I had to cross the busy junctions of the large busy roundabout. Whilst waiting for a break in the relentless stream of traffic I noticed the building with the large bill board had large bold letters above the doors, "REGAL". The front of the building had a Art Deco design which looked out of place tucked between the other buildings. Having negotiated the roundabout I made my way back to the hostel ready for the evening meal.

The evening meal was warm over cooked Macaroni Cheese. I sat at a table with some other back packers sharing their travel experiences. They talked about some places they had visited in India. Saying I had only been in Bombay a few days the others offered advice of where to visit on my journey around India.

"Avoid Goa, all white people were considered hippies" one backpacker suggested, "to show their disgust at the behaviour of the hippies some shop keepers refused to serve white people. One person was tied to a tree by some locals and left". I was also advised to only use my right hand when eating; the left one is meant to be used for your bottom, this was advice that could have waited until after the meal.

Someone asked if I had travelled overland to India, replying I had flown and suggested that it would be difficult travelling overland after the Russian invasion of Afghanistan and the attacks by the Mujahidin. Someone mentioned that it was possible as long as you don't wear any clothing of a military appearance and you speak English. Someone had heard about some travellers who drove through Afghanistan, they painted their car pink to make it obvious it was not a military vehicle.

After several other travel stories we joined the other backpackers on the wide veranda furnished with two long leather sofas. From here you could look out on to the street below with all of the noise of passing traffic and pedestrians. An American brought out his guitar and played some songs while others talked. Talking to John, an Australian in his 50s who had been in Bombay during the Independence celebrations said "the crowds became violent and some people were shot by the police".

23

Someone commented on his man bag; John joked about this and said he could not do without in India because he knew everything was safe but he could not take it back home to Australia, "I would never live it down".

Announcing he was going to the Taj Mahal Hotel, "I want to see what it is like, does anyone else wanted to come", I declined but several others went with him.

Once they had all gone I decided to take a walk in the cool evening air and explore around the local area, and made my way to the main road. Even though it was relatively late the traffic was still busy and surprisingly shops were still open. One large three storey building was lit up by hundreds of light bulbs draped over the front of it. Some of the light bulbs had blown which were being changed by a young lad who had climbed up the front up the building using the small ledges without any form of support or safety harness, Hanging on he unscrewed the bulbs and changing them whilst they were still lit which he did with great dexterity.

The lad had attracted an audience and I must admit it was compulsive entertainment as the shop owner directed which bulb to change and showed little concern for the safety of his assistant. The young lad eventually changed all of the bulbs that needed replacing and came down to terra firma safely to the exuberant applause from every one.

A short distance along the road I came to a junction where a road lead off down a dark alley between two tall buildings, it looked very dark and sinister but at the far end people were silhouetted by some bright lights. I just

24

had to see what was happening.

Walking down the dark alley I could make out the light was coming from small open fronted shops lit by lanterns that silhouetted the pedestrians and shop keepers. Emerging from the darkness in to the bright white light I saw some of the shops had glass cabinets with silver and gold jewellery set with a wide variety of gem stones, silver ingots and ornaments that glistened in the shimmering light of the lanterns. Walking further along the road I realised all of the shops were jewellers.

Some shop keepers beckoned me in but I declined and just looked in awe. This back road seemed to be devoid of any westerners but I did not feel threatened or out of place.

Suddenly there was a cacophony of musical instruments and shouting. Out of a dark alley came a procession with dancers followed by musicians blowing trumpets, banging cymbals, drums and strumming stringed bows. Men carried lamps held aloft on long poles to illuminate the way. The procession was preceded by several people gyrating as they performed a wide swirling dance.

The noisy and lively procession slowly made its way through the crowds with the din of all of the instruments drowning out any conversation. The procession lasted for some time and then faded away into the darkness and life returned to normal with people selling, bartering and buying. With all of the excitement of the evening I had lost track of the time and thought I should get back to Mereweather road before the hostel door was locked for the night.

When I got back the group that had gone to the Taj Mahal had just returned. They were all excited, John asked me to guess who they had met at the Taj Mahal. Of course I couldn't, "it could have been any body, was it somebody well known?"

"Yes it was" John replied excitedly, "we walked in to the foyer of the Taj Mahal, this guy walked in and we realised it was Muhammad Ali".

I could not contain my surprise, "you must be joking!".

"We also got to shake his hand".

To say I was envious was an understatement and wished I had gone with them, "what did the Taj Mahal look like?

"It is the plushest and grandiose hotel you could imagine with a marble floor" replied John.

John asked where I had been, explaining that I went for a walk and ended up down a side street and found some small jewellery shops. John said that was not a good idea, anything can happen down these back streets.

"It felt safe enough, there was a deafening musical procession that appeared from no where".

The other backpackers were starting to drift off to their dormitories and decided to do the same.

The dormitory I was in had about ten beds and one shower. The guy in the bed next to mine was sitting bolt upright with his eyes closed and totally silent, which struck me as being a bit strange but nobody paid much attention to him and I had no intention of loosing any sleep either and soon fell asleep.

Waking the next morning, everybody else appeared to be asleep except for the guy who was still sitting bolt upright. Deciding he was definitely weird I got up for a shower before the mad rush and went down stairs and sat on the veranda sofa listening to Bombay's morning chorus. A gong sounded to announce breakfast, to my surprise it was sausages, eggs and toast followed by cereal as well as a pot of tea. If needed there was a second round of toast which was too tempting, also a refill of tea.

After breakfast I got my things together and set off in to the bright sun light to explore Bombay, starting at the Waterfront. The sea gently lapped against the boats by the Gate Way to India as they were readied to ferry tourists out to Elephanta Island. Pigeons were cooing as seed was scattered on the pavement for them, which struck me as strange considering the people begging close bye. The market stalls were already set up for the day's business. Amongst the crowd I noticed the guy who had sat up all night and seemed to be walking in my direction, "hi how are you doing?" he asked with a distinct Australian accent,

Cautiously I replied "I'm okay thanks".

"My names Chris" and held out his hand. "I'm going out to Elephanta Island, have you been there yet?", "No not yet".

Chris suggested we could go out there together, half-heartedly I said "yes, why not". It didn't seem to be such a bad idea, even if Chris was a bit weird.

We boarded a boat and once full of passengers it set off out across the bay giving us a panoramic view of the Waterfront, taken up mostly by Taj Mahal Hotel and Gate Way to India. The boat journey took about an hour, it felt relaxing to get away from the hustle and bustle.

We talked about our planned trips in India. Chris was only staying in India for a short while and then flying on to Pakistan.

" my plan is to travel south and see what happens, I will take things as they come".

At Elephanta Island we all disembarked at a jetty and walked under the low trees to some caves. The caves had been hewed deep in to the rock, carved pillars supporting the ceiling. Inside were various carvings of gods, including Shiva. It was remarkable that the ancient caves had been created so long ago with primitive tools.

After looking around the caves we decided to have something to eat at a tea shop. Being the only white people we were very conspicuous and Chris seemed very conscious that we were attracting some attention, especially when he pointed out I was eating with the wrong hand. After the meal we walked around the forest along the busy track passing several families; women dressed in brightly coloured saris and the men wearing bright white starched shirts.

Returning to the jetty after a few hours we boarded the boat back to Bombay. At the Gate Way to India I said bye to Chris and set off to explore Bombay.

I wanted to visit the Prince of Wales Museum. Inside the museum was large and airy with ancient Indian artefacts and sculptures dating back before Christ. There were displays of the British colonial era as well as contemporary Indian art.

With so much to see I lost track of time looking at the

28

displays. Feeling that I should have a cup of tea I left the museum and found a lively and crowded tea shop full of white people not too far away. The only space available was at a table with a guy sat with a small black box in front of him.

"Is the seat taken?"

The guy looked up from his small black box, "no!" after a brief pause added "my name is Rick".

"Good to meet you Rick" We talked about our experiences of Bombay, not that I had much too relate to. Rick mentioned he was backpacking but seemed quiet negative complaining how dirty and busy it was. Rick explained about his phobia of drinking the water in India, "This is my battery operated water purifier" pointing at the small black box. Rick had already started purifying his glass of water which he had poured in through a spout and it slowly trickled in to a receiver via a filter. The purifying process was laboriously slow, much akin to watching paint dry.

I mentioned about no body asking if I wanted a tea, Rick told me I need to shout out Chai and they will bring one over. This sounded rude but decided to try it. Calling out Chai one of the tea shop waiters almost immediately brought a glass of milky tea to the table. With the tea arriving so quickly at the table I could not see why boiled water was not good enough. Rick insisted that there were still impurities in the water and he did not want to take a chance.

As I had nothing better to do while I drank my tea I watched Rick's water purifier laboriously filter the water drip by drip.

"What happens if the battery runs out?"

Rick thought about this and I felt this had not really crossed his mind but then said "I do have some spare batteries". Eventually Rick became excited and announced his water had been purified and he can drink it. I thought that if the temperature was at 120 degrees thirst would take over and the purifier could become redundant. Having finished my tea I said fare well to Rick and his purifier wishing him the best of luck with it. Along the crowded pavement was a Sadhu with a painted face and a large python around his neck who I got to pose for a photo, he looked surreal amongst the pedestrians busily making their way to where ever they might be going and ignoring him as if it was an everyday thing. Not much further I almost literally bumped into an Indian gentleman. He was about 5½ feet tall, middle aged and wearing an old grey suite that had been carefully looked after and a white shirt open at the collar. He asked me if I knew where the Quakers office was; replying I did not, he then explained that he had come to Bombay by train to meet the Quakers who had been recommended by a friend.

He showed me his letter of introduction "I have been trying to find the Quakers for a few days now and not had any luck". He asked if I could lend him a few Rupees. His story sounded genuine but felt slightly suspicious and made the excuse that I did not have any spare cash and had to get to the bank. The Indian gentleman smiled, said okay, wished me luck and walked off in to the crowd.

Making my way to the Floral Fountain I took the road straight ahead and came to an area with modern corporate style buildings with radio masts and microwave dishes on the roof. I found that I was the only westerner around and felt conspicuously out of place as everybody else was wearing a suite except for an elderly man who was sitting on the pavement with an open umbrella shielding him from the sun. The man was repairing a shoe, tacking a new heel on to it whilst three others patiently waited their turn.

I followed the road for some distance passing a variety of old and new buildings, it was not so busy around this part of Bombay and a lot quieter. I got the impression not many westerners walked through these streets but nobody paid any attention to me.

Eventually I came to a shore line edged with old Indian and colonial style buildings that looked as if they had been neglected for some considerable time with their grey weathered walls facing out to sea. Just off the shore, some 300 metres away was a white domed walled building with a tower, leading to it was a cause way lined with lamp posts. A number of people were walking out to it, the women's brightly coloured saris fluttered in the sea breeze. It looked like a procession, unable to curb my curiosity, I had to have a look.

Either side of the causeway were a number of beggars, I noticed one of them was defecating in front of everyone but no one paid any attention him. Seeing all of these beggars made me realise that if you gave money to each one you came across you would very soon end up with no money and I made a conscious decision that I would only offer food, if they refused the food then they cannot be that needy.

The causeway led to an ornately decorated archway which entered in to a court yard. Inside was a small white washed building topped with the large dome, the towers were slender minarets, one on each corner. Walking around the grounds it felt like a place you could calmly rest and reflect, even though it was quite busy. I made my way back along the causeway, turned left and followed the road for a short distance past old weathered buildings and came to some pristine white hoardings that appeared to screen some sort of large enclosure, skirting around the fencing I came to a large arched entrance through which I could see a large expanse of green well-kept grass edged with white railings and stands at one end.

Walking under the arch I stepped on to a horse racing track. It seemed so bizarre having a race track in the middle of the city. Nobody was about but it looked perfectly maintained, if I wanted I could just walk on to the track. This was a stark contrast to the rest of the fields and parks I had seen so far which were more beige than green, no doubt a place for the wealthy. Leaving the race track I followed the road, not sure where it would lead to then came across a mosque with two tall minarets and two domed towers situated in the middle of the road with a river of traffic and pedestrians either side.

It was getting late and I decide to try and make my way back to Mereweather road. Not sure where I was going but somehow made my way back to the Floral Fountain

32

and headed to the Waterfront.

The pedestrian and road traffic was as busy as ever, everyone seemed to be making their way home. Stopping at a road with a zebra crossing I checked the traffic. Cars were waiting at a set of traffic lights about 20 yards away. It looked perfectly safe to cross, boldly stepping out in to the road when suddenly the traffic lights changed.

The waiting vehicles, mostly yellow Ambassador Cabs, instantly accelerated around the bend with out any intention of slowing down for the zebra crossing; I could not run either way to avoid the vehicles they were travelling too fast. My only chance was to stand still, positioning myself side on and hopped there was enough room either side for this risky choice as they hurtled towards me; if a car moved left or right just a fraction the wing mirrors would catch me. Instinctively standing on tip toes and with my arms up in the air to avoid getting caught I stood stock still and waited as the cars raced towards me, still accelerating. What seemed like a miracle the cars passed either side with just centimetres to spare. Once the cars passed I ran over to the pavement and decided there and then that it was time to move on and leave Bombay as soon as possible.

After the evening meal whilst sitting on the veranda I described my close encounter with the Bombay traffic which made everyone laugh, someone mentioned how lucky I had been, "someone must be watching over you". I wanted to get some evening air and walked towards the Floral Fountain to see what it was like at night. Considering the time it seemed quite busy, a number of people were walking towards the park and I followed them and found there was a fun fair with two Ferris wheels, a carousel and several stalls. The lights glowed against the pitch black back drop.

The stalls were traders selling various Indian crafts of various descriptions; some were similar to those sold down by the Waterfront. One stall in particular had some intricate wooden carvings and woollen knit craft. The owners of the stall were from Kashmir, they asked me where I was from, and what I was doing in India. "I am going to try and travel all over India",

they became excited and told me that I must visit Kashmir, "it is the most beautiful place in all of India with mountains, rivers and in Srinagar you can stay in a house boat on Dal Lake". They made Kashmir sound very exotic and told them I will do my best to get to Kashmir.

They bought me a tea and waxed lyrically about the Kashmir Valley as I looked at what was on their stall. Picking up a travelling chess set they told me to open it and smell the wood. "it is made of Rose Wood, Sandal Wood and Ebony". There was a distinct exotic aroma of the Sandal Wood, the small chess pieces were intricately carved and would be an ideal way to while away the hours and bought it. Before saying good bye I shook everyone's hand then made my way back to the Salvation Army Hostel.

The next day I was up early, at breakfast I found out that I needed to catch a train from Victoria Station of all places if I wanted to travel anywhere in India. Quickly finishing breakfast I set out on to the busy street which did not feel so claustrophobic, maybe I was getting accustomed to Bombay, except for the cough I had developed which I put down to the vehicle fumes that made me even more determined to get out of Bombay.

On the way to the station a woman spat on to the pavement bright red saliva which looked like blood. A snake charmer wearing a large turban sat on the pavement played his flute with its bulbous end. He had two baskets with cobras reared up and dancing to his tune and a large python lying across his lap as several people stood close by watching. Taking some photographs it struck me how strange this was with so many people walking past and two potentially poisonous snakes on the pavement, the python seemed to get bored or did not like the snake charmers flute playing and started to slither away.

Arriving at Victoria Station I was astounded at the imposing building with its ornate yellow brick Gothic Style façade, either side of a grand main entrance were two towers and arched windows. The entrance itself was below a large veranda with five high archways and a small tower at either end of the veranda.

Inside it was as busy as out on the street. People were queuing for their train tickets at a kiosk. Passengers sat down with their luggage in the middle of the station concourse, families sat around their trunks stacked like pyramids. Porters dashed backwards and forwards with sack barrows or carried luggage on their heads, including hefty trunks.

I joined a queue which moved very slowly and noticed why; people were barging in at the front. As I patiently

35

waited two women, each with a bundle of thin sticks in their hands started arguing which became more vocal and heated until out of the blue a man dressed in a beige uniform armed with a three foot rattan cane walked up to them, shouted and then hit both of them with his cane, then waved his hand as if to dismiss them. Quietly and without another word they went their separate ways. Eventually arriving at the front of the queue where a man dressed in a beige uniform sat behind a iron grill. Asking for a ticket to Bangalore the ticket man shook his head and said "no, no not here, you need to go to the office for tourists in the main station".

Utterly amazed that I had been queuing all of this time for no reason I begrudgingly went in to the main station, the wide open space looked as if it could house the Albert Hall. With so many offices it looked impossible to find the right one. After enquiring in an office I was directed to the right one. Explaining to the clerk I wanted a train ticket for Bangalore; "no you are in the wrong place". Go outside the station, turned right. About 50 metres along the pavement there is a set of wooden stairs. At the top of the stairs is an office, you can buy an Indrail ticket there". The clerk explained that the Indrail ticket was for tourists and it would entitle me to get a place on a train any time in first class. It also allowed me to use the first class waiting rooms at stations. Thanking the clerk he shook his head and smiled.

I found the office which was quiet and had a fan blowing a welcoming cool breeze. Joining a small queue and was quickly at the front and asked for an Indrail ticket.

"How long for?" the clerk enquired,
after some consideration I asked for a month.
"What class, first or second?"
Deciding on first class I was asked for $95 which took me
by surprise, luckily I had enough American Dollars with
me. I was given a green A6 size ticket with one month
printed on it and the date it expired. On the opposite side
were the terms and conditions which had precise details
of how much luggage could be carried by various people,
including children who were allowed half of the weight of
an adult.

At last I had my train ticket but was mystified when the
clerk told me I had to book my train, then said he could
book it for me which was a relief; I was not in the mood
to join another queue. The clerk booked me on to the
evening train to Bangalore which left at 7:30 pm. "You
must check the notice board on the platform for your
carriage, bogie and booth number". This is important he
said with a smile and a shake of the head. Not sure what
he meant by bogie and booth but wanting to get away I
said thank you and went out in to the hot sun.

Having bought my train ticket next I needed to post some
post cards and found that the post office was almost next
door to Victoria station. The Post Office was a huge
building, inside it was cavernous, the floor was marbled
but even more impressive was the high domed roof that
looked almost identical to St. Pauls Cathedral in London
with a gallery leading around the dome and pigeons flying
around in the high ceiling. The postal counter was a large
circular island in the middle of the floor with a marble

facade. It was busy but I did not mind queuing, it gave me chance to admire the magnificent grandeur of this opulent post office.

At the desk I asked to send my post cards to the UK and was given the stamps. Licking the back to stick them down and found the stamps were not tacky. The postal clerk pointed out that there were pots of glue for sticking the stamps down. This struck me as unusual and amusing, what if the letter stuck to another going somewhere else? I returned to the Salvation Army hostel to pack up my things not wanting to miss the train. I was excited about leaving even though I had come to enjoy Bombay; no day was ever the same. I wanted to make the most of the last few hours in Bombay after having something to eat and went to the Water Front for a last time before catching the train. The excitement of leaving Bombay filled me with trepidation at what might be waiting out there in such a large country, what adventures would I encounter? I had a tea under the Gate Way to India feeling this would be the last time I will see it and wanted to remember the moment.

After drinking the tea I returned for my rucksack and set off for the station. It felt strange having to carry my rucksack through the busy streets knowing that I was leaving to travel out in to the wide expanse of India like an intrepid explorer. The station was even more crowded than it had been earlier with islands of luggage doted about the concourse with the owners waiting to board their train. I found the main notice board with the list of trains leaving that evening. Running my finger along the list I found my train to Bangalore with the platform number, departure time with the carriage and the bogie number. Boarding the train I was surprised to see metal bars at the windows. Settling in to my first class compartment I sat on one of the very well-padded plastic covered seats. Above the seats were two metal frames with a hook holding them in place. In the corner of the compartment was a small fan. Relaxing, I was now ready to start my exciting journey, where ever it might take me.

A surprising encounter on Chamundi Hill.

The train pulled out of Victoria Station with a sudden jolt
then slowly built up speed clattered long the track,
rocking side to side. It was starting to turn dark and I
thought there would be little to see travelling over night to
Bangalore some 550 miles away. The outer urban fringes
of Bombay gave way to a rural Indian landscape. It
looked exciting, from what I could see by the faint light of
dusk and wondered what it was like out there with very
little protection from the wild animals roaming about.
After some time the ticket inspector came round, showing
my Indrail card, it was acknowledged with an approving
nod. As he was about to leave I asked where toilet was.
"At the end of the carriage" he replied and left the
compartment.
Making my way to the end of the carriage I found a small
room, the toilet was the same as any other I had used so
far in India, it was a hole in the floor with two place
markers to put your feet. It was hard enough getting used
to squatting down to the use the toilet when stationary but
having to balance whilst the train was rocking about was a
whole new skill to be mastered. Having over come the
difficulties of defecating whilst bobbing about I was
surprised to see a large shower head with a handle on a
chain, thinking how civilised this was I decided to have a
shower in the morning before arriving in Bangalore.
The train stopped at several stations, they struck me as

40

being similar to the old Victoria stations in Britain, except the signs were in Hindi. At one station another passenger came in to my compartment and sat down. I said hello but got no reply, presuming the other passenger did not understand me I carried on looking out of the window in wonder at what looked like a barren landscape without a glint of light from any habitation. After some considerable time of staring out in to the Indian wilderness I started to feel drowsy and tried settling down to sleep on the seat, the other passenger pointed at the metal frame above my head, said something in Hindi and used the hands to indicate sleep, I realised this metal frame was a bed.

Releasing the latch I pulled down one of the two top bunks and climbed on to it. I was a bit apprehensive, there was just a chain each end to take my weight which did not seem strong enough. Throwing caution to the wind and thought that if it did break I would not fall too far, just five feet. Using my large rucksack as a pillow I clung on to my small rucksack containing my passport, traveller's cheques and camera, pulled it in close to me with my arms through the shoulder straps to prevent it being stolen. Before long the gentle rocking of the training sent me off in to a deep sleep.

I was woken the next morning by what sounded like a frantic crowd of people. Sitting up to see what the commotion was I found that two other passengers were also sleeping in the compartment. Looking through the metal grilled window the train had stopped at a jam packed station. People were struggling to get on to the train but were being prevented from doing so by the people getting off. At the same time children were walking up and down the platform holding up trays of food and small ceramic pots of water that they were trying to sell to the passengers. The train was at the station for at least 10 or 15 minutes then the whistle sounded. Passengers jumped on just as the train started to pull away with vendors at the windows still handing over their merchandise.

Gradually picking up speed the train was out in the country side passing fields being ploughed with ox drawn wooden ploughs and dried paddy fields. Small make shift huts dotted the landscape. Women were working dressed in saris, some carried pots on their heads. The arable scenery went on for hours but I did not tire of it, the view was fascinating, I was getting to see the real Indian, every day life away from the cities from the safety of the train. Each time the train pull in to a station I attracted an audience that gathered at the window. As the day wore on I thought we should be arriving at Bangalore soon but the evening turned to night. At one point the train slowed down then came to a halt in the middle of the country side. It was pitch black outside with no sign of any buildings or lights. After about 15 minutes some of the passengers got off and started to walk beside the train. I could hear them talking but there was no sign of the train moving.

After about half an hour some of the passengers got back on the train which I took as a good sign but another 15 minutes went by without any movement. The engine started to make a puffing noise as if it was building up steam but the train still did not move. Regardless of the long wait no one seemed too fussed or bothered. Suddenly a whistle sounded, the passengers standing next to the train scrambled back on as it started to move and we were on our way again.

It didn't look as if we were liable to arrive at Bangalore any time soon, getting a bunk down I turned in for the night. The rocking motion of the train was very therapeutic as I drifted off to sleep.

I woke with the sunlight gleaming in to the carriage I did not know what time it was but it felt early. Looking out of the window the country side was rolling bye and looked very similar to what I had seen the previous day with people working the fields. Gradually more buildings filled the landscape; the roads by the railway track were busy with cars, buses and pedestrians. Eventually the train gradually slowed down and then stopped at a platform with a large yellow sign, Bangalore. I quickly got my things together and rushed off the train,

The train journey had taken two days to cover some 500 miles (800 kilometres), even though it was an express train. This journey was a culture shock and made me realise I should not expect to get anywhere too fast by train. As I walked along the platform I stared in disbelief, people had got off the opposite side of the train and were nonchalantly walking along the railway track with their luggage.

Making my way to the station entrance I found myself in a large airy hall with a marbled floor. It was not very busy

43

and was a complete contrast to Victoria Station in Bombay. Whilst trying to get my bearings and deciding what I needed to do next I saw another white guy in dungarees with a large rucksack who looked equally lost. Deciding it might be a good idea to see if he knew of somewhere to stay in Bangalore I walked over to him, he must have thought the same and as we met we both shook hands and introduced ourselves. Rolf was slim, slightly taller than me and looked as if he had been in India for some time. Rolf explained he was from Frankfurt and was studying Psychology. He had travelled Bangalore too see a local faith healer who practiced just outside Bangalore. After the brief introduction Rolf suggested we should take a taxi and ask for a suitable hotel or guest house.

Climbing into a waiting Ambassador taxi the driver said he could take us to a good hotel and drove us across Bangalore on half empty roads.

Bangalore was very different to Bombay, its wide roads looked deserted in comparison to Bombay and considerably less pedestrians.

After about fifteen minutes the taxi pulled up outside a white three story building which looked well kept. The taxi driver indicated that this was the hotel and once we had paid him and retrieved our rucksacks out of his vehicle he drove off. Inside it was clean and had an airy atmosphere; the hotel staff was polite and friendly. Agreeing that this would be a good place to stay we decided to share the price of a large room to save money, it made sense. After dumping our luggage in the room we set off to explore Bangalore. Buying a map from a book stall Rolf pointed out the botanical garden not far away which we felt deserved a visit.

The botanical gardens were enclosed by metal railings with a wide metal arched entrance. A wide tar macked path lead its way around the park past neatly cut lawns and laid out flower beds. There were small shrines dotted around dedicated to various Hindu deities. In the centre was a band stand but unfortunately no one was playing. A number of people were idly walking around the gardens, several carried metal churns who appeared to be working in the garden.

We spent some time exploring the Botanical Gardens but were unable to find some where to have a drink or eat. Leaving the botanical gardens we walked around the streets and found our way to a part of Bangalore that had several tea rooms. All of them were busy but we found one with a few empty seats. After sitting down and calling chai we were soon joined by a young man. He asked us our names and then told us he was from Burma.

We found it strange that he was here but he explained that he had been persecuted back in Burma by the military authorities and had to flee for his life. This sounded melodramatic but when he explained what life was like in Burma; it sounded extremely draconian and oppressive. As we ate our rice meal and ordered another tea our friend told us more about life back in Burma for those persecuted by the military regime. Our friend finished his story by saying "one day I hope to return to Burma", Rolf and I wished him the best of luck and hoped that he will see a democratic Burma one day. Our friend asked us where we were going to visit in Bangalore. Replying that we were not too sure because we had just arrived; he suggested we should visit Old Bangalore and look around the market, "it is not far from here". After buying our friend a meal and saying good bye we set off.

We found our way to the market, it was surrounded by a white washed wall which was entered via a small arch. Inside there were a large number of small stalls raised on a concrete platform selling a variety of goods. One sold dry coloured powder neatly piled up on metal trays. Others sold fruit and vegetables, hand crafted metal work and spices. Under a large canopy brightly coloured garlands were being made for offerings at the temple by people sitting on a raised platform, when finished the garlands were hung up ready for sale. There was the now familiar fragrant smell of Joss sticks in the air mixed with the sound of Hindi which made it feel extremely exotic.

We left the market and wandered out on to a busy wide street with auto rickshaws, cars, bicycles and Enfield motorbikes. Busy narrow roads lead off from the wide main road and were packed with small businesses. A man was sitting outside an open fronted shop with a type writer and talking to somebody, they seemed to be pawing over a sheet of paper. It appeared that the man at the type writer was a scribe drawing up a letter for his client. Down another road a number of people sat at old Singer sewing machines similar to what my mum had used, it seemed strange seeing them here in India.

Each side road was cram packed with pedestrians, cows, carts and vendors with hardly any room to move but all

46

managed to keep moving. Further along the road by a corner we came across a young boy no older than ten sitting on a large paving slab with a cobbler's anvil and a hammer repairing a pair of shoes. He was being watched by a young girl and an even younger boy. It did not seem right that he should be doing this work but maybe this was necessary for his family to feed itself. We watched the boy as he deftly repaired the shoes showing a skill far beyond his years.

As the day was drawing to a close we tried to find somewhere to eat, not that there was a shortage of places but they all looked crowded with people who had just finished work. We opted to eat where we were staying which seemed to be more convenient.

The meal was served on a plate which was much better than a palm leaf. Rolf mentioned that he was going to visit a faith healer the next day to watch him heal the faithful. The faith healer was very popular and Rolf had heard about him in Germany. I was curious and a bit sceptical about faith healing and wanted to see if it worked.

The next day we caught a bus out of Bangalore having been reassured that it was the right one. After about half an hour the bus stopped on a road by a walled compound on one side and several make shift shelters opposite which turned out to be tea shops. We entered the compound through a wide gateway. Inside was a large whitewashed single storey building and a large crowd sitting on the ground patiently waiting.

One of the faith healers disciples walked amongst the

crowd talking to individuals who appeared to be giving him money. This went on for about half an hour then the disciple stopped walking amongst the seated crowd which created an air of excitement in anticipation the faith healer would appear.

Waiting for about ten minutes the disciple suddenly made an announcement in Hindi which excited the crowd even more. Rolf and myself talked about what we might see when people were healed and cured.

We anticipated that somebody would be selected and then miraculously be able to walk or see. After about fifteen minutes a man appeared from the house, holding up his hands everyone fell perfectly silent as he made an announcement.

It was obvious the crowd were not happy with what they had been told. Rolf asked somebody what was happening. We were told that the faith healer was not well enough to heal anybody to day. We were obviously disappointed but not as much as the people who had travelled so far in a hope of being cured, maybe of some incurable illness, with this faith healer being their last resort. Even though he was not going to meet the crowd a disciple walked amongst them taking donations. Whilst waiting I was suddenly overcome with a feeling of nausea and a throbbing head ache. Feeling a tea would help alleviate my nausea I crossed the road too one of the tea shops. Once inside though I needed to lie down on the wooden bench. As luck would have it one of the faith healers disciples was close by and asked what was wrong. Explaining that I did not feel well; he instantly asked what symptoms I had. Having told him he announced he could cure me. Even though I did not feel like standing up I forced myself doubting this was going to work but could be entertaining. The man asked me to kneel on the wooden bench which I found difficult as it wobbled, and felt uncomfortable. The man then placed his hands on top of my head and pressed down firmly. I could feel my neck and ankles straining from the force as he chanted in Hindi for about a minute.

Once he had finished he asked me if I was better.

" No!" I replied.

He told me to stay where I was and placed his hands back on top of my head; pushing down harder I could feel the pain in my neck and ankles. He chanted even louder than before for about three minutes. He then suddenly stopped, dramatically lifting his hands as if they were being scorched and announced I was cured.

He looked at me in amazement when I told him I did not feel any better. He dramatically announced "I will try one more time". A large crowd had gathered at the tea shop, now he had something to prove.

This time he placed his hands on my head with so much force it caused intense pain down my back as the tendons in my ankles strained under the pressure, I felt he was now taking a kill or cure approach. Chanting at the top of his voice in Hindi for a good four minutes, his arms flew back as if he had been electrocuted by several thousand volts and asked me how I felt.

"I feel worse", this caused an almighty roar of laughter from the gathered crowd. Even though I felt worse from my experience I was glad to have made so many people laugh. The faith healers disciple made what sounded like a disgruntled comment, broke through the gathered crowd and quickly retreated across the road to the compound. Once he had gone somebody told me there was a medical centre just up the road some 300 metres away. Rolf mentioned how poignant it was having two types of medicine so close to each other. At the medical centre I was seen by a doctor almost immediately, asking what was wrong, I explained my symptoms and told him about the faith healing I had received, the doctor smiled and said "I doubt that it helped". He prescribed some tablets and asked me to come back the next day.

Rolf said he had found my faith healing interesting and could write it up when he gets back to Frankfurt.

We arrived back in Bangalore at a bus stop close to a shrine. Even though I still did not feel well we visited it hoping it might help me recover from my ailment and the hands on treatment. In a white washed court yard, there was a large enclosed shrine with a statue of Nandi, the bull god, in side. This was painted white and had a pair of large black wooden gates. The statue of Nandi itself stood about 3 metres high and painted black. Several garlands were draped over it, various other offerings such as flower petals, joss sticks and small candles had been placed just in front of it, coloured candle wax adhered to the statue. A Sadu stood next to the statue dressed in a white sarong greeted us by putting his hands together and bowing. The atmosphere was quiet and serene, ideal for gathering your thoughts. Having paid our respects to Nandi we made our

50

way back to the guest house where I laid down and fell asleep.

Later that night Rolf arrived back, he turned on the light which woke me up with a start. He had gone out for something to eat and had been talking to someone about a city not far away called Mysore which had its own Maharaja and tourist attractions. Mysore sounded interesting.

I suggested leaving the next day but Rolf reminded me that the doctor wanted to see me again. I was feeling slightly better and said I should be okay and didn't want to go back again just to be told I was better.

The next morning I was definitely feeling better and we packed our things, had some breakfast then went to the station and drank tea as we waited.

The train for Mysore arrived on time and we found a seat in first class. The train sedately puffed its way through the Indian country side with palm trees nonchalantly bowing and people working in luminous green paddy fields. The train passed several stations including one called Seringapatam, I pointed out to Rolf that the fort looked interesting but he was not the slightest bit interested. Soon we arrived in Mysore Station. It looked just as it might have been when the British ruled India with a Victorian style wooden fretwork on the stations awning, wooden benches and heavy wooden doors. The platform was crowded with passengers, porters and vendors wheeled barrows selling tea and finger food. Rolf and I made a quick exit out of the station to find somewhere to stay. We did not have to walk far when we found a guest house that looked well kept and comfortable. The interior was constructed of pine with a wide staircase, upstairs there was a large landing and several rooms, it felt ideal. Once we had booked in and dumped our things we went off to explore Mysore and find somewhere to eat. Close by was a busy tea shop packed with Westerners which we took as a good sign for being a suitable place to eat. Sitting at a large crowded table we joined in the conversation with everyone talking about their travels and experiences in India; the conversation was happy and full of laughter. Having eaten a rice meal some one said I should try the Lassi. Having not come across a Lassi yet I decided to try one. Lassi is a Ghee (yoghurt) drink with ice which tasted sweet and refreshing, ideal for the hot Indian weather. The back packers at our table gradually left the tea shop, Rolf and I decided to do the same, even though the atmosphere was exciting we wanted to explore Mysore. Wandering around the streets we came across Silver Street. All of the shops sold jewellery made in both silver and gold, some had precious and semi-precious gems set in them of a variety of colours.

At the end of Silver Street was a roundabout with a white marble statue of a man in traditional Indian dress standing under a white dome. The statue was of the Maharajah who had recently died, not too far away was a very majestic building with large gold domes. This was the Maharajah's palace where anybody could walk around the grounds.

There was a small pyramid type temple with various Indian deities decorating it. Outside guarding the palace

were two black life size Tiger statues facing out on to a perfectly cut four hundred yard lawn. Walking around the peaceful grounds I tried to imagine what it must have looked like at the height of the Indian Raj. Rolf said he was feeling hungry and went back to the tea shop.
I stayed for some time soaking up the tranquil atmosphere. Walking back I came across some craft shops selling a wide variety of wood work, papier-mâché, metal craft, bone carvings, Hookahs and some Ivory work. The one thing that attracted my attention was the bone and Ivory carved chess sets; they were very detailed with each chess piece carved as a traditionally dressed Mughal Indian. The King was a Maharaja seated on an elephant, the Queen and knights were on camels. The temptation to buy a chess set was great, but being quite expensive, and decided my small Kashmiri travelling chess set was good enough. After spending some time browsing around the craft shops I headed back to the hotel.
The next morning Rolf said he was going on a bus trip but I wanted to visit the palace again. Setting off by myself I wandered through the streets. At the Palace I wanted to take a panoramic photograph of it and walked down the long wide gravel path to a set of gates.
As I stood there framing the palace in the lens a uniformed man marched towards me carrying a rifle. He wore a beige uniform with puttees up to his knees in a similar fashion of the troops from World War One, shiny boots that glinted in the sunlight and had a turban on his head. Arriving where I was standing he asked what I was doing. "I want to take photographs of the palace and then

asked if I could take his photograph in front of the palace. Swiftly standing to attention he puffed out his chest and held his rifle against his right leg, the left arm absolutely rigid. Quickly taking the photograph I said thank you and he marched away. After taking several photographs I realised it would be easier to find my way around with a map.

Looking around the shops I found a book stall that sold a paper tourist paper map of Mysore and also one of Kerala with a hard cover. Looking at the Mysore map I noticed that there was a zoo and felt I should visit it. Winding around the roads I eventually arrived at a set of iron gates. Once inside I could see it was not a big zoo but had a large number of cages and pens. By the entrance were two large glass fronted vivariums.

The first one had a python in it. The next one appeared to have another python but when I read the information plaque it was a King Cobra. I could not believe the size of it, the body was thick, some 4 inches in diameter and with a broad head and looked at least fifteen feet long, I decided there and then this was a snake to avoid at all costs especially having heard the stories when I was younger that a King Cobra's bite can kill and Elephant. Walking around there were leopards and tigers in cages without a barrier, you could walk up to the cage and put your fingers through the wire mesh. There was an Indian Rhinoceros, again you could lean over the enclosure wall and reach in. The biggest surprise was at the end, a pen was surrounded by a railing low enough to step over. In the pen were several Gavials, (long snouted crocodiles), one was at least 3 metres long. The zoo was about to close and visitors were asked to leave, it was late afternoon and I made my way back towards the town. One feature that stood out when walking around Mysore was a high hill on it's out skirts and felt I should try and climb it the next day.

Back in Mysore after having eaten I visited the craft shops again. One was very busy with Indian tourists admiring the craft work especially the tables with wood and mother of pearl inlays, carved book rests, wooden plaques with inlay images of gods and animals. I found one of a tiger sitting by a lake with a tree in the back ground. The wood inlay was detailed, outlining the tiger and set in Rosewood. It was hard to resist buying some thing typically Indian that would remind me of my time in this wonderful country. As I browsed around the craft shops I lost track of time and felt hungry. After a rice meal with its small spice dishes and poppadum's which I crushed up and sprinkled on to the rice I went window shopping for the rest of the afternoon until it got dark. The evening atmosphere in Mysore was pleasantly cool and friendly; many of the Indians walking around the streets were young and appeared to be on holiday. Eventually some of the shops started to close which was a sign that it was getting late, not knowing what time it was I went back to the hotel. Rolf was already asleep and after I collapsed on to my bed it did not take me long to dose off.

The next morning over breakfast I told Rolf about the zoo but hc did not seem too bothered. Having finished eating I set off for the hill which my map named as Chamundi

Hill. Walking out of town towards Chamundi Hill I passed people working in some of the fields and a large pond covered in water lilies where several people were washing their laundry or taking a doosh which I had found out was the phrase for washing one's self.

At the foot of Chamundi Hill were some wide steps with buildings either side. Beyond the buildings the steps narrowed rising straight up as far as I could see.

The climb was quite steep, either side were low trees which gave some shade. Every now and then I stopped to rest and admire the scenery across Mysore and the distant barren landscape. Just outside Mysore was a large white building that looked like a palace. Climbing higher I could see the far distant parched Indian landscape where it vanished in to the haze of the midday heat, the ground was beige as far as I could see. Further up the steps the view took in the whole of Mysore with its white washed roof tops and the palace that looked like a toy for a train set.

With the sun high in the sky it felt extremely hot and hoped that I could make it to the top soon. Every now and then the steps were intercepted by a road which did not seem to lead anywhere in particular. Some way up Chamundi Hill I came across a large carved Nandi that was at least 10 feet tall surrounded by bushes and trees. It was black and had carved ornamental decorations around its neck. Suddenly I remembered seeing this statue before. At home we had a set of encyclopaedias dating from the 1930s and there was a picture of this statue with a caption saying it had been carved by the elements. It was such a surprised to come across something that I had seen so many times in the encyclopaedia when I was younger. Sitting on a low wall to rest and admire the craftsmanship I stared in wonder and disbelief having come across this statue. An elderly Sadu walked up the steps, he stopped in front of me, put his hands together and bowed. I stood up and bowed in return. Then without any hesitation he knelt down and kissed my feet and silently carried on up the steps. I stood there in amazement as he carried on towards the top. I was so humbled by this gesture and wondered why he might have done this.

The temperature now felt as if it was at least 30° C which was making it harder to climb the steps but after another half an hour I made it to the top stepping on to the flat tarmac summit where there was an extremely large statue holding a snake and a sword.

There was a small temple and some shops where I bought a well deserved drink.

To one side was a bus terminal, a bus would have been easier but I would not have seen the statue of Nandi. Standing at the edge of the walled summit I looked out in to the hazy distance; the parched ochre ground was almost hypnotic gazing out across the Central Indian Plain from this high vantage point.

After staring in to the distance for some time I walked back down the steps admiring the view as I descended. It was a huge relief making it to the bottom step, the whole day had been an exciting experience and had managed to climb 1008 steps to the top, seen the statue of Nandi, never imagining I would ever see some thing like this from the encyclopaedia.

Back in Mysore in the late afternoon sun I sat in a park to have a rest by some huge trees. These had high broad branches, the sheer size made me think these were ancient, being some few thousand years old. After resting my legs I headed for the nearest tea shop for a well deserved meal.

The next day I told Rolf about my hill climb, Rolf had done it in a bus the day before and could not understand why I had walked up the steps.

The next day I had decided to catch the train to Seringapatam and visit the fort. The journey through the vivid green countryside did not take long to arrive at the quiet station. Inside the fort were some stalls selling fruit and vegetables. As I went to buy some mangoes a cow ambled up and helped itself. The vendor picked up a thin stick and to my surprise hit the cow. I thought the cows had a right to go where ever they wanted, obviously there were some exceptions.

The fort still had most of its battlements intact and there were small buildings with in the court yard. It was very quiet an ideal place to get away from the noise of any city, not that Mysore was noisy, well not as noisy as Bombay. Walking around I found out that Wellington as a young subaltern fought with the East India Company here when the British captured the fort from Tipu Sultan in 1799, an exploit that was to help propel the young Wellington to fame and fortune. After several hours I caught the train back to Mysore and met up with Rolf. He had decided to catch the evening train; wishing him the best of luck I hoped we might meet up again. After packing his things he headed for the station. I needed to move on and explore the remote distant India I had seen from the top of Chamundi Hill and decided to catch a train the next day for the coast.

Lakeside camping, The Periyar Wild Life Sanctuary

My time in Mysore had been enjoyable with its calmer
atmosphere without feeling hassled by venders to buy
their goods; but all good things come to an end and
booked my seat on the train heading south. At the station
a queue of people were booking their tickets, but the
queue was static as people walked to the front, leant in
front of the person being served, asked for their ticket
and were served by the ticket clerk.
After some considerable time with my nerves gradually
getting frayed by those pushing in I made it to the kiosk
and placed my large rucksack on the kiosk desk to my
right to block any one from push in, my small rucksack
was pulled up over my left shoulder which I hoped would
be some sort of deterrent. As I leant forward to talk to the
ticket clerk a man tried to get in front of me. He put his
head between the bars of the kiosk and my rucksack.
Taking a slight step backwards I let the rucksack slide
across my back, then swiftly jerked my shoulder forward
propelling my rucksack with some force.
It caught the man in the side of the head pinning it against
the bars whilst I carried on talking to the clerk. The
weight of the camera and other contents seemed to
sufficiently deter the intruder from trying any more.
I did not have to wait too long for the afternoon train
which headed towards Bangalore at a reasonably sedate
pace through the lush green countryside with the familiar

rice paddies being worked by farmers.

After a lengthy stop at Bangalore where passengers got off to replenish themselves with water and food, the whistle signalled the train to leave and passengers raced to get back on as the train pulled away. After leaving Bangalore the train picked up speed following the railway track as it looped out in to the parched Indian countryside past the many towns and villages in central India.

As the evening closed in the countryside faded to a dark indigo screen. Unable to see anything in the murky landscape I decided to turn in for the night. I drifted off in to a deep sleep rocked by the train as it clattered along the railway track.

The next morning I woke with the bright Indian sun shining in to the carriage. The porter came around to let everyone know the train will be arriving in Olavakkot soon. Looking at my map of Kerala I had bought in Mysore Olavakkot was not on it, but I decided it might be a good place to stop and break my journey to the coast. The train gradually slowed down as it approached Olavakkot and stopped with a jolt. I picked up my two rucksacks and went to step off the train but there was no platform and had to jump down on to the gravel. There were few buildings, most appeared to be wooden make shift constructions, apart from the one next to the station; the road leading from the railway track was sand and gravel, I felt excited thinking this is the real India.

The brick building next to the station was a tea shop which was just what I needed, a cup of tea and something to eat. Entering the busy tea shop I instantly attracted every ones attention and wondered why.

After having eaten and had a tea with everyone in the tea shop taking cursory glances at me I asked at the till where I could stay in Olavakkot. The man tipped his head to one side and pointed down with his index finger and said "here". Asking to look at the room the owner took me to the back of the tea room along a short corridor and opened a wooden door to a small room. It was bare except for a large concrete block with a mattress on it, the room was very Spartan, but as I planned to just stay for the one night it was sufficient and asked how much. The man told me it was 10 rupees (about 55p) and could not believe the price.

I asked about washing and was shown a separate room with a large sink. Pausing briefly I decided for 10 rupees what can you expect and said I will take it.

I put my large rucksack in the room and walked off down the sandy track to explore Olavakkot. Beside the wide sandy road on one side were various shops which looked more like sheds with the wares laid out in front. On sale were clothes, metal pots, bowls, plates and jugs.

I quickly attracted a merry band of followers of various ages who were all smiling and laughing.

A middle aged man sitting outside a tea shop beckoned me over to join him for a tea and politely accepted. Introducing himself he asked me my name, where I was from and why I was in Olavakkot. Explaining that I needed a break from the long journey and thought it would be a good place to stop. "There is not much to see in Olavakkot it is just a small town". Pointing at my entourage the man added "not many white people stop in Olavakkot. The last time a white person stopped here it was an American on his motorbike about three months ago. He stopped for a cup of tea and then left".

This was the India I had come to see away from the cities, a glimpse of what few Westerners get to see first-hand. We talked for a while with my audience watching and listening intently. Now and then the man translated for the growing crowd which made them all laugh and smile.

After a tea and biscuit I said good bye and set off with my entourage in tow which gradually dwindled to a few individuals but every now and then as I walked by people stared in surprise.

I followed the dusty road and arrived at a partly dried up river lined with tall palm trees. There were a number of people along the river bank doing their washing and watering horses. I sat down on the river bank to take in the serene rural view with its calm and peaceful atmosphere of this small part of India; a big contrast from the bustling cities.

Having sat watching the people working by the river I had built up an appetite and set off back to the Olavakkot guest house for a large rice meal off a palm leaf which I ate with my hand.

After eating I set off again to explore more of Olavakkot. I walked along the wide sandy road and came to a junction with a road leading off through some fields and took it to discover where it went. Across the fields were a row of small houses. A few people were standing and talking in the road when some one saw me approaching;

more people appeared from the houses and made way for me.

A smiling congregation followed me, some asked me my name, and others asked where I was from. As I walked along the road the crowd grew larger until there were about 30 people of various ages. A middle aged man sitting in a door way called out hello then suggested I should come inside his house, "if you stay long enough the crowd will lose interest and go away". Taking up the offer I ducked down to get through the low door way and stepped in to a single room with white washed walls and two small windows. There were two seats and a low wooden table. Joss sticks burnt in a small statuette filling the air with an exotic aroma, my host appeared to almost apologise, "it is time to burn my offerings for my god". Smiling I said it was okay and commented that it smelt nice.

My host asked if I wanted a tea, not wanting to offend I said yes please. To my surprise he poured the tea in to a china cup with a saucer then handed it to me. We talked about Britain and what it was like, then my host remarked he would like to visit one day. I asked about the best places to visit on the west coast but he just said it is nice on the coast even in Cochin. Having finished my tea we noticed how quiet it was, "I think they have gone now". Thanking my host for the tea I shook his hand and said goodbye.

Opening the door and to my utter amazement I was confronted by an even larger crowd of some seventy or eighty people. Stepping out of the small house the crowd parted and allowed me to walk between them, as I carried on walking along the road the large crowd followed cheerfully laughing and chatting.

I felt that if I tried to tell anyone about this they might not believe me and decided to take a photo of my followers. Turning around I held up my camera and said I wanted to take a photograph of everyone. Calling out loudly so they could all hear, "get closer together so I can fit you all in to the photograph". I did not have to ask them to smile for the photograph as everyone huddled together and stood still, just as I took the photo a large number of the crowd in front move forward each trying to get to the front and were out of focus which was disappointing but I knew the photograph had captured the atmosphere of the moment with the sea of smiling faces.

Waving good bye to everyone I made my way back to the guest house for something to eat just as the sun was setting. The row of small make shift shops were now lit up by Tilley lamps, the metal work glistened in the shimmering light. I noticed that nobody was taking an interest in me, maybe because I was not so conspicuous in the night light or the novelty of a white person in town had worn off.

The next day I found out that there was a bus that went out to a dam, the Malampuza Dam. The idea of a dam in what seemed to be such an arid area seemed peculiar and wanted to visit it. The bus did not leave until the afternoon so having time to kill I exploring around Olavakkot. I had come to wonder why anybody wanted to live in such a dry place. It seemed to be so far away from any accessible water supply except for the river and that seemed to be drying up, maybe because of the dam. I checked the times for the trains, the next train was the following day which gave me plenty of time to experience this remote part of India until I caught the bus out to Malampuza dam. I leisurely walked around Olavakkot occasionally drawing some attention but not as much as the previous day.

The journey to the dam was about forty five minutes travelling through dry parched country side with stunted trees. The other passengers were smartly dressed, the women in their brightly coloured saris and the men in trousers and shirts. The bus pulled up in what seemed to be in the middle of nowhere, it looked very dry, sandy and was silent. The other passengers walked off along a path towards some hills, they all seemed to know where they were going so I followed behind. Walking a short distance over a rise in the ground I stood in front of a large expanse of water. At one end was the dam with the lake stretching off for some distance; on the opposite side of the lake were the hills. Half way across the dam were two towers, below the dam was a garden where most of the other visitors were walking to.

Following the path I came to a sign which said the garden was dedicated to a Hindu deity. In amongst the pathways were small shrines and statues where you could give offerings such as fruit, flowers or light joss sticks. It seemed to be an idyllic spot to have a place dedicated to a god or for a picnic. The women in their saris contrasted with the reddish sand and the green of the park, they looked so elegant.

As the sun started to set the bus driver called for the passengers to board the bus which took a little time, some of the passengers did not seem to be in much of a hurry and the other passengers did not seem to mind waiting, including me.

It was such a nice place to sit and watch the sunset. The bus travelled back to Olavakkot as the last vestiges of the sun light vanished below the almost perfectly flat horizon and the light faded to an almost inky blackness. In Olavakkot the vendors Tilley lamps lit the shop fronts with a warm glow that stretched out across the sandy road where a small crowd had gathered. Being inquisitive I had to see what the attraction was. A tall man was the centre of attention. He had a short beard and dressed in a long purple flowing robe with yellow or gold trim and wearing a black turban, he looked like a character out of the Arabian Nights. The lights from the shops reflecting off his long satin cloak which contrasted with the side in shadow making him look quite sinister and almost menacing. Standing next to him was a shorter man who appeared to be an interpreter. They had small bottles. Their sales pitch was entertaining as they appeared to extoll the virtues of the bottles contents as the crowd silently listening. It just seemed surreal as the two men attempted to sell whatever they had in the bottles out in the middle of the Indian plain. Nobody seemed to be interested in buying whatever was in the small bottles. The tall man became impatient and his sales pitch more dramatic as he held up the bottle aloft above his head and pointed at it. It all seemed futile, no one was interested. After some time I went off to my guest house for something to eat realising I had not had a proper meal all day, then settled down for the night ready to catch the morning train.

Over breakfast the next morning I looked at my maps to decide where I was going next. On the back of my Kerala tourist map was some tourist information describing various places of interest.

As I mulled over the different places two stood out Nilambur and Thekkady.

Nilambur was described as "renowned Elephant training camp that was easily accessible from Calicut with dense teak plantations". Thekkady was described as, "a town situated near the Periyar Wild Life Sanctuary holding pride of place among the tourist attractions in Kerala. A cruise on the Periyar Lake provides a unique opportunity to relax in the cool clime and see wildlife in natural habitat. Species generally seen are elephants, bison's, antelopes, Sambur Deer, wild bear, tiger, etc."Thekkady sounded like an opportunity too good to miss and be able to see those animals in the wild, especially a tiger.

Two hotels were recommended that were run by the Kerala Tourism Development Corporation. I decided that the best way to see these animals, especially tigers was to be there first thing in the morning and late at night. To do this I decided to camp out on the wild life sanctuary. After this I would go out to the coast and visit Cochin, first I was going to visit Nilambur. Booking my seat on the next train was straight forward being the only person catching

68

the train that day. I needed to change at Shoranur then catch the train for Nilambur which was the end of the line. Sitting in the train gave me a majestic view of the dry landscape which looked absolutely barren, devoid of any life but out there I knew people were living in their small huts, somewhere and wild animals were roaming around. The countryside changed and became greener.

Arriving at Shoranur's small station late in the afternoon, the countryside was a lush green with trees including tall palms, rampant vegetation and the rice paddies.

The steam train for Nilambur soon arrived, it had basic carriages with wooden benches which added to the rustic appeal of the journey. The train steadily trundled through the bright vivid green landscape and arrived at the quiet station of Nilambur.

I made enquiries about the elephant training camp and was told it was some ten kilometres away, but there were no buses; there was only one thing for me to do, walk! Leaving the peaceful station behind I soon found myself out in the country side with paddy fields either side of the narrow palm tree lined road, the sun was high and hot. After a few kilometres I came across some women who were filling up their jugs with water from a hand pump that was by a small brick built house, when they saw me they shielded their faces by pulling their Saris up over their heads. I took a quick photo of the group to remind me of the moment. Further on I came across some more women who were carrying fire wood who did the same when they saw me.

Eventually making it to the elephant sanctuary to find it

was not open. A notice had been posted saying that the elephants had been found homes in various national parks. It was totally peaceful out in the middle of the countryside amongst the trees, but there was nowhere to stay and had to make my way back to Nilambur in the afternoon sun along the hot road. Glad to arrive back at the station I sat in the shade and waited for the train to Shoranur. It was late afternoon by the time the train arrived and had to wait another several hours for the train to Kottayam which gave me time to have a long shower and some food after my day's exertions. Reflecting on my disappointing day I hoped that Thekkady and the Periyar Wild Life Sanctuary would be more rewarding. By the time the train arrived it was dark. Once in the carriage I climbed in to a bunk wrapped my arms through my rucksack straps and dozed off. The train arrived at Kottayam early the next morning, excitedly I got off the train and went straight to the bus terminal which happened to be just outside the station. Before long I was on the bus to Thekkady, the urban landscape gave way to open rolling countryside of palms and low beach type trees. After several miles the road narrowed and changed from tarmac to a gravel surface that climbed through a distinctly hilly landscape.

The road weaved its way around the hills at times with a sheer drop of few hundred feet, with the wheel right on the edge. Higher up in the hills were tea plantations either side. The scenery was very different to what I had seen so far from the dry arid landscape to these lush green hills and notably cooler temperature. After about five hours we came to a small town, the houses and shops were mainly constructed of wood with corrugated steel roofs; this was Thekkady.

Getting off the bus I thought it would be a good idea to buy some food if I was camping out. After browsing several stalls I bought some rice and eggs. The eggs were for breakfast and the rice was to see me through the next few days. At the same time I asked for directions to the Wild Life Park. Being told where the road was I found a wooden sign pointing down a single lane road to the Periyar Wild Life Sanctuary.

The road was lined with tall over hanging trees, after a few kilometres I came across a small wooden hut with several park rangers sitting in side. I asked if it was okay to camp in the park, they all smiled and shook their head side to side in agreement, one of the rangers waved his hand and said "of course you can". Beside the hut was a large wooden carved sign that depicted the animals you could encounter in the Animal Sanctuary which included an elephant, deer, buffalo and a tiger.

The carved sign gave me a sense of excitement as I followed the narrow road until I came to a cleared area with a picnic table under the trees with a scenic view of a lake. Sitting down on the bench I marvelled at the view of the lake nestled between high forest covered hills. Tops of semi submerged tree trunks protruded out of the lake like the masts of sunken sailing ships. Grass bordered the lake giving a wide barrier between the waters edge and the tree line. The grass was surprisingly short and looked as if it had been mown, perfect for pitching a tent.

As I sat contemplating my camp site an American guy
arrived, "hi, what are you doing?"
"I was thinking of camping here and wondered if I would
get to see any tigers".
I was in Uttar Pradesh for a week with guides trying to
spot tigers but did not see any. I doubt if you will see any
but it was a nice place to camp".
After a brief conversation he walked off.
It was starting to get dark, I needed to pitch my tent
before the light went and get a fire going.
By the time I had my tent up, found some fire wood and
lit the fire it was dark. There was no moon and the only
light was from my camp fire. I cooked the rice in my
small pot which seemed to take an eternity to boil and sat
by the fire warming myself as the evening cooled and
listened; it was dead quiet, not a sound from any human
or animal. I reflected on when I first left Bombay and
seeing the people out in the countryside, wondering about
the wild animals that might be about and here I was
camping on a Wild Life Sanctuary with various wild
animals about, including tigers possibly lurking in the
shadows. After eating I let the fire die down, the faint
light from the glowing embers gave off enough light for
me to climb in to my tent. Covering myself up with my
large towel I soon fell asleep.
Early the next morning the chilly air woke me and
decided to go for a walk in a hope too catch a glimpse of
some of the wild life by the lake and warm myself up.
Without thinking that a tiger might be sitting outside my
tent I unzipped the flap and stood admiring the view, my

72

tent was in the shade but the far end of Lake Periyar and the distant hills were bathed in bright sunlight giving the trees a yellow tint. I made my way from the chilly shade of the trees to a cutting bathed in sunlight. I instantly felt the suns warmth and stood still looking and listening for any wild life.

The only animal about was a large kingfisher perched on a branch on the edge of the lake. It suddenly darted off, dived in to the water and resurfacing with a catch and perched back on the branch to eat its food. I stood still, quietly listening for some time hoping to see or hear something walking about but nothing appeared.

Eventually succumbing to hunger I returned back to my tent to boil my eggs and use the boiled water for a cup of tea.

Whilst eating I heard a noise in the trees just behind me. Looking around I couldn't see anything but I could hear something rustling the leaves, a branch moved high up in a large tree where three black monkeys were sitting. They must have been watching me all of the time, I tried to get a closer look at them but they were being elusive and climbed to a higher branch.

After breakfast I took advantage of a stream that lead in to the lake and washed my clothes, beating them on a large convenient rock next to the stream; it was perfect, the latest mod cons.

Whilst washed my clothes I noticed several large black aquatic animals wriggling in the water. Scooping one up I realised that it was a tadpole but not any type of tadpole, this was about five inches long, this must have been what

73

the Kingfisher was catching earlier in the morning. Putting the tadpole back I carried on with my washing, thrashing and beating my clothes on the rock to ensure they were clean when I heard the foliage rustling and twigs breaking. Turning around I saw an elephant that was being ridden heading straight for my tent; dropping my washing I ran towards the elephant waving my arms and calling out in an attempt to prevent it from trampling my tent, but was unsure how I would stop the elephant in its tracks.

Just as I got up to my tent the elephant veered off to one side. The man riding the elephant did not react to my frantic efforts and seemed to be totally oblivious or asleep. The pair of them ambled off in to the distance around the edge of the lake, much to my relief.

By the time I had finished doing my washing a number of people had wandered down from Thekkady. Being in need of some food I set out for Thekkady to buy some provisions.

Some were local people who had the same idea as me were doing their washing, others were tourists. Further up the stream a film crew was set up comprising of the camera man, sound recordist, two actors, the director and two helpers. I watched them as they filmed the scene which seemed to be a typical Indian style romance with the attractive actress looking dreamily in to the actor's eyes and every few minutes they were being interrupted by the director. Surprisingly this did not attract any attention from any one walking past.

Further along the stream a group of women were doing

74

their washing, a young pretty woman from the group walked up to me, licked her finger then wiped it down my dark suntanned arm then held it up for the others to see, they laughed and commented in Hindi. Realising what she was doing I licked my own finger and did the same and shook my head, this made them laugh even more.

Arriving in Thekkady's long high street, a single road leading in past the shops and out at the other end in to the surrounding countryside Most of the shops sold fresh vegetables, a few sold touristy type carvings and of course there was the obligatory tea shop but nowhere to cash a traveller's cheque. Whilst buying my food at a stall I asked if any Tigers wandered off the Animal Sanctuary, "yes! Tigers occasionally roamed in to Thekkady from the sanctuary" the smiling stall holder replied.

The surreal thought of a tiger doing a bit of window shopping amused me. The stall vendor assured me that nobody had come to any harm and there was a remote chance of seeing a tiger which excited me. Having a tea and some rice I headed off back to my tent.

A large number of people were now out in the animal sanctuary; all of them were Indians. The peace of the forest and lake was broken by people shouting in the distance which was coming from the tourist boat at the far end of the lake. The noise was enough to deter any animal from coming out of the cover of the foliage.

After putting the shopping in my tent I set off to explore. Following the edge of the forest that backed on to my tent I walked by the edge of the lake. The forest ended and I came to the wide avenue between the forests which gave me a clear view for what appeared to be several kilometres.

A few hundred metres away at the forest edge was what looked like a small cat, similar in size of Scottish Wild Cat. It sat at the edge silhouetted as if waiting for some prey to walk by. I waited, hoping it would walk down towards me but it stayed where it was. As I started making my way up the avenue the foliage began to rustle with large branches and trees swaying about on the edge of the forest.

There could only be two animals in the park that could move the trees that much, an elephant or buffalo, from experience in Africa both can quite easily become angry. I waited to see what would emerge from the forest but nothing did, looking back up the avenue the cat had disappointedly gone.

I carried on around the lake stopping now and then to listen for any wild life, the noisy tourists in the boat were quiet and peace had returned and hoped there was some prospect of seeing some animals, but even with it being quiet none were lured out in to the open.

It got to the point where it was getting late and didn't want to be far away from my tent when it got dark. Just as I was getting close to my camp site I spotted a snake several yards from me slithering through the short grass. It was slim and about six feet long. I stopped, not being a snake expert I was not sure if it was poisonous, the snake also stopped which gave me time to see it more clearly. It had a yellow mottled pattern, the snake remained motionless for about three or four minutes then slithered off in to the forest.

Back at the tent I collected some fire wood and water to cook with, by which time it was getting dark. I lit my fire to keep the bugs away and cook my rice.

Sitting in the dark warmed by the flames licking up around my cooking pot, reflecting this could be the most exciting camping I had ever done. The rice had cooked and I boiled up some water for a tea.

Slowly eating and drinking I wondered how conspicuous I was and if any animals might be attracted to the fire. There was not a sound except for the fire crackling, and definitely nothing could be seen beyond the light of the fire in the dark night. As I looked around in to the darkness I noticed a large fire up on the opposite hillside. I wondered if it spread out of control across the hill side and was transfixed by the orange glow lighting up the surrounding trees. I was convinced there were some people silhouetted by the large flames.

The fire did not spread and was still burning when I eventually turned in for the night with the intention of having another early morning walk and maybe catch sight of some wild life.

Some time during the night I was suddenly woken by a noise, then a loud splash. I gingerly pulled down the window flap at the end of the tent and peered out in to moon lit night. I could see clearly down to the lake and waited in anticipation for something to move. For an hour or so I sat waiting to catch a glimpse of any animal, the splash sounded relatively close but nothing moved and eventually I dozed off.

Waking the next morning I set off for the early morning walk by the lake. It was peaceful, not a sound could be heard. After walking by the lake for an hour or so I went back to my tent for some breakfast and a cup of tea. By the time I had finished it was still quite early and quiet, no tourists were about and thought I would take a walk up through the forest behind my tent. Crossing the road I had arrived on a few days ago the ground sharply rose up through the forest, it was steep but the vegetation was not too thick and was easy to navigate my way through it. Treading carefully and trying to be as quiet as possible ensuring not to rustle the leaves or snap a twig, paying attention to where I put my feet to avoid treading on a snake. Every now and then I stopped to look around and listen. Apart from the sound of some birds not much could be heard.

Having climbed up hill for some distance the ground started to level out at the crest of the hill, pausing briefly to listen to the sound of the forest. Suddenly a bush a few yards in front of me abruptly parted as a huge deer sprang out from its cover directly towards me, it veered to the left and bounded away in to the forest, the suddenness left me rooted to the spot with the excitement of the moment. It showed how a large animal can so easily hide in the forest and not be seen until you were almost on top of it. Standing still for a minute or so to regain my composure I listened for any more movement, the forest was peaceful again. Contemplating whether to go on I decided to walk back down the hill the way I came, being more vigilant but hoping to see more animals. Once out of the forest

78

and back by the lake I walked around the edge for a mile or so but not much was stirring in the midday sun except for the sound of distant voices. Back at the tent I checked my finances, I did not have much money and needed to pay for the journey back to Kottoyam and reluctantly decided to leave the next day.

I walked up in to Thekkady for a tea and something to eat whilst the tourists trekked down by the lake. Returning later to my tent knowing it would be quieter I walked and listened but unfortunately I did not get to see any more animals.

As the light started to fade I lit my camp fire and cooked the last of my rice and wondered how long I would have to stay to see a tiger but reflected on the cool night air and how uncomfortable it was in the early mornings, I wanted to get down to a lower and warmer altitude out on the coast.

After the meal and a tea I sat by the warm fire until there were just the glowing embers left then settled down for the night.

I slept through and woke at first light. Wanting to make the most of my last morning in the Wild Life Sanctuary I went for a walk in hope of seeing some wildlife but nothing seemed to be stirring, not even a distant grunt. Eventually hearing people talking in the distance I decided it would be best to go back for some breakfast and pack everything up.

Having packed my tent away I walked up to Thekkady, it seemed like an anti-climax after the excitement of camping for the last three nights out on the sanctuary, my

Periyar Adventure had come to an end but I still lived in hope of catching sight of a tiger in the wild with so much more of India to see. Whilst waiting for the bus I looked at the various shops and drank tea until it arrived around midday. The packed bus weaved its way down the forested hills, past the tea plantations too Kotoyam. My next stop was the sea.

Life's a beach; The West Coast and Far South.

It was late afternoon when the bus arrived at Kotoyam, I did not have to wait long for the train to Cochin. I whiled away the time watching other passengers on the platform as they waited for their train and had something to eat from the platform stall which served up finger food and tea in my metal mug. Once the train for Cochin arrived there was a frantic rush to get on it, the passengers dragged their luggage through the doors Children who had made it on were being directed through the barred windows by the parents.

I found a seat available in first class and felt happily secluded as I looked out of the barred window at the busy platform. Once everyone was on board a whistle was blown, the train jolted then slowly gathered speed. The train journey was over night, the bunk felt a lot more comfortable than being on the ground in a tent, and safer. Early the next morning the train arrived in Cochin. It halted at the end of the railway line directly next to the sea. The sea air felt fresh, a welcome change to the dry heat of the last few weeks, and the cooler temperature of Thekkady. I got off the train, not far away was a jetty where small ferries waited to take the passengers across Cochin Harbour to various destinations. Nearby were two broad scooped fishing nets which were dipped in to the sea and then pulled up once there were enough fish in the net. I had a basic map of Cochin in my Kerala guide showing some of the islands.

I decided to catch the ferry for Vypeen, a long narrow island that faced out to the Arabian Sea. I wasn't in the mood for being in the more crowded part of the city, but wasn't sure if there would be a guest house on Vypeen. The ferry journey across Cochin Harbour took about ten minutes giving a panoramic view of the harbour.

The single road on Vypeen was sandy and lined with various buildings. Homes, shops and a guest house which was a bit more palatial compared to what I have been staying in since leaving Bombay. There was a bed with a proper mattress and clean white sheets. The room was of a good size and quiet. Down stairs there was a dining room. Once settled in I set off to explore this peaceful coastal out of the way retreat.

I followed the road to see where it might lead to and came across a narrow lane that led under some trees, I could not resist finding if it went it went out to the beach. There was some shouting from behind the foliage lining the lane which turned out to be a game of football, what surprised me though all of the players were kicking the ball in bare feet.

Weaving my way along the narrow foliage covered lane I caught a glimpse of some shimmering light in the distance. As I got closer there was the sound of the waves breaking on the beach, sun light glinted off the waves as they rolled in.

Blocking the path was a small lagoon and considered wade or swimming across it. Stepping in to the water I noticed a hump protruding out of the water at the far end

82

of the lagoon. At first I thought it was a log but noticed it had a pattern similar to that of a large python. The amount that was visible would have made it an extremely large python, not wanting to tempt fate I erred on the side of caution.

Whilst deliberating how to cross the lagoon and wondering if I was just being paranoid a young lad paddled across the lagoon in a dugout canoe "do you want to go to the other side?" he called,

"Yes" I replied and climbed aboard his canoe once it was at the bank. "What is the large lump at the far end?",

"snake" he replied,

"is it a python?"

"Yes, we killed it last night" he said in a matter of fact way.

This brought home to me how you cannot take things for granted and also how these people even though it is relatively built up there was the danger of animals close by.

Once on the other side I paid a few rupees for the boat ride and walked out on to the soft sand which stretched for miles in one direction. The beach was lined with palm trees, a typical tropical beach that you would see in any holiday brochure but without the high rise developments. In the other direction were some boats on the beach, their sails flapping in the sea breeze with a large crowd standing around them. A boy ran past me towards them, I felt that this must be worth seeing, drawing closer I heard the excited sound of the crowd.

At the boat I could see why, the boats were full fish.

Every one seemed to be haggling over the price. Some were quite large, almost as big as a Grouper whilst others were not so majestic. Impulsively picking up a fish, suddenly I felt like having fish for a meal and called out "how much?" When a man told me the price I did not haggle but just paid what was asked. The excited atmosphere of the crowd was almost electric, I could not resist hanging around listening to the haggling and bartering. Once the fishermen had finished selling their catch I set off for the guest house armed with my fish to get it cooked. At the lagoon I found the young lad with his canoe waiting to transport me back to the other side and paid for the return journey. Making my way back to the guest house I puzzled over how it was going to be cooked and felt I had been impetuous rather than practical.

I asked the guest house proprietor if he could cook the fish and serve it up with some rice. He shook his head in agreement, "I will do it straight away". The prospect of eating fresh fish that had been caught just a few hours ago excited me and didn't have to wait long. The fish had been cooked whole, head and tail as well and served with a large pile of rice. I was given some small spices dishes to go with the meal. The fish tasted wonderful and was cooked just right with the meat flaking off.

After having eatenI thanked the proprietor for cooking the fish and asked how much I owed him, expecting to be charged for the rice and the chef's time. When he told me the price it was obvious I was being charged for the fish as well. I objected and we ended up having a long discussion over the price which attracted an audience, the proprietor turned and talk to his customers in Hindi, I felt at a disadvantage and was being judged. Maybe I was and the audience was deciding which story to believe making it a bit one sided. Objecting that I had paid the fisherman on the beach and just wanted it cooked. Eventually the proprietor relented and charged for the rice and a nominal price for cooking the fish.

After the lively confrontation I went for a walk to relax, there was a gentle breeze that you only get on the coast that feels cooling and refreshing. There was not much else to see, just a few homes, mostly constructed of wood but some were sturdier and made with breeze blocks. I came to the conclusion that I did not need a lot of the clothes in my rucksack. The weather so far had been about 25°C and felt I could send the winter clothing I arrived in home. First I needed some brown paper and tape to wrap up the clothes. There were a number of shops that looked as if they would sell what I needed, one even called itself an Emporium; the sort of place that sold everything you would ever need.

Finding a shop that sold the brown paper was quite easy but the sticky tape proved to be a bit more difficult, even asking by a trade name I was greeted with bemused smiles. When I tried describing what I wanted this created a lot of excited discussion which at first gave me some hope that somebody would know what I wanted but each time there was the shake of the head, "no" and a broad smile. Having tried several shops somebody mentioned one that might have what I wanted.

The shop was very small but was stacked with an array of merchandise, it looked the most unlikely place to have any type of tape let alone sticky tape. Even so I asked the shop owner, he thought for a little while and then rummaged about in the back of his small shop as I waited expectantly; from underneath a pile of boxes he produced a discoloured, crumpled box with 'Sellotape' written on it. I was jubilant and was overcome with joy, not that I normally get excited over Sellotape but this eureka moment warranted the jubilation.

I rushed back to the guest house and wrapped up the clothes I wanted to send home. The parcel was quite large but it gave me a lot more space in the rucksack and made it a bit lighter. It was late and decided to post the parcel the next day.

After breakfast I caught the ferry across the harbour to the main city of Cochin to find a post office. The boat ride was pleasant as it glided over the perfectly flat water under the hot sun.

Not far from the jetty was the strangest sight. A Fakir was upside down, his legs stuck up in the air and his head buried in the sand with a bowl in front of him so people could donate money to him. I was transfixed, this was not something you expect to see every day and could be considered sensible. As money was thrown in to the bowl the Fakir waved in appreciation.

Though transfixed I managed to drag myself away remembered why I was in Cochin. Finding the post office not too far the quay, it was a white washed building that looked as if it was newly built. Fans blew a cool breeze

making it very comfortable. Joining one of the long queues I waited for my turn which took some time but eventually arrived at the desk. Explaining that I wanted to send the parcel to the UK,
 the clerk said "no, no, no", thinking I was in the wrong queue I looked around. The clerk pointed directly at the parcel and said "it is not wrapped properly".
Questioningly I looked at the clerk and then the parcel. It was wrapped in 2 layers of brown paper and securely sealed with whole role of Sellotape.
He explained I could not send a parcel wrapped in brown paper, "it might tear open".
Reassuring the clerk I was willing to take a chance but he repeated his self "no, no, no, you must wrap it properly".
I was lost, what on earth did he mean by 'wrapped properly', "how?" I enquired.
"You must wrap everything in cloth, sew this up and then use sealing wax on the sewing" he said with a self-satisfied smile.
I looked at the clerk in utter disbelief, my mouth dropped open not knowing what I should say. I felt myself staring at him goggle eyed thinking he could not be serious.
After a pregnant pause I managed to regain some sort of composure and asked where I could buy these things thinking he might tell me of a shop close by.
The clerk looked at me, smiled and simply said "in a shop".
Slowly I replied "of course"; turned around to be confronted by the rest of the queue who had all been listening to the conversation, each person seemed to have

87

a bemused smile. I was obviously not over the culture shock yet.

Finding a shop not too far away that sold what I needed to send my parcel home I felt it was not really worth the hassle.

Sitting outside the Post Office I wrapped the brown paper parcel in a sheet of linen cloth, then laboriously sewed up the seams with a stitch that was not too loose just in case this was considered insufficiently secure and was asked to resew it. I melted the sealing wax using a box of matches, burning my fingers in the process. At last it was done and I re-joined a queue.

Once at the front of the queue again I presented my wrapped parcel and announced I wanted to post it to the UK.

The clerk repeated "UK?" and then asked me "where is the UK"?

Realising the abbreviation might be a problem I said "the United Kingdom". The clerk then asked "Where is the United Kingdom".

I replied "Great Britain",

the clerk looked at me reached out for a book, flicked through the pages and then said "we do not have a Great Britain in our list".

By now I was losing my sense of humour. Trying hard keep a sense of proportion "is there England on the list?" He flicked through the pages and announced "yes England" as if it was a sudden revelation. The parcel was weighed and I was handed the stamps. I was instructed to paste the stamps on to the parcel properly and hand the parcel back at the counter.

Placed around the post office were small pots of glue to adhere the stamps to the parcel, having slapped the glue on the back and front of the stamps I handed the parcel in at the desk with a huge sigh of relief and decided this was the first and last time I was going to post a parcel.

Most of the day had been taken up with posting my parcel and felt I had seen enough of Cochin and looked at my tourist map of Kerala over a tea. Do I go north or south? Reading about Cannanore to the north, it was described as being well known for its historic fort dating back to the colonial past with a lovely beach. If it had a beach it must be perfect.

After booking out of the guest house later that afternoon I went to Cochin station and asked for a seat on the evening train to Cannonore. A platform attendant told me there were not any seats available and I needed to book a seat first.

"I have an Indrail ticket which allows me to board a train without any previous booking",

the platform attendant paused " the seat will cost 20 rupees".

Feeling indignant at being black mailed replied "I did not have to pay for the seat".

The platform attendant shook his head and smiled uneasily "I have to charge you".

Calling his bluff replied "I will pay at the ticket desk and went to walk away".

"Okay, I might be able to find a seat". Within minutes a vacant seat had been found and I was aboard the train.

The journey to Cannonore did not take long and the train

arrived late that evening. Making my way through the winding streets it was relatively easy to find somewhere to stay. I booked in to a small guest house with modest sized rooms, net curtains hung in the window which opened out on to the busy street below. The room was clean, with a small sink in the corner, a dressing table plus a comfortable bed, absolute heaven.

The next morning I woke with sunlight filtering in to the room through the net curtains. Opening the large window to let in some cooler air at the same time the street noise flooded in.

Before going out to explore Cannanore I decided to sit at the dressing table and write several brief letters whilst eating a large pineapple I bought the previous day.

Having finished and pleased that I had been so industrious I set off to post the letters and find somewhere to eat. Close by was a tea shop that was not busy, it looked like the ideal place to eat without an audience. As I stepped inside the proprietor held up the palm of his hand, "no, closing!" Why would he be closing at midday?

Not being too concerned I found another close by; again I was told they were closing. Opposite was a tea stall and thought this was as good as any but the stall owner said he was not selling any more food. I offer to buy some boiled eggs he had on his stall but he refused to sell them to me.

I began to despair about where I could eat. It was then I noticed the streets looked almost empty and were definitely quieter which left me perplexed and wondering why.

Not to be put off I set off to find some where on the way

to the beach. Everywhere was the same, in fact it was even quieter as I got further away from the town and became obvious there was no where to eat. The road to the beach was empty, no pedestrians or vehicles of any kind were about.

As the inviting beach came in to view with the rolling surf washing up on to the yellow sand I noticed a man sitting on a low wall. We greeted each other "my names John" and shook hands. Striking up a conversation I impulsively said, "I was trying to find somewhere to eat but everywhere was closing".

"You will not be able to buy any food now it is past midday".

Almost a dumb struck at this comment quizzically asked "why?"

"There was going to be an eclipse" and shook his head as if to emphasis the comment.

I looked at John in disbelief not sure what to say. John quickly explained "it is believed to be bad for your health if you are outside during an eclipse, especially for pregnant women. It is believed you should not eat just before or just after an eclipse".

This is the first time I have ever heard anything like this, "In Britain we don't stay indoors during an eclipse", then pointed out that he was out doors. He looked at me, smiled and said he felt it was a load of mumbo jumbo. We both laughed.

John asked where I was going and replied "to the beach". John said he would walk with me and added he wanted to see the eclipse. The beach looked just like the idyllic

91

picture post card sandy tropical holiday destination. Miles of sandy beach fringed with palm trees as far as the eye can see, and completely deserted.

We sat under a thatched awning with just the sound of the waves. John looked at his watch and said the eclipse will be happening soon. Within minutes the light started to fade as the moon travelled across the sun, birds started to roost and a bird of prey swooped down on to the beach as the temperature cooled slightly which felt pleasant. This lasted for a few minutes then it brightened up and became warm again.

As we sat talking on the wall a small procession arrived along the road. Several men were pushing a bright yellow covered cart with garlands hanging from it and came to a halt just before the beach. I stared mesmerised when John said it is a funeral and asked if I want to have a look.

Taken by surprise at this comment I said they would not want strangers intruding in their funeral.

"It was okay", he got up and walked towards the group of men. I apprehensively followed and felt uncomfortable when I saw them taking the dead person out of the covered cart.

As we approached they all looked towards us then carried on with placing the draped body on the ground. It was a man wrapped head to toe in a cloth with just his face showing; he was slim and did not look very old, about 50ish. There was a small pit where the men placed medium sized logs, then place the dead man on top. Pausing as if saying a prayer we all stood silently for a few minutes then they built up the pyre, covering the dead man with logs and coconut shells. Once completely covered one of the funeral party lit some kindling and place it in a hollow underneath the dead man. The logs caught light straight away fanned by the sea breeze. It was not long before the whole pyre was ablaze engulfing the dead man underneath. Everyone stood silently; I just stared in amazement at how quickly the fire took hold engulfing dead man. The flames started to die down then John suggested we should leave.

Walking away leaving the six men with their dead relative John asked where I was going when I left Cannonore, "I was going to travel south". "You must visit Trivandrum; there is a nice beach where you can watch the sun set". I asked where Trivandrum was and he told me it was on the train line south of Cochin.

After saying good bye to John I made my way back to Cannonore. It was late in the afternoon and some shops were starting to re-open and much to my relief found a tea shop and ate a large palm leaf of rice. After the days events I had lost interest in sight seeing and thought about travelling south. I went to the station to check the train times and found there was a south bound train later that evening, rushing back for my things I quickly packed everything up made it back to the station with plenty of time before the train arrived and had several teas from a tea stall on the almost empty platform. Once on the train I fell straight to sleep.

Waking the next morning, there was still some way to go before the train arrived at Trivandrum. I watched the country side roll by with fleeting views of Kerala's sleepy

93

backwaters edged with palm trees, it looked very inviting. At long last the train pulled in to Trivandrum, disembarking I followed the signs for the beach, on the way passing a number of walls daubed with a large red hammer and sickle with large writing in Hindi next to it, they obviously took their politics seriously in Trivandrum. I came to a sign for the beach that pointed down some wooden steps which descended under a tree canopy. The steps turned sharply to the left to be met by a glorious wide beach with gentle waves lapping on to the sand, edged with tall over hanging palm trees. On the right at the bottom was an open fronted tea shop, three large windows faced out on to the beach.

Stepping down on to the soft warm sand and went straight in to the tea shop and sat down at a wooden bench by one of the windows with a panoramic view looking up the beach. Some four hundred yards away were a group of white people by a thatched roof hut. Having finished eating and needing some accommodation I walked up to the thatched hut to see if any one knew where there might be somewhere to stay for a few nights.

The crowd was lively and looked as if they were having a beach party. Before I had the chance to talk to anyone a guy held out his hand "hello I'm Tom, do you need somewhere to stay?"

Taken by surprise I replied "yes".

Tom exclaimed there was a spare bed in the hut he was staying in and pointed to a small low walled structure that was about eight feet tall topped with palms, it was not much bigger than a large shed. Looking in side it was

94

very basic with one window and a flimsy looking wooden bunk. I tentatively asked how much it cost per night, "I will go and find out for you". Tom vanished in to the rear of the thatched hut and soon reappeared, "5 rupees". Enquiring where I could wash, Tom pointed to a well, "there", at 5 rupees what could I expect, it was on a beach less than 50 yards from the sea. "I'll stay" but felt a bit reluctant about my things maybe being stolen but decided to take a chance.

Now on Trivandrum Beach the first thing I wanted to do was go for a swim in the Arabian Sea. Fishing my goggles from my rucksack in a hope there was some thing worth seeing under the water. I was surprised that no body swimming, it then crossed my mind that maybe this was a common haunt for sharks but throwing caution to the wind I dived in to the clear water. Close by was a large rock that jutted out from the beach for about 30 yards, waves rolled up over it.

The force of the waves buffeted me towards the rock but I managed to keep away from it and dived down in to the marine world.

The sea floor dropped away quickly and soon found myself in about 20 feet of water. The rock was teeming with small vividly coloured fish bobbing about in the current. I could not believe my luck, they did not rush off to hide but stayed where they were.

Staying under water for as long as I could watching the fish as the waves rocked me backwards and forwards making it difficult to keep still in one spot. I resurfaced, took a deep breath then swam back down again. Each time I tried to get as close as possible to the fish conscious of the sharp rock. I don't know how long I spent diving around the rock; loosing all sense of time with the excitement. Eventually getting out of the water I walked up the beach to the thatched hut, somebody sarcastically asked me if I had found any treasure.

Excitedly I explained there was a large shawl of fish down by the rocks but the reply I got was a nonchalant "Oh really".

After my exhilarating swim and a quick wash with the cold water from the well I walked along the beach beyond the tea shop. Here the beach vanished in to the distance with hardly anybody else about. There were dugout canoes and wooden planks lying out on the sand. Walking along this stretch of beach it felt like a different place from the other end of Trivandrum Beach with hardly any body about, just like a tropical paradise with a gentle sea breeze and the waves breaking on the sand. I ambled along the beach for some distance feeling the soft sand between my toes. The sun was starting to dip in the sky and made my way back to the tea shop for something to eat.

As I sat in the tea shop crowds gathered at the water's edge to watch the sun set as it vanished over the horizon casting its last rays of sunlight. As the last glimmer of sun light faded the crowds dispersed leaving an almost empty beach. The crowd by the thatched hut were now silhouetted by the lanterns. I joined the boisterous crowd and bought a cold drink. There was a multitude of accents from around the world; it was hard not to get carried along with the light hearted atmosphere as it went on until late when the revellers started to leave. It got to the point where I was feeling tired and decided to turn in. Without any light I fumbled about in the dark but managed to find my bunk and settle down to a peaceful sleep.

The next morning I got up unsure what time it was. Using the water from the well I poured a bucket of very cold water over my head then washed myself then threw several more buckets of water over my head. Feeling refreshed I went for some breakfast. Having eaten I decided to do some more snorkelling on the rocks, not wanting to miss the opportunity of watching the fish. I spent several hours snorkelling around the rock swimming out to the far end, even though it was not too far out the water was quite deep.

When I had finished snorkelling I decided to go back in to Trivandrum to find out about the train times. There was a train that evening at 11p.m. heading south to Cape Comorin (Kanyakumari), the very southern tip of India and decided to catch it. I went back to the hut and packed my things in to my rucksack ready. I hung around the hut with the other backpackers making most of the time on Trivandrum Beach. Everyone was talking about where they were planning to go next, most were travelling north, none seemed to have been to Cape Comorin which was disappointing, I had hoped to find out where I could stay. Saying good bye to several back packers I made my way to the station and waited on the platform, I didn't want to miss the train and waited in the first class waiting room. The waiting room was large and airy with a shower which was a welcome relief. I bought some food from a tea stall on the platform. Asking for my metal mug to be filled up, the stall holder refused, asking for three glasses of tea instead and poured them in to the mug much to the amusement of the stall holder. The train eventually arrived and seemed to be half empty which I thought was a good omen; there should be plenty of room available in the guest houses at Cape Comorin.

The train arrived at a quiet Cape Comorin station early the next morning; being so early I felt there should be a guest house with an empty room. No rooms were available in the first one; they were booked up for the week.

Unperturbed I went to the next guest house, they said the same thing.

Trying several other guest houses and hotels I got the same answer each time, no rooms were available. I had been looking forward to sleeping in a comfortable bed but this was not going to happen.

Contemplating what to do I followed a path that led round by the sea to some sand dunes that towered above the road, the reflected light from the pale sand and sea was dazzling. It occurred to me I could camp out in these sand dunes, it seemed as if it would be safe enough. Making my way across the sand I noticed an elderly man walking towards me, he called out "how are you?" then inquisitively asked where I was staying. I told him that there was no where to stay in Kanyakumari so I was going to camp in the sand dunes. He smiled, "you will not find a room, many pilgrims will be arriving this week, Cape Comorin is an important place for Hindu's".

You must not camp in the sand dunes, without saying why he suggested I could stay at his guest house. This sounded like good news, I was going to sleep in a bed and maybe have a shower. He pointed to a small palm leaf structure in the middle of the sand dunes all by it self. It was about the size of a family tent with an apex roof. I found it inconceivable that somebody would be living here let alone having guests.

"Come, have a look".

Walking towards the small structure it looked well-constructed and sturdy.

Inside there were several compartments divided by palm leaf panels. The owner of this very modest shelter had his own small room which faced south. I asked how much he charged, he smiled and said "nothing! All you have to do is get up early each morning to watch the sun rise".

Feeling there must be a catch but was reassured this is all I had to do, watch the sun rise; The owner asked if I smoked Marijuana,

emphatically replied "no",

"good, we get raided by the police now and then".

Having agreed to stay I was surprisingly asked to book in and an official visitor's log book was produced.

The owner of the guest house pointed out the different nationalities of his visitors; they were German, British, American, Mexican, French, Australian and many more. Looking down the list I saw one guest who called "Just in Space". Next to the name was a cartoon of a dustbin with crossed eyes and stars swirling around the lopsided bin lid. Reading the comments many said how much they had

99

enjoyed staying here. I was shown my own compartment which was six feet long and about four feet wide, just enough room for me and my rucksack. At this point it crossed my mind that there were no washing facilities, realising it would be a silly question I refrained from asking where they were. Having organised myself I set off for town.

Kanyakamari was a small town. Just outside of Kanyakamari in view of my guest house at the water front was the Mahatma Gandhi Memorial, a large pink and white building with a curved roof with an Art Nuevo appearance. Once past the memorial I was on the edge of town close to the bazar with its arched entrance. Inside the bazar were market stalls selling a variety of crafts such as hand woven lamp shades, paper machete boxes, and religious carvings.

Several children tried to sell me necklaces they had made from small shells, the work looked intricate but I didn't really want to buy any. As I went to walk away they insistently brandished their craft work with broad smiles. It was obvious that I was not going to get away without buying any. Pretending to look at each necklace I chose five and paid the few rupees they wanted. After looking around each market stall I left the bazaar to look at the temple which Cape Comorin is famous for, The Devi Kanya Kumari Temple built on a large rock some 500 yards off shore, which struck me as an amazing fete of engineering.

By now I was feeling hungry and found a suitable tea room to eat, entering I shouted Chai, picked up a large palm leaf to show I wanted to eat some rice and a waiter came over with a large bowl and ladled the rice on to the palm leaf, after several scoops I had to tell him to stop. I attracted some quizzical glances; possibly some of the Indians were surprised to see a white person in Kanyakamari. Having been the centre of attention so many times I ignored them and ate my meal instinctively with my left hand.

Having eaten I set off to explore the town and try my luck at the guest houses again for any available room. After several frustrating enquiries I gave up and made my way back to my austere accommodation. Just above the Mahatma Gandhi Memorial I sat down on the warm sand, the sun was starting to get low in the sky as I soaked up the warm evening sun, the sea breeze gently cooled the evening air.

A number of people gathered on the shore line to watch the sun set as it slowly dropped down in to the sea, lighting the sky with a vivid orange hue, a fitting end to an interesting day. Back to the palm leaf hut I checked my large ruck sack and as promised it was all still there. It was still relatively early and seemed a shame to not make the most of my time at Cape Comorin. Walking back in to town I headed for the bazaar. It was lit up with hanging lanterns. It was busier and had a vibrant exotic atmosphere with the aroma of joss sticks wafting through the covered market. It was an atmosphere that I had not experienced anywhere else, it felt relaxing. Everyone was so friendly here in Kanyakamari, maybe because it was a place of Hindu pilgrimage.

101

After wandered around the streets and stopping at several tea stalls to sample their biscuits I made my way back to the palm leaf guest house, a lone lantern shone in the inky blackness like a beacon showing the way through the undulating sand dunes. The other guests were sitting around and talking. All were western nationals; I was the only British person. I recognised Miguel, a Mexican who me and Rolf met in Mysore. There were 2 American's a German and an Italian. We all exchanged our experiences of what we had seen so far and where was the best place to go next. One of the Americans mentioned that he had come over from Sri Lanka via the ferry. Quizzing him about this I asked where the ferry sailed from. "The ferry leaves Ramaswaram each day" Looking at my map by the light of the lantern, Ramasweram was not far along the coast from Kanyakamari, as the crow flies. By train I would have to go via Madurai.

After a long fascinating conversation about Sri Lanka I decided to go there. It sounded so nice, the idyllic break from India. All of the others were heading north either back to Bombay to fly home, over to Calcutta or up to Nepal. Calcutta and Nepal sounded like exciting options to Kashmir. Eventually we all turned in for the night, someone spotted my large towel as I fished it out of my rucksack and asked where I got it from.

"I bought it in El Salvador",

everyone laughed, "they must be very cosmopolitan in El Salvador to sell towels with Egyptian hieroglyphics printed on them" came a reply. Once the lamp was out I quickly fell asleep on the soft warm sand, the best mattress ever.

The next morning I woke just as the sun was starting appear over the horizon. Everybody else was up sitting out on the sand cross legged waiting for the sun to climb up over the horizon. I was asked to have a look at the sun by the guest house owner.

"I can see the sun from here laying down",

"you need to be sitting up to appreciate the full experience" came the reply. Not wanting to disappoint my host I got up and joined the others, the sun warmed my face, arms and legs and added to the visual experience with the anticipation of another idyllic warm day.

The sun rise felt just as spectacular as the sunset, painting the sky in a bright luminous orange which silhouetted the Devi Kanya Kumari temple off the shore. The sky changed to a yellow and then a pale blue. It suddenly struck me travelling due south from Cape Comorin across the Indian Ocean the next stop is the Antarctic. If you travelled east there was Australia and west there was Southern Africa.

Once the sun was up in the sky I organised myself and set off in to town for some breakfast. Whilst eating and checking my map to see where Rameswaram I decided there was not much else to see in Kanyakumari and might as well catch the train to Madurai and then to Rameswaram. I couldn't wait to travel to Sri Lanka.

At the station I tried to book a seat, producing my Indrail Ticket the booking clerk pointed out that it had expired, "you have to buy a proper train ticket". Disappointed I reluctantly bought a 'proper train ticket' for the 9 pm train to Madurai. Deciding to travel second class because it was a short distance and unlikely to be too uncomfortable. This gave me more than enough time to look around Kanyakamari and be at the station on time. I reflected on having been in India for over a month, the time seemed to have flown by and had been exciting.

After spending the rest of the day ambling around the streets I went back to collect my things and say my good byes which surprised everyone. After explaining I wanted to go to Sri Lanka, they all understood.

Thanking the guest house owner for letting me stay for such a memorable experience which I will never forget I made my way to the station. Checking the information board for the correct platform, carriage number and bogie and found the train already waiting and already packed full.

There did not seem to be any space on the wooden benches or on the floor but a family made room for me and offered me a seat on the already packed bench. I struggled to squeeze my large rucksack in which I laid under my feet so my knees were up almost under my chin and kept my small rucksack on my lap.

The carriage was stiflingly hot with so many people crammed in on the benches and the carriage floor. I became the centre of attention; people were talking excitedly in Hindi and touching my arms. I tried to brush them off with a smile at first but this made them laugh and touch me even more. Deciding it was best to ignore their unwanted attention and eventually they lost interest in me.

As the train pulled out of Kanyakamari Station some families started eating whilst others settled down to sleep. They obviously had all done this before as the families arranged themselves so they could sleep comfortably. Holding on to my rucksack, I wrapped my arms through the straps making it as inconspicuous as possible that I was guarding it. As the evening wore on passengers started to settle down to sleep. Eventually fatigue took over, no matter how much I tried to stay awake and drifted off to sleep with my head leaning on the rucksack.

Rameswaram; the Gateway to Sri Lanka

Waking suddenly in the dark, the carriage was stiflingly
hot, it felt excruciating. My T shirt was drenched with
sweat, but reassuringly I was still holding my small
rucksack. Every one appeared to be asleep; it was
surprisingly quiet considering how many passengers there
were sleeping on the benches and the floor. Sitting still in
the dark I appreciated the silence of the packed carriage
but looked forward to arriving in Madurai. Even though I
felt tired my cramped position and the excitement of
visiting Madurai kept me awake, unsure what to expect
but knew it was going to be interesting and exciting.
After what felt like an uncomfortable eternity the first hint
of light lifted the dark veil in the carriage, slowly other
passengers started to wake and the quiet chatter gradually
grew louder. Nobody was paying any attention to me
now, they were interested in their families and eating. As
the sun rose higher in the sky the carriage became warmer
until it was almost unbearable.
At long last the train arrived in Madurai. Not many
passengers were getting off and I had to climb over those
sitting on the floor, some waved good bye. Politely
waving back I breathed a sigh of relief to be get off. It felt
pleasantly warm standing on the platform after having
spent the night on the stifling hot train. I needed a shower
and even though I did not have a first class ticket I
thought I would go into the waiting room where I knew

there would be one. Luckily no body questioned me and had a long cold shower; it felt so good to be clean and to cool down. Reluctant to come out from under the cool water, it felt like the best thing in the world but Madurai was waiting to be explored. Putting on clean clothes I found a tea stall on the platform which sold hard boiled eggs; that was breakfast sorted.

After dropping off my large rucksack at left luggage I bought a tourist map and left the station to be confronted with roads jam packed with pedestrians, the sort of crowds I had not seen since Bombay. The only difference here the roads were a lot narrower. The noise was almost deafening with the traffic, people talking, the clatter of the cart wheels and music. A temple was prominently marked on the map and headed for it closely following the streets on my map, weaving my way around the narrow crowded streets avoiding the rickshaws, carts, pedestrians and the cows on the pavement was a feat of nimble foot work.

Turning in to a plaza I was confronted by a large imposing pyramid shaped tower that over shadowed the surrounding buildings. The tower had hundreds of hand painted gods and deities set on it looking down at those below as if passing judgement from above.

I found the entrance to the temple and walked in side, it was instantly peaceful and a lot cooler. Surprisingly I was the only white person.

Inside the temple were murals and statues of different gods. One mural was dedicated to Krishna showing his life story, it also had some text in English explaining the

107

life of this god.

I spent a few hours in the temple soaking up the Hindu culture, it felt serene and relaxing, so different to the hustle and bustle of Madurai outside. Having only had the boiled eggs for breakfast I needed some sustenance and find a place to stay for the night. Once outside the noise of the street hit me and seemed even louder, how anybody could live in such a noisy place was beyond me.

Finding a crowded tea shop to eat, it felt uncomfortable sitting opposite someone just feet away as they ate their rice. Quickly eating I collected my ruck sack from the Stations left luggage to find some where to stay. This seemed virtually impossible, no hotels or guest houses were marked on my map. My map showed a bridge scross a river, I wondered if there was a hotel on the other side. The long low bridge was busy with every type of traffic imaginable and pedestrians but crossing it I noticed how quieter it was. Once on the other side all of the deafening noise was just a distant buzz. It felt much more peaceful, looking back at the crowds on the other side of the bridge going about Madurai I did not feel like going back too soon.

Looking around all I could see were open fields, no buildings and wondered where I was going to stay for the night. In the distance I saw what looked like mountains and realised this was the Western Ghats, it did not look to far away and headed off towards them along the quiet straight road; also in hope of finding a small guest house along the way.

Having walked for several kilometres the mountains were

not getting any closer and there were no sign of any buildings until I came across a road side vegetable stall, several men were standing next to it. Smiling, they all said something in Hindi which I took for a greeting and said hello back. Choosing some vegetables I impulsively decided to camp out for the night in the middle of the Indian countryside. I bought a several small potatoes and some eggs and carried on walking towards the mountains. The sun was starting to get low in the sky and I needed to find a suitable place to camp. I came across a dry paddy field with a small pond set back from the road. The water looked clean and did not taste strange so I decided this would be the ideal spot. Gathering some twigs and small branches for a fire, collected some water in my can then placed the potatoes under the fire wood. I didn't feel like putting up my tent especially when the ground was rock hard and impossible to driving a tent peg in.

The small fire crackled creating embers which covered the potatoes. By the time they were ready it was dark. I fished the potatoes out of the embers then placed the billy can amongst them. The potato skins looked black, felt crunchy and tasted of charcoal on the outside but in side they were perfect, a welcome meal. By the time I had finished eating the water was hot enough to make some tea. Sipping my tea in the pitch black I looked up at the stars directly overhead, they sparkled brightly, there were so many. The embers eventually fizzled out leaving me without any light; it was time to settle down. Pulling my large towel up over my head and using the large ruck sack as a pillow I soon drifted off to sleep.

The early morning chill woke me just as the dawn was starting to break. Getting up I lit a fire to boil the eggs. As the sun rose in the sky it warmed the air and felt more comfortable. Once the eggs were cooked I used the water to make a tea, whilst drinking it I deliberated over whether to carry on walking towards the mountains or walk back to Madurai. Eventually I decided to walk back to Madurai where I could catch the train to Rameswaram for the Sri Lankan ferry. Having eaten I got my things together and set off along the now busy road. All of the traffic was heading towards Madurai, most loaded with vegetables but some carried hay and other goods.

By the time I arrived back in Madurai it was mid morning, the noise was just as intense as the previous day which convinced me that I should get the next train out of town. At the station I battled with the usual queues but now I was more adept at crowding out any one pushing in by putting a ruck sack either side of me and deftly leaning in the direction of any miscreant. For those who were a bit more persistent I raise my elbow up which seemed to do the trick.

The train to Rameswaram was that evening giving me some time to look around Madurai a bit more but once I got my ticket I could not find the energy to walk around this noisy city and sat around on the platform watching the different people going about their business as passengers got on and off the trains, porters carried heavy luggage on their heads and those standing at the tea stalls. Some looked calm as if they had everything organised, others appeared quite frantic and where there were groups such as families appeared to sit and deliberate at great length without really going anywhere.

Observing all of these people going about their daily business gave me bit of an insight in to the Indian psyche. After numerous teas the train eventually arrived, it seemed as though the whole platform was trying to get on to the same carriage as me, I could see why the carriages had metal bars at the windows when things got this frantic I imagined a lot of people would climb through the window. I squeezed in to the crowd that was getting on to my carriage and was literally pushed on to the train from those behind me in a similar fashion as a herd of cattle might nudge and barge. Once on the train I surprisingly managed to find a seat and flopped down on to the wooden bench, glad to be leaving Madurai as thoughts of Sri Lanka filled my mind, wondering what it was going to be like and will it be a hectic as India. First I had to get to Rameswaram for the ferry.

The journey from Madurai to Rameswaram is not far, just over hundred miles but it still took all night to get there. I got some sleep but kept waking up, maybe the thought of somebody taking my things played on my mind. The train arrived at Rameswaram early the next morning. The station was Spartan with just a platform and lighting, different to the stations I had seen so far where they had waiting rooms and some where to eat, there wasn't even a tea stall. The walk from the station in to Rameswaram was a few hundred metres along a wide tarmacked road which had a dusting of sand. The buildings looked as if they had just been planted straight on to the sand either

111

side of the wide road. Street venders selling tea lined the road, more than I had seen in other towns. The buildings varied from modest dwellings made of wood and palm leaves to large multi-roomed homes and guest houses. I noticed that there was a faint aroma of seaweed or fish which I put this down as the smell of the sea. A young boy asked if I needed somewhere to stay and before I could answer he said "follow me", not knowing my way it made sense. Following my guide through Rameswaram I saw some white people which took me by surprise and found myself staring at them as they waved. One thing that stood out above all of the other buildings was a temple spire, this towered above the roof tops, even of the two story buildings, we seemed to be heading in its direction which was exciting. Wandering through the streets it felt my guide was taking me on a guided tour of Rameswaram as we weaved around various streets past numerous shops. When I asked if it was much further he assured me that it was not far and sure enough it wasn't. We reached the far end of town, turned a corner and standing alone on the shore was a building painted bright red, white and yellow, it would not be out of place on any British coastal resort. In side it was light and airy with windows all around, a patio door lead out on to a fenced off patch of sand. Thanking the boy for his help I gave him 3 rupees which was his cue to run off leaving me at the reception desk where a middle aged man was standing.

"Yes! Can I help you?"

"Do you have any rooms" I asked in expectation.

He replied with a smile and a shake of the head "I am afraid there are no rooms".

Disappointed at not having a bed to sleep on or a shower, and not in the mood to walk around Rameswaram to find another guest house I asked if it was possible to pitch my tent out on the patch of sand.

The man shook his head and beamed "yes of course". "How much?"

after a short pause he said "four rupees",

smiling to myself in almost jubilation replied "thank you".

The view from the guest house and my tent looked amazing. Rameswaram sat on a long sweeping bay that stretched for over a kilometre, I had a view of the waterfront with the white or light beige buildings and moored boats. In the distance I could make out what looked like the ferry terminal. The bay was edged with almost pure white sand with palm trees dotted along the bay.

Having pitched my tent I went to book my ticket for the Sri Lankan ferry. Following the road back towards the train station, past the buildings and tea stalls, the temple with one of the tallest spires I had seen so far in India, which I had too visit.

Just past the turning for the train station the buildings were more modest, wooden structures with corrugated roofs. Each one had a small stall in the front and appeared be a home. At a junction a sign saying "Ferry" pointed left, the smell of seaweed or fish was distinctly stronger. Turning the corner the ferry terminal was directly in front of me, it was a low metal structure with a corrugated roof. The bottom half of the structure had corrugated boarding around the outside and wire fencing between the boarding and the roof. There was a small queue of mostly white people with a mixture of European, Australian and American accents. Not long after I had joined the back of the queue a man in a beige uniform shouted "No more", pulled across a shutter with a jarring of metal against metal then the sound of a pad lock and chain as it was secured.

The disappointment from those who had been waiting for some time was very audible, one person in the queue made a comment about missing the ferry again. I was surprised that the queue for the ferry was suddenly cut off, how did I get a ticket? Calling through the metal wiring I got the attention of one of the Beige Uniformed men and asked how I could buy a ticket for the ferry. He replied "you have to queue in the morning and wait. If you are early enough you will get on the ferry".

I asked if I could buy a ferry ticket now ready for tomorrow.

Smiling retorted "no tomorrow!"

The others who had been queuing had already left which was disappointing, I was hoping to find out where they were staying and if they knew if there were any rooms available. As I had to wait until the next day I felt there was just one thing to do, explore Rameswaram.

Turning left at the sign post junction I followed the sandy road further around the bay. After a short distance I came across a small temple with one entrance which led to a

114

walkway leading around a central pool. The water did not look inviting at all, it was coated in green alga and had branches protruding from it. What was interesting about this temple were the carvings. They were typically Indian but covered every part of the temple; the pillars, ceiling and arch ways. Inside the temple it was cool giving a welcome relief from the late morning heat and stayed for some time making the most of the cool shade. A few people walked around the temple but then left.

Eventually leaving I made my way back through the streets towards the guest house stopping of at various shops along the way. Some sold Indian woodwork and craft work. I had seen a lot of Indian carving and woodwork especially in Mysore, here it looked equally amazing such as tables with inlays and intricately carved legs, elephants of all sizes, wooden inlayed pictures similar to the one I had bought in Mysore of the tiger by the lake, a typical image I had hoped to have seen at the Periyar Wild Life Sanctuary. Other work included chess sets with the pieces carved out of bone depicting ancient Indian soldiers on foot, elephants and camels.

Occasionally stopping at various tea stalls, not so much to try the tea but to sample the coconut biscuits which were the best I had tasted so far in India. There was one stall in particular that had the best biscuits, they obviously had a secret recipe.

As I slowly made my way around the streets I kept noticing the temple spire which hogged the Rameswaram skyline, subconsciously I was drawn towards it and found myself at the entrance. It had a large stone carved

115

archway with a low stone balcony to one side. Sitting on the balcony was an elderly man who looked like a Sadhu with his face painted white and a red mark down the middle of his forehead. He appeared to be guarding the doorway, as I went to walk inside he said "no!" Looking at him with a surprised expression, tilted my head to one side and held out my hands with the palms facing up as if to ask "why". The man pointed at my feet which confused me at first then I realised he wanted me to take my sandals off.

I handed the man my sandals with their heavy lorry tire soles and was given a numbered token back. Walking under the high arch in to the temple from the hot sun there was an instant chill that made the hairs on my arms stand up. Inside the temple the light was subdued, it looked cavernous with its high ceiling. Broad stone pillars were tall and intricately carved and had a girth similar a Giant Redwood tree trunk. They followed the corridor every twenty feet or so leading around the edge of the temple and supported a ceiling decorated with a floral design. I followed the corridor where it turned right and was instantly awestruck to see the corridor stretched for over a hundred yards with more pillars with the same detail. I stopped to admire the view thinking that the temple had been built several centuries ago with all of the carving which must have taken thousands of people to construct it. Eventually the cool temperature though welcome was starting to feel cold and decided to leave.

At the door I felt through my pockets for the numbered token but could not find it, looking around it was not on

116

the floor either. Retracing me steps in the temple it was nowhere to seen. Thinking it wouldn't matter too much I explained to the man I had lost it, smiled and asked for my sandals. The elderly man asked for my token. Shrugging my shoulders I reiterated that I had lost it and again asked for my sandals.

The man then exclaimed "no sandals!"

Explaining again that I had lost the token and pointing at my sandals I said "those are mine" thinking this would help prompt him to hand them to me.

He said "no token, no sandals".

Pointing at the sandals I exclaimed "look at the others, they are different", making it obvious the other sandals were the typically Indian thin soled style but his expression did not change. I suggested that he should let me try them on to prove they fit, then planned to walk away.

But replied "no!"

By now I thought this was getting ridiculous and had to come up with a way of persuading him to give my sandals back, I thought about just grabbing the sandals but there was a chance he might report me to the police which could be awkward. Asking the elderly man if he remembered when I arrived, he replied "yes", "what sandals did I give you?"

He pointed to my sandals. Exasperatingly I asked "if you know they are mine why can't I have my sandals back?" He replied "you don't have a token". Inquisitively I asked who he was going to give the sandals to, he looked at me, paused and said "you when I have the token".

117

Out of desperation I reluctantly asked "can I pay for the lost token",
immediately he said "yes";
"how much"?
"5 rupees" he replied. Reluctantly I handed over 5 rupees, slipped the sandals on and walked off to find myself a tea stall
Remembering that there were a row of tea stalls in one of the streets not far away I headed for them. Whilst the stall owner was making my tea I pondered what biscuit to have with it. Being undecided what to choose from his display I had one of each which took the stall owner by surprise. He handed me the biscuits which I slowly ate as if testing them. One of the biscuits was made with coconut which tasted so good. Having drunk my tea and eaten the best coconut biscuit ever I headed back to my tent with the intention to go down to the beach just beyond the guest house for a swim.
Grabbing my diving mask from my rucksack I rushed off along the beach. On the beach hidden behind the sand dunes were some small rafts made of four wooden planks that were strung together; similar to those laid out on the beach at Trivandrum. Nobody was about for me to ask if I could borrow one. Thinking it would be okay to take one out to dive from I hauled it to the water's edge. I found a paddle hidden in the long grass, it was a pole with small rounded flat blades secured either end. Digging a hole in the soft sand amongst the grass I buried my small rucksack and placed my sandals on top to mark where the rucksack was. As I hauled the raft down to the water I

118

wondered if it would float. It bobbed about on the small waves as I gave the raft a hefty push, at the same time waded out and climbed on board.

Paddling the raft was considerably easy to control as it floated out from the shore, looking down the water was absolutely clear and about 15 to 20 feet deep. Some fish were swimming around a large boulder, it looked ideal for snorkelling. Looking back I was some 200 yards from the shore.

Placing the paddle on the raft I slipped in to the surprisingly warm sea and dived down to the sandy sea bed. Large symmetrical boulders some 3 or 4 yards across dotted the sea bed as if they had been lobbed there. Resurfacing to get my breath I dived down to one of the boulders, it was covered in barnacles, sea urchins, shells and small corals. Swimming in between the crevices were small brightly coloured fish. Hanging on to the side of the raft I noticed it had drift away from the shore, and realised I had to kept an eye on it whilst diving. Back under the water it amazed me how clear it was, I was able to see for some thirty maybe even fifty yards and would be able to see a shark prowling about. This was something that had not crossed my mind so far but it would be exhilarating and a bit precarious if one did happen to come wandering by. I swam around another boulder looking at the small fishes and coral that populated the rock.

After having dived down several more times I climbed back on to the raft and noticed that it had drifted further from the shore, a good 400 yards or so. Paddling back to the shore I noticed somebody on the beach who seemed to be watching me. Pulling the raft out of the water on to the sand was a struggle. The boy who had been watching me walked over and told me I had taken his uncles boat. Apologising I explained no one was about and thought it would be okay to borrow it.

"I am sure my uncle would not mind" he replied.

Pulling the raft up to where I had found it was difficult because I had been paddling and diving, also the raft was wet. Looking for my sandals the boy pointed to where they were. Glad to have found them I dug up my rucksack. The boy pointed out that nobody would ever take my sandals, they were far too heavy which made me laugh then said fare well and walked back to my tent letting the sun dry me off.

I was feeling hungry now and wondered if the guest house did any meals. Asking at the desk I was given a menu, the usual Indian meals such as Biryani were on it and some western style food such as omelettes, fried eggs, boiled eggs which tended to be hard boiled and fish with vegetables. I asked for the fish, having only eaten rice and fruit since Cochin. My meal arrived with steam rising from it, the fish had been slightly grilled with the head left on; the meal was one of the best I had so far in India. After finishing I set off to find out what Rameswaram was like at night.

Rameswaram was just as lively at night if not more. There were more tea stalls and shops were still open lit with lanterns which creating a carnival atmosphere. I wandered from stall to stall sampling the biscuits popped in to different shops and came across somebody selling reed mats which most people used in India to lay on, especially those who had to sleep on the pavement. Night life was lively in Rameswaram which was surprising considering Rameswaram was a small town. People were sitting at tables in tea shops talking over a glass of tea but I just wanted to enjoy the cool evening air and walked from shop to shop. Being conscious I had to be up early the next day for the ferry and made my way back for an early night.

Waking the next morning the sun was already up, the inside of the tent felt warm. Realising it was late I rushed around packing things away, took down my tent and shoved it in to my rucksack. Rushing to the ferry terminal I grabbed food from a stall on the way. By the time I arrived there was a long queue but felt sure I would get on the ferry.

There was lively chatter between the people in the queue with so many different accents. American; English, both southern and northern; German; Australian and New Zealand, there was also a large number of Indians and Sinhalese. Every now and then there would be a disgruntled comment as some one pushed in at the front of the queue which was moving slow enough as it was. This all added to the lively atmosphere and excitement of getting on to the ferry.

Some vendors sold snacks and drinks, an elderly woman was working her way along the queue asking for Paisa and was given some money by several backpackers as they off loaded their small change. The queue was getting shorter and the anticipation of actually being able to get on the ferry was showing as conversations became livelier. Then suddenly, just like the previous day a man called out that the ferry was full. Some at the front of the queue tried to negotiate and be allowed on but the gate was pulled across and pad locked.

Feeling disappointed and unable to believe I was not up early enough decided to find a room close by. A man in a sarong asking if anybody wanted to stay in his hostel but nobody paid any attention to him. He asked me if I needed somewhere to stay. Replying "yes" thinking he was working for a hotel or guest house near by, "where is it". The man flung out his hand and pointed to a palm leaf constructed hut that was very similar to the place I had stayed in at Cape Comorin but this was taller and wider. "Can I look inside",

"yes, look" and followed the man through the wide entrance. In side I could see it had a rudimentary wooden frame, light filtered through the gaps between the palm leaves making it easy to see inside, surprisingly there were wooden bunks. Being opposite the ferry terminal it was ideal, and there was a bunk to sleep on; perfect. Asking how much he charged the man replied five rupees a night, "I'll stay!" I had to sign in the visitor's book and noticed that Justin Space had been here. There were a few other staying, saying 'hi' to each other we exchanged stories about our time in India. I told them about Olluvakod, they all seemed to be surprised I had stayed in such a place. After placing my rucksack under a spare bunk I went for a walk around this end of Rameswaram. Running alongside the customs office jetty was a quay jutting out from the shore. The smell of the sea weed and fish here was extremely strong. Some boats were moored up at the far end and a number of men stood as if to be deliberating over something. Unable to curb my curiosity I walked down to them, they appeared to be looking at what seemed like a pile of debris on the wooden boarding. There was an assortment of shells in amongst wet seaweed, not saying anything I bent down, picked up a mollusc shell and raked in amongst the shells and seaweed, one of the shells had a pattern similar to one indigenous to the Indian Ocean known to be poisonous. Then I noticed a small stone fish with its ugly bulbous eyed face and long thorny dorsal fin, it was surprisingly small and could easily be missed if you was walking along the beach. One of the fishermen called out "no!" and reached down to stop me touching it, not that I intended to. Picking it up carefully by its tail fin he deftly threw it in to the sea. I was disappointed at first but appreciated his concern for my safety.

I hung around on the quay listening to their joyful banter and wondered if they did boat trips but they shook their heads. Eventually saying good bye to the fishermen; they all smiled and waved as I left them. Leaving the quay I headed towards the high sand dunes on the edge of town which towered above the buildings. The road was lined with palm trees as it left the last dwellings behind. A horse was being washed down in a pond by its owner, a little further on I left the road and climbed the high sand dunc. It took some effort walking on the soft fine sand, with each step I slide backwards but eventually I made it to the top. Looking back I was standing high above Rameswaram. In the other direction the sand dunes undulated off in to the distance for several kilometres jutting out in to the bright blue Indian Ocean. There was no shade at the top; the sand was exposed to the direct sun light which scorched my feet. Directly below the sand dunes were three women in bright pink, red and yellow sarees. They had red clay pots and looked as if they were sitting at a well. I had a clear view of the small pond where the man was standing up to his waist as he washed his horse. Sitting on the sand I watched these people doing their daily chores and took in the tropical landscape; it was calm, quiet and relaxing, but hot. I thought of trying to walk out to the far end of the sandy peninsula but decided against it, it didn't look like a place to suffer from heat exhaustion. After admiring the scenic view I headed back in to Rameswaram for something to eat, drink and to be in the shade.

I found a small tea shop which was a lot cooler than the sand dunes, calling chai as I collected a palm leaf to eat off, soon a refreshing glass of tea arrived at the table. My palm leaf was piled high with rice and I was given three spice dishes for adding to the rice. Quickly eating the rice I left the tea shop to get away from the numerous flies and headed back to the palm hut.

The other back packers were sitting in the shade of the hut keeping out of the midday sun and exchanging travelling stories. I was asked about some of the countries I had visited. Everyone was particularly interested in Kenya and Belize. The stories went on in to the evening whilst we drank tea from a shop close by. It was late and having to be up early in the morning for the ferry I made the excuse I needed to get some sleep, the hut owner said he would wake me up in time for the ferry.

Early the next morning I woke, got myself organised before a queue for the ferry had started. The hostel owner asked me if I wanted to leave my luggage with him, explaining that some people who planned to return to India leave their heavy luggage with him so they don't have to carry it. I declined the offer and thought why would you leave your thinks here? But asked if I could have mail sent to his hut, he said this was okay and gave me the full address. It was surprising that a temporary building like this would have a proper address; it showed how organised things were in India.

Signing out in the visitor's book I joined the ferry queue. There was the usual banter about various places some of the backpackers had been and where they were going in Sri Lanka. Most of the other passengers seemed to be heading for the surf at Colombo. Being so close to the front of the queue I felt excited and soon made it to the ticket kiosk, producing my passport and paying for the ticket I was able to board the ferry, third time lucky. Having bought my ferry ticket I followed the directions of the customs officials and walked out of the cool interior on to the long Quay.

We were directed to climb down the wooden steps on to one of the three moored barges tethered together. As I climbed down a couple with a large BMW motorbike were being helped by the crew to lower it on to the barge.

The couple looked concerned and instructed the crew helping to be careful, "don't drop it in the sea". With the care anyone would give a baby the motorbike was slowly lowered on to the barge. Once all of the barges were full we were towed out to the waiting ferry some four hundred yards off shore. Climbing aboard most of us made our way to the top deck where I made myself comfortable and settled down to write some long overdue letters, there was a lot to write about and of course to let everyone know of my contact address at the palm leaf hut.

Once the last passenger was on board the ladder was hauled up. There was a faint rumbling sound from the ferry's engine as it started up. After a pause it started to move gently turning south in the direction of Sri Lanka. A cheer went up from the back packers as the ferry slowly set sail on a perfectly calm sea. At long last I was on my way to Sri Lanka, not knowing what to expect and where I was going but looking forward to whatever adventure might be waiting for me.

Part Two
My brush with Buddhism

Tea with George, a font of knowledge

The ferry arrived in Sri Lanka after dark at Mannar
Island; the excitement was tangible as the ferry docked
alongside the quay. Passengers hurriedly disembarked
down the gang plank and were met by the waiting
customs officers on the station platform. Passports were
checked with a cursory glance then we were directed to
board the waiting train. Backpackers jostled for a seat in
the dimly lit carriage as we stowed our baggage where
ever we could. I managed to find a seat close to the door
in one of the carriages which quickly filled up with back
packers and their luggage, including an Australian with
his surf board.

The last few passengers boarded the train, a whistle blast
broke through the excited chatter and with this signal the
train suddenly jolted then slowly pulled away from the
station. I decided on the boat after talking with other back
backers that I would start my journey around Sri Lanka at
Anuradhapura, a city in the north of the country. Many of
the other backpackers were making their way to
Colombo, the coastal capital of Sri Lanka. Having

considered how slow the trains were in India and thinking it would be some time before the train arrived at Anuradhapura I tried and get some sleep whilst the train travelled south through the moonless night, the trees that lined the train track were just black shadows.

After an hour or so the train slowed down and eventually came to a halt at a dimly lit station, a large sign read Anuradhapura. At the same time the station attendant called out the name of the station. Quickly picking up my rucksacks I left the boisterous carriage, stepping out on to the dark platform I looked around and saw a few other passengers had also got off. The station attendant waved his lantern to signal to the train to carry on its nocturnal journey. The engine blasted smoke up in to the air as it took the strain then slowly moved, with each puff of smoke the train gathered speed. I watched as the pact carriages trundled past until the last one left the station and gradually faded behind the dark cloak until it was totally silent.

The others who had got off the train walked along the platform to the exit whispering to each other which seemed appropriate, it was just as quiet as the Periyar Wild Life Sanctuary. We left the platform through an arch in to a covered area that opened out on to a road, nobody was about, or a dog could be heard in the eerie silence. I asked one of the others what the time was, it was 3 am. Not knowing where to go and without any street lighting along the road we all thought it was best to wait until day light. Rolling out my reed mat, I pulled my large towel out of my rucksack. Laying down and pulling the towel over

128

my head with my rucksack as a pillow I fell asleep. Waking to the low chatter of voices, I pulled down the towel I could see the faint light of dawn; the others had been awake the whole time I had slept. Getting up I packed my towel and reed mat away, said good bye to the other back packers and followed a road that lead to some buildings.

Even though the day was breaking it was still quiet, unlike India where the roads would be busy by now and pedestrians going to work. After a short distance a Sinhalese man who was walking towards the station stopped and asked if I needed some where to stay. Replying that I did but was not sure where to go. "You can stay at my house".

Asking where it was he said "follow me; it is not far". As we walked along the road he asked me where I was from. When I told him I was from Britain this triggered an avalanche of questions about England and Britain. I did my best to answer them without sounding too blasé. We passed a pond and came to a row of homely sturdy wooden buildings with small front gardens with a low wooden fence and gate. Stopping at a gate my guide told me this was his house. I asked how much he would charge if I was to stay to which he replied 15 rupees a night plus food. An unbelievable price at less than 30 pence a night. He told me he will have to tell his wife first.

Replying that this was okay, "in the mean time I will walk further along the road to see if there was any other place to stay",

"there was no other place along the road" he quickly

replied.

Not to be put off I told the man I will look any way. Not much further along the road I came across a large two storey white building with a large lawn in front of it, large windows and a wide wooden door, it looked like a hotel or guest house. Letting myself in I was met by a friendly Sinhalese man.

"Can I help?",

"yes, I have just arrived in Anuradhapura and was looking for some where to stay".

The man told me to wait and he vanished through a door way behind a wooden desk. I could hear him talking in Sinhalese then he returned and said "we do have a spare room for a few days".

I was shown to a large room with a high ceiling and a single bed draped with a pure white mosquito net in the middle of the room and a sink to one side. The room was painted white with out any decoration but had a large sash window, it looked perfect. The man asked if the room was suitable, smiling I replied it was and asked how much he charged. The price was a little more than the house but this looked luxurious. "Do you want any meals, they will cost two rupees, not believing the price it was too hard to resist and said yes. Putting my rucksacks down and paying for the room I then had a strip wash before going out to exploring Anuradhapura.

Making my way back towards the station I saw a sign for the Ruwanwelisaya Stupa, I followed a narrow path with a well manicured lawn either side. A stark white spire crowned with a large golden orb towered above the trees.

Getting closer I could see the spire sat on a plinth which was on top of a large symmetrical bell shaped structure. To one side were smaller Stupa's. As I approached the Stupa I found myself looking almost straight up at the sky. Having never seen any thing like this before I was over whelmed by the magnificence of the edifice and stared in wonder. This all sat on a platform some eight feet high surrounded by carved elephants. Each side of the platform stretched for about 150 metres. To say that this structure was tall would be an under statement. I sat down on a grassy bank to admire the monument.

Whilst starring at the magnificent structure a man sat beside me and asked if I wanted to buy a genuine antique. Without waiting for a reply he showed me a small ornament with a dusting of soil. It looked as if it had just been dug out of the ground, taking a closer look I wondered how old it might be but declined to buy the antique. He told me it was hundreds of years old and how sacred and special it was. Again saying I was not interested he changed the conversation asking me if I was English or Australian. Saying I was English he told me he could do a good deal. Smiling and shaking my head again said no. The man smiled, shrugged his shoulders, "I will sell it to another tourist" he said optimistically. Just at that moment a coach pulled up and with an even larger smile the man announced that the German tourists had arrived. Enquiring how he knew, "they look like any other tourists you might see getting off a coach". Replying "I can tell" he leapt up and ran over to them. I watched as he gave his sales pitch and showed the small soil encrusted statuette

131

to the tourists, hoping he will sell it and soon enough one of the tourists paid the man who showed the others his purchase. I did not find out if they were German tourists though, they were too far away for me to hear them talking and wasn't concerned if they were.

Watching the tourists taking photographs of the stupa with themselves in front of it felt voyeuristic but entertaining as they adopted touristy poses. I walked across the neat lawn surrounding the Stupa to look at it more closely and admire the workmanship that had gone in to the carved elephants surrounding the platform.

Whilst crossing the lawn I saw several white upright posts that looked like giant fingers pushing up out of the soil; drawing closer I could see they were narrow pillars that could easily be mistaken for an art installation. Close to the pillars was a smaller pure white Stupa which looked just as magnificent as the larger one.

Between the trees and ancient structures were a group of people, one was a monk in his bright yellow robe standing under a tree. My curiosity got the better of me and walked towards them to see what was so interesting. The tree was surrounded by a fence, a sign was attached which read 'This is the Sacred Bo Tree which was planted in 288 BC The Sacred Bo Tree had been brought to Sri Lanka by King Asoka's daughter. The nun Sanghamittra, brought a piece of the Sacred Tree with her to Sri Lanka from Bodh Gaya in Northern India where it is continuously growing until this day in the island's ancient capital'. The thought that this tree could be over two thousand years old was difficult to comprehend. The sign went on to read 'The original Sacred Bo Tree in Northern India which Buddha sat under when he is said to gained enlightenment'. It made me contemplate that this tree had a distant connection with Buddha long before Christ was born. The atmosphere under the Bo Tree in the dappled shade was peaceful and serene, similar to that in a church or Hindu Temple, I envisaged Buddha sitting under the tree in India in similar peaceful surroundings.

Walking around the ancient site made me think that I was walking in the same footsteps of the Buddhist monks all those centuries ago. Wondering if it was just as tranquil then as it was now amongst the ancient city ruins where everybody seemed so calm and talked in a low tone. The sun had dipped down below the trees and my stomach reminded me it was time to eat and made my way back to the guest house. By the small ponds that I had passed earlier that morning a woman and young boy were selling coconuts, they chopped the tops off for customers so they could drink the water inside. Feeling thirsty I bought one; the liquid in side was cool and refreshing perfect for the hot weather. A cow ambled up to the coconuts and sniffed them, the boy deftly fended off the cow whilst crouching down protecting the produce totally unperturbed by the cows' persistence. Finishing my drink on the way to the guest house I arrived just as it was turning dark. In doors I was chastised by the proprietor for not carrying a torch. Replying that it was okay "I could see where I was going".

"It is not about being able to see where you are going, it's so you can see the snakes".

Replying nonchalantly "it was okay",
The proprietor rolled his eyes as if to say "tourists!"
The evening meal was rice with various spice dishes to mix with it which tasted slightly different to that I had eaten in India. It felt strange eating off a plate and using a fork, though I felt tempted to eat with my hand. After having something to eat and talking to the people in the guest house I could feel my comfortable bed calling and said good night. Lying on the bed I felt myself sinking in to the soft mattress, any woes and worries faded away as my muscles relaxed and I drifted off to sleep.
The next morning I woke; seeing the white draped canopy around the bed made me wonder where I was, then remembered it was the mosquito net. After a strip wash I was ready for breakfast. There was a middle aged couple already at the large dining table, saying hello they told me their names were Hannah and Thomas. I could not place their accent and asked where they were from; something I had tried to avoid doing in India, even if was a bit clichéish it seemed an appropriate question to ask. They were Dutch and said they were in Sri Lanka to study batik design. Explaining that they had already been to Indonesia to study the batik there and wanted to see how they were made in Sri Lanka. Hannah explained "they use a different type of wax in Sri Lanka. The wax used in Indonesia was softer and did not crack giving a smoother quality when dying. In Sri Lanka the wax is more brittle which allowed for the unique individual designs". They asked me what I was doing in Sri Lanka,
"Whilst travelling through India I was told about Sri

Lanka and felt I should pay a visit and caught the ferry. I intend to travel around the country for about a month". After a long breakfast Hannah and Thomas showed me some of their work, there were large sheets of cloth hanging up with various designs. The thought of doing some batik work excited me and wanted to learn how to do it myself. Eventually Hannah and Thomas said they had to get on with some work, replying that I had to get out and explore Anuradhapura I grabbed my small rucksack and set off in the hot tropical sun. It was much more peaceful than India and felt I could quite easily settle in Sri Lanka. Heading for the ancient city, I needed some more time looking at the ancient monuments which were meant to contain sacred relics and represented Buddha.

The quiet serene atmosphere felt that the ancient place was detached from the rest of Sri Lanka or even the world and had been preserved in its own tranquil bubble for millennia. The local inhabitants mirrored the peaceful atmosphere looking outwardly calm and not showing any signs of anxiety. After walking around the stupa's and grounds I decided to sit down to fully appreciate the calm surroundings in the shade of some large trees. Every one walking about whether they were Sinhalese or tourists talked in a low pitched voice, there was no shouting or loud noises. It felt like the idyllic place to live without any audible intrusion. After some time my stomach broke the silence as if to protest and indicate that I needed to have something to eat and a tea. Setting off to find a tea stall or shop, not too far away was a stall that sold a variety of handmade biscuits. It was difficult to choose which one to try with my tea so I bought one of each. Sitting down on a bench close by I took my time to compare the flavour in turn and how they compared with those in India, the coconut biscuit was my favourite.

After my biscuit tasting I walked around the town to find the post office to post the letters I wrote on the ferry, and to find the bus terminal. I had decided that I would start my journey around Sri Lanka the next day. Not sure where I was going and thought I should ask for some advice from the people at the guest house. The post office was easy to find, it was airy in side and not too busy, they had heard of the UK. The bus terminal had several bus stops with each one going to a different destination across Sri Lanka, such as Polonnaruwa, Sigiriya, Trincomalee, Batticaloa, Kandy, Galle, Colombo and Nuwara Eliya, I definitely needed some advice of where to go next. After walking around the shops I went back to the guest house for some lunch and asked where would be the best place to visit next. Each person had their own opinion where I should go. Polonnaruwa was suggested, it was not too far to travel. Somebody suggested Sigiriya because it is an ancient monument, Batticaloa was agreed by everyone because of the coral reef. The idea of getting out to the coast appealed to me but after much deliberation I opted for Sigiriya. After a rice lunch I sat on the veranda overlooking the lake and forest at the back of the guest house. It looked like an ideal place to wander and gather your thoughts. Hannah and Thomas came out on to the veranda for their afternoon tea and we spent an hour or so talking about our travels. They mentioned the cave temple at Dambulla, it sounded exciting with several statues of Buddha either reclining or sitting inside the cave and decided to add Dambulla to my list. After our conversation I visited the ancient site once more and experienced Anuradhapura night life. The late afternoon sun was warm with a still air. A few people were walking along the road, some cows stood beside it nonchalantly ignoring the passers bye. In the ancient city there were a number of tourists, it was so quiet you could hear the click of their cameras.

I aimlessly wandered amongst the ancient structures experiencing the ambiance and trying to envisage what they would have looked like. The light started to fade and I appeared to be the only person about; remembering the warning about not being out after dark without a torch I started to make my way back to the guest house. On the way I came across a tea stall and felt obliged to have one. As I reflected on the taste of the tea, it tasted different to that in India and far better than what you can buy in the shops in Britain, even though it was served up by the side of the road. I could not resist one of the biscuits from the stall which helped to make the experience so special, drinking Ceylon tea in Sri Lanka by the side of the road which might have been picked and dried only a few weeks ago. I idly chatted with the vendor who asked where I was from, then asked what Britain was like as if he had long forgotten memories of home. Finishing my tea I said fare well and slowly made my way back to the guest house for an evening meal with the intention of an early night, I wanted to be up early to catch the bus for Sigiriya and start my journey of Sri Lanka.

Distracted I stayed up late drinking Ceylon tea and talking with the staff at the guest house about Sri Lanka, it gave me a picture of what to expect. They told me about the ancient palace on top of the large rock at Sigiriya, there was the Temple of the Tooth in Kandy, the monastery on top of Adams Peak and Diyaluma Falls. With so much information about where to go and what to see I was torn between so many different places and felt it would be best not to have a planned itinerary and just see how things worked out. Eventually retiring to my room I very quickly fell in to a deep sleep.

The next morning I woke to a dazzling bright sunlit room. Had an egg breakfast and talked to Hannah and Thomas about the best place to visit and see batik being made. They suggested I should ask at any place that sells a wide selection as they will have their own workshops. After breakfast I packed my rucksack, said good bye to everyone and headed for the bus terminal where there was already a long queue for the bus to Sigiriya and wondered if I would be able to get on. Soon a dust covered red bus arrived already with a number of passengers. Somehow everyone got on whether they stood or sat, luckily somehow I got a seat by a window. Leaving Anuradhapura behind and out on the open road the bus conductor started to take the fares from the passengers talking to each in Sinhalese, after a brief conversation each time he was handed the fare and he whirled the handle on his ticket machine. When it was my turn to pay

he asked in English where I was going,
"Sigiriya" I replied.
The conductor looked at me in bemusement and asked
again but more in a questioning way. "Where are you
going?"
Repeating "Sigiriya" the bus conductor smiled, turned to
the passengers in the bus and spoke in Sinhalese and
imitated my pronunciation of Sigiriya which sounded
more like "Sigeereeah" which made everyone one laugh, I
smiled along with them even though I did not know what
had been said but had a rough idea.
After the laughing had subsided a passenger inquisitively
asked me where I wanted to go, I deliberately pronounced
Sigiriya slowly hoping that he might understand.
"Ah! You want to go to Sigiriya" which he pronounced
with a rolling R. It did not sound too different the way I
had pronounced it but obviously had caused some
confusion. The man said I should always say the letter R
as a rolling R, he then invited me to try again.
I repeated myself, "Sigirrrriya". Everyone one cheered
and applauded and I could not help myself smiling as the
conductor said "that is better you said it the right way",
gave me a ticket, took the ten rupee note and gave me a
handful of change. I had so much change I felt that he had
not taken the right farer, it seemed too cheap. The journey
was jovial, everyone happily talking and smiling.
Every now and then the bus would stop to let people on
who were standing by the road side, even though there
was no obvious bus stop or any houses in sight. It looked
as though you could just stand by the road and the bus

would pick you up which struck me as a marvellous idea. I watched the relatively flat, almost luminous green country side pass by with the dry rice paddies and beyond the blue distant hills. Cows and people walked beside the dusty bumpy road as they made their way to work or market. After a few hours in the distance above the trees was a large domed mound. The road weaved its way through the green landscape and then back in the direction of the large mound. It was obviously much larger than what it appeared from a distance.

Eventually the bus stopped almost next to this huge mound that looked just like a giant tree stump. The conductor called out to me "Sigirrrriya" with a smile, everyone laughed. I got off the bus and stepped into the hot midday sun and stared up at this huge rock in the middle of flat countryside. My awe struck gaze was interrupted by "hello!" looking down I saw a little girl of about ten with a broad smile on her face, almost ordering me she said "you need some where to stay, come with me". The girl's perception was uncanny knowing I would need some where to stay, bemused I followed as she skipped off pointing and added "my house is there". At first I could not see any buildings but hidden behind some large trees was a white washed building with a red tiled roof and white window frames. The front door was made of dark brown wood and had a door step. It looked very homely from the outside. The girl opened the door and told me to come in. I stepped in to a large room with a rug on the floor, a large sturdy wooden dining table and several wooden chairs in the middle of the room and a large fire place. A slim woman came out from an adjoining room and the girl excitedly spoke to her in Sinhalese. After she had finished talking the woman softly asked if I needed a room. Saying I did she showed me to a modest bedroom with a comfortable looking bed. The room was ten rupees a night and the price of the meals were separate; I was not even going to haggle over the price it would have been mean to even try.

Having found somewhere to stay I headed for the large rock and the Sigiriya Palace on top. I followed a well worn dusty path lined with low bushes and trees that led towards the rock. As I got closer the enormity of the rock became even more apparent with it towering about five hundred feet above me and just as wide, if not more. The rock face itself had a mid-grey granite appearance. Beside the rock was a wooden scaffold some fifty feet high with a platform and steps leading up to it with some people on the platform looking at the rock face. The dusty path weaved round by the side the rock in to some sort of court yard surrounded by low walls that appeared to be excavated remains of old buildings. People were wandering about, women in flowing saris and men wearing striped sarongs and white shirts, a stark contrast to the parched foliage and reddish sand. A sign at the foot of some narrow wooden steps said in Sinhalese and English that the steps lead up to the top of the rock. Narrow wooden steps were supported by a metal frame work, wire cable was anchored to the rock face as a hand rail. The steps looked precarious but the urge to climb to the top for the view was too hard to resist. The steps

141

proved to be quite sturdy and before long I was on the top platform stepping onto a grassy verge admiring the view of the jungle in one direction and in the other what looked like a water garden with the country side leading off to the distant pale blue hills.

The top of the rock was not entirely flat, it looked as if there had been a series of terraces at one time which sloped down towards the far side. Grass covered stones marked the foundations of a large building showing where the outer and dividing walls were. There was no rubble to indicate what the building might have looked like but the amount of rock that would have been hoisted up to the top must have taken a considerable amount of effort. Sitting down and admiring the view I imagined what it must have been like living up on top in the palace. The jungle stretched out in to the far distance, with a green canopy covered the jungle floor without a break and wondered what wild life was down there walking around, hiding or resting in its shade. A few more people arrived at the top but other than that no one else seemed willing to brave the climb to for the majestic view. The water gardens had several ponds and paths between them, obviously the inhabitants liked their gardens which made me wonder what plants had decorated them. After spending some time at the top I remembered the other structure on the side of the rock.

The decent was relatively easy, unless you happen to suffer from vertigo or it was a wet day when the wooden steps would be slippery and quite dangerous. Making my way around to the other structure I spotted a largish rock

142

sparkling in the sunlight, picking it up and looking closely I could see it was covered in tiny white and bright red crystals. The red crystals looked like tiny rubies and the tiny white crystals sparkled like diamonds. Even though the rock was relatively heavy, weighing about a kilo I decided to keep it as a memento of my visit to Sigiriya. At the wooden frame work I climbed the ladder leading up to a narrow platform with a railing on the outside. High up on the rock face were some ancient frescoes. They consisted of several images of half-naked buxom women holding what looked like fruit, one wore a head dress inlayed with semi-precious stones and looked as if she could have been a princess or queen. The artist had managed to depict the women in a 3D style rather than a flat 2D rendition similar to the ancient Egyptian drawings. What was so amazing that the art work had lasted so long on the rock face with the colours still relatively vibrant. Pulling my self away from the ancient art work I went to find some where for a drink. Making my way back to the guest house I noticed at the end of the road some sort of covered eating area. Walking from the hot sun in to the cool shade was a welcome relief, an idyllic place to sit and drink tea.

A slim elderly Sinhalese man sporting a moustache sitting at one of the large wooden tables called out "hello how are you doing it is so good to see you, come and sit down". He made the greeting sound as if he had just bumped in to an old friend that he had not seen for a long time. He stood up, held out his hand and with a wide smile and said "my name is George, what is your name?"

Shaking hands and telling George my name to which George said "It is good to meet you Peter, take a seat", unable to resist the invitation I sat down in the high backed wooden seat. It looks like you need a drink, what would you like? I asked for a tea and George called over to a man dressed in a smart safari type trousers and jacket and asked him to bring two teas.

"Well Peter how are you finding Sri Lanka" George enquired.

"I'm having a wonderful time",

"Good! Sri Lanka is a lovely country".

"It is a lovely country" I replied in agreement.

George explained that he was manager of the national park and organised trips in to the jungle, he then added "don't go in to the jungle by yourself there are a lot of dangerous animals living there such as Buffalo and Leopards. The buffalos will chase you and not give up and you will not see the leopard until you are right next to it".

I told George the advice we were given in Kenya about leopards when on exercise whilst serving in the British Army. The guide from the Kenyan Rifles told us not to play with leopards. George laughed "that sounds like very good advice".

George told me a lot about his self, Sri Lanka and Ceylon as it was previously called. George was posted at Trincomolee or Trinco as he called it during WWII as an anti aircraft gunnery officer. The Japanese had bombed Trincomolee so they defended it with a lot of anti aircraft guns.

144

George asked where I was planning to go. I mentioned Pollonaruwa, Kandy and the coast. George told me I should visit Kuchchaveli, "it is just north of Trincomolee and has a deserted beach with just a few people living there". If you go to Kandy you must visit my friend who owns a craft and gem shop. It is near the botanical gardens just outside Kandy on the main road and wrote down the address for me. George asked me a lot of questions about England which I did my best to answer which made me reminisce a bit. George asked me where I was staying, when I said at the guest house where the bus stops, George replied "I now them, they will look after you there".

We talked at length until it started to get dark then thought about going back to the guest house, I mentioned to George about the advice I was given in Anuradhapura about carrying a torch so you can see the snakes; "that is good advice, we have many dangerous snakes in Sri Lanka". Saying good night George said "good bye, I hope you enjoy your trip in Sri Lanka".

Once in doors I met the woman's husband who was slim and wore a sarong who asked if I wanted something to eat, I could smell the rice was already cooked and said yes. The rice was served on a plate with some small dishes with various spices in them.

Whilst eating the man asked about my journey. Mentioning that I had come over from India on the ferry they were curious about what I thought of India. Being diplomatic I told them that it was an interesting country which was very big, had slow trains and some places were

145

very noisy. They laughed and asked me if I was going to stay in Sri Lanka. They were surprised when I said I will be going back to India and travel north. After eating I noticed there was a chess set on a shelf and asked if anyone could play. One of the children said yes, after having set up the chess board it was obvious that the girl could not play chess and offered to teach her which took up the rest of the evening much to the delight of the parents. During the chess lesson I asked if there was a bus to Dambulla, there was one at about 9am and decided to go there next and visit the Buddhist cave temple. As much as I was enjoying the evening with this family I wanted to get some sleep and said good night.

The next morning I was awake early, packed my things away, had some breakfast then said good bye and waited on the dusty road for the bus to Dambulla. When it arrived several tourists got off gawking at the giant rock in a similar way that I had, we said hello and I got on to the bus. The half full bus waited for a while and then trundled off along the dusty, bumpy road through the foliage covered countryside. After about two hours we arrived at a parade of make shift shops. The bus stopped and the conductor called out "Dambulla". It was a relief not having to quickly get off the bus before it quickly dashed away like the buses in India. There was a sign pointing upwards to a rock saying Rock Temple. At the top I could see a small white building with a red roof. Steps were carved in to the rock leading up to the building; the climb was not strenuous, even with my rucksacks.

The white building had two fake yellow window shutters either side of an entrance which was similar in size to a door for a house, a sign asking for sandals to be left out side. The entrance led in to a large cave some 20 yards wide by 50 yards. Along one side of the cave was a ledge where several Lord Buddha's of various sizes were perched. Each one was either painted gold or covered in gold leaf. In the middle of the cave was a small stupa about six feet high. A Buddhist Monk wearing a yellow robe stood to one side, as if guarding the temple. The cave was spectacular especially the huge reclining Buddha, some 20 feet long and too large to have been brought in to the cave in one piece. Obviously a grand engineering fete had taken place over a thousand years ago and made me wonder how advanced the civilisation was to manage this marvellous achievement. The ceiling was painted with an intricate design of red and gold. Some of the Buddha's had various types of offerings placed around them such as flowers and food. What amazed me the most was that this place has been in continued use since the 1st century BC where many people had come to pray and monks had lived when other civilisations had crumbled.

Finally pulling myself away from the cave and its magnificence I stepped back out in to the bright sun to be presented with a panoramic view of the parched ochre country side below. The land was mainly flat except for several distant hills, one hill looked just like a huge pyramid standing in the middle of the plain. Directly below smoke rose from the forest. The view was spell binding and kept me anchored to the spot, I did not want

to forget this scene and stood still taking it all in.
Eventually making my way down the steps to the road
and walked past the parade of shops with various crafts on
sale, such as jewellery, carved brightly painted masks,
pottery, batik and block printed clothing. Whilst browsing
I decided to stay the night unsure if there was some
accommodation.

Along the road I could see what looked like a sign for a
guest house, knocking and letting myself in side I stepped
in to a large dimly lit room with a table in the middle and
several chairs around it. A woman who was sweeping up
with a bundle of hand held sticks, looking up she said
hello. I asked if she had a room available,

"yes, it is that one there" came the reply pointing at the
door next to me. Opening the door I stepped in to a
spacious room with a large bed and some furniture. It
looked ideal, comfortable and homely. Saying I wanted to
stay for one night the woman said that was okay. She
mentioned she had two other guests in the next room and
asked me not to make too much noise at night. I put my
large rucksack down in the room, paid for the room and
then went out to carry on browsing through the craft stalls
and to find some where to eat. Not much further along the
road I came across a tea shop with benches outside.
Sitting down a man came out through a door way and
asked what would I like? I asked for a tea and some rice,
almost instantly the tea arrived and soon after a large plate
of rice. Instinctively I started to eat with my fingers, the
man arrived back with a fork and looked surprised as he
offered it to me, waving my hand to indicate I did not

need it I carried on eating. Sitting outside the tea shop gave me the chance to watch life pass by and people go about their daily business. Life seemed so much calmer in Sri Lanka compared to India. Things were done at a slower pace which seemed appropriate considering how warm it was, it made me wonder if there was a need to rush about any way. Who decides the need to rush all of the time? What is not done today can always be done tomorrow.

By now the sun was starting to get low in the sky and was struck with the idea to watch the sun set from the top of the steps by the temple. After my tea I made my way up the steps and waited, before long the sky gradually turned yellow, purple shadows were cast by the trees and the hills. As the sun sank lower the shadows grew longer like giant fingers reaching out across the countryside sinking the landscape in to a dusky purple haze.

The sun sank below the distant hills colouring the sky in a bright crimson hue that silhouetted the distant hills. The sky gradually transformed to Alizarin Red then to dark blue allowing the first stars to glimmer in the evening sky. Having watched the fantastic sunset I made my way down to the road. The shops had lit their lanterns creating a luminous trail which looked like a giant fluorescent caterpillar which created moving shadows as people walked in front of them. The light cast from the lanterns gave the masks a scarier appearance than what they had during the day, almost bringing them to life and would not be out of place in a horror movie. I came across a shop that sold mosquito coils which and felt would come in handy at some time to keep the irritating pests at bay. I had a final cup of tea then set off back to my guest house where a faint light outside helped me find the front door. Once through the door I said good night to the owner and then settled down to a long peaceful night in my cosy bed. The next morning the bright sun filtered through the yellow curtains tinting the room with a warm glow. After a quick wash I sat down for breakfast, scrambled egg with bread, it tasted so good. The other two guests came out from the adjacent bedroom. They were a young Swiss couple who had been in Sri Lanka a few weeks. As we exchanged travel stories they asked where I was going next, without hesitating I said Polonnaruwa. This seemed to be logical place to go as it was quite close to Dambulla. The owner of the guest house mentioned that there wasn't any where to stay in Polonnaruwa, but explained that I had a tent and could resort to camping. Finishing breakfast I got my things together and waited by the side of the road for the bus for Polonnaruwa.

Thomas and his family, the perfect hosts

The bus eventually arrived and managed to get a seat by a window. The bus rumbled along the dusty road on a journey that took longer than anticipated, stopping frequently for passengers waiting by the roadside. When we arrived at Polonaruwa I was not exactly sure which direction to go. There were not many signs and definitely none for places to stay, to my surprise I was rescued by a young lad who told me if I needed somewhere to stay he cold show me. He then instructed me to follow him and lead the way along a gravel path past what looked like ancient temples. As we turned a corner I could see some small palm leaf huts in the distance. As we drew closer the boy said I could stay here and told me he was going to get his mum. He vanished in to one of the huts, a few minutes later a woman came out. She told me if I needed a place to stay I could stay in the hut behind me. Turning around there was a palm hut was some eight feet tall eight feet long and six feet wide. Opening the wooden door I could see it looked very similar to the palm leaf hut I stayed in at Rameswaram and thought it was home from home. There were no windows but it looked sturdy and would keep out any rain, not that any was expected having been very lucky so far with the weather. The bed was made from a wooden frame with canvas stretched over it, looking relatively comfortable, it was better than sleeping out in my tent. On the floor there was a large

151

reed mat which made it feel homely. I noticed on the floor a small oval glass jar with some liquid in it and string sticking up from a stopper. At first I thought it was a perfume bottle, asking what it was she replied "it is a lantern, just light the string". The woman looked worried, maybe she concerned I thought the hut was too rustic or austere, but it was ideal and said "okay" with a wide smile. She smiled back then told me that I could wash from the well outside; there is nothing like amenities that are guaranteed to work and not break down. The door did not have a lock on it but so far I had not had any problems with my unattended belongings and just shrugged off this problem.

I asked about food and the woman said she could cook some rice, it sounded perfect and paid for two nights which I thought would be enough to see the ancient city. Having some where to stay and eat I set off to explore the ancient ruins which seemed to be in such good condition considering the age of them dating back to about 1000 AD. The buildings appeared to be constructed of granite and looked as if they had been temples. Some of the buildings had relief carvings that had stood up to the ravages of time and stupa's in various stages of dis-repair. A free standing statue of a man some ten feet tall holding what looked like a large slice of water melon was being admired by a large group of tourists, which looked familiar then realised the statue was on a Sri Lankan bank note. This grand imposing statue turned out to be of a king. Also there was a giant statue of the reclining Buddha that equally attracted some considerable attention.

Several well dressed tourists were visiting the ancient site. They appeared to be following a guide who was rushing, maybe to ensure they got to see everything on their itinerary. It seemed a shame to have limited time to visit a place like this, unable to soak up the ambiance and atmosphere, but felt sure they would not be too happy staying where I was.

Just like Anuradhapura it was very peaceful and calm, it felt like a perfect place to spent a few days to help you gather your thoughts. Whilst wandered about the large ancient city I came across a stall where a man was selling antiques and crafts. He had a wide selection of wooden carvings, metal craft work, jewellery and gemstones to choose from. He ignored me browsing through the artefacts whilst he talked to two customers. I noticed a purse made of very small, intricate stainless steel chainmail links with a metal hasp. A fashion accessory that harped back to the 1930s which would not be out of place at a Christies or Sotherbys auction.

One thing that stood out was a carved wooden box in the shape of a book with an elephant design on the lid. It resisted my attempts to open it no matter which way I pulled or pushed, the vendor stopped talking to his customers, took the box from me then slid down the spine, pulled it backwards which allowed the lid to slide out revealing a hollow interior. The vendor returned to his customers who were very interested in buying some jewellery and doing their best to haggle the price down. Neither seemed to be gaining an advantage or giving away which appeared to aggravate the customers.

Deciding that the elephant puzzle box would make a great present I asked how much it was but the vendor ignored me, he was obviously determined to sell them what they wanted but at a very good price.

The haggling went on for a good five minutes and then the vendor agreed with their price. The two customer's seemed mean considering the price they were haggling over was pence even if it sounded a lot in rupees. The vendor seemed happy with his sale and bid his customers farewell.

Turning to me he apologised for not telling me how much the box was and told me that he did not want them to know he was going to give me a good price for anything I wanted to buy, I do not want to charge you the same price as them, pointing over his shoulder. The vendor then said "you can have the box for twelve rupees. This seemed far too cheap and decided to buy something else to make it worthwhile for the vendor's generosity. There were two wooden fruit plates with intricate carving around the edge and in the centre. The vendor said how much they were which again seemed far too cheap but I happily paid and we shook hands. He asked me if there was any thing else I wanted to buy, "I noticed you picked up the purse", he obviously did not miss a thing. I told him it looked nice but I don't know any one who would like it and declined his offer even though the price was very generous. We talked for a while until some potential customers stopped to browse, saying good bye as he said hello to the well-dressed tourists, at the same time gave a sly wink.

154

Walking away I hoped that the smartly dressed tourists would be very benevolent to him and not haggle too hard. I walked around the ancient site for another hour or so admiring the ancient architecture and reflecting on the people who walked around the buildings such a long time ago in their brightly coloured costumes, robes and dresses with their richly decorated jewellery. I made my way back to my palm hut for something to eat and found the rice had just been cooked and was still hot. I fished out my bowl from my rucksack filled it up with rice and sat on the grass in the evening sun with my meal and tea. It was very relaxing, hardly a sound disturbed the peaceful evening as the setting sun cast a luminous yellow glow across the sky which turned orange and gradually faded to a mid-blue and then indigo. I thought about writing a short letter home by the light from the small lantern, having lit it there was barely enough light to see let alone write. Deciding to have an early night I lit my mosquito coil to ward off any bugs and settle down on my canvas bed which felt like any other camp bed I had previously slept on. Putting out the flame from the small lantern the hut was plunged in to total darkness and very soon I was asleep.

The next morning I was woken by clatter and banging. Getting up I collected my washing things together and walked over to the well for a wash. The woman was working outside and seemed to be tidying up. Waving hello then pointing to the well indicating I was going to have a wash. She pointed to the small bucket attached to a long rope beside the well and said I should drop the bucket down the well for the water. The bucket dropped to the bottom with a splash as it landed at the bottom, the bucket floating on top then slowly sank as it filled up, once full I hauled it up. At first I used the water in the bucket to wash my face and under my arms, the cold water felt refreshing, then I poured the cold water over my head. The woman had been watching me and laughed. Filling the bucket again I hauled it back up and poured the water over my head which made the woman laugh even more. I was not sure what was making her laugh but I felt clean and had managed to brighten up somebodies day. After drying off I was ready for breakfast which turned out to be two hard boiled eggs and a tea; now I was ready to explore Polonnaruwa.

I could not resist visiting the ancient city again in case I missed any of it and look more closely at the relief carvings around the temples. Many of the buildings had elephants and fake windows carved in to the exterior walls. All that remained of some of the buildings was the supporting pillars similar to those in Anuradhapura. One group of pillars looked similar to North Indian totem poles from a distance. I came across a tea stall and sat down on the grass to drink it whilst watching the tourists eagerly dashing after their guide trying to cram every thing in their hour or so visit. They all looked smartly dressed with pressed shirts, blouses, shorts skirts and wearing socks and shoes, a stark contrast to my attire; Khaki shorts a T shirt and sandals from El Salvador made from old tyres. Several of them carried an SLR camera with a large telephoto lens and a camera bag slung over their shoulder, no doubt holding more lenses. Some complained about how warm it was and after a short time several returned to their air conditioned bus. I wondered how much they had paid to come out on their day trip, and the holiday in Sri Lanka only to be defeated by the hot weather and felt obliged to sit in the bus to escape the heat.

Having finished my tea I went to explore the surrounding countryside. Feeling there must be more to see and followed the gravel path away from the ancient site and came across a large spectacular lake fringed with palm trees. A wide, gravel road circumnavigate the large lake which I found irresistible to follow. There was an occasionally building beside the road, some were painted white with tiled roofs. One looked as if it could be a small temple with a brightly coloured design on it. I came across an elderly man wearing white robes and had a long white beard slouching on the step of a memorial stone, he seemed to resting in the shade away the mid-day sun. I said hello but he did not reply, only stared at me with his sad eyes. He had a small bag and a walking stick which seemed to make a poignant statement about his own long journey. I wanted to take his photograph to remember this moment, lifting my camera I asked if I could take his photo but he just staring at me dejectedly. Without any further comment I took his photograph, said thank you and walked on.

The countryside stretched away from the lake in a patch work of rice paddies separated by interspersed trees, in the far distance was a large mound. Small huts dotted between the rice paddies and workers tended to their crops. Further along the gravel road I came across a team of three workers tilling the soil with long handled cleavers. I raised my camera to take a photograph, as I did they stopped work and posed with broad smiles. I could not help laugh at how they automatically stopped when the camera was pointed at them, after explaining that I wanted a photo of them working, they straight away resumed their digging for a perfect photograph. Having taken the photo I called out thank you, they stopped waved and said something in Sinhalese, in reply I told them they are doing a good job which made them all laughed.

After walking some considerable distance under the afternoon blazing sun I concluded that most sensible people were sitting in the shade. Oscar Wilds phrase "only mad dogs and English men go out in the mid day sun" came to mind which was very apt in my case. As the sun started to dip in the sky I turned to walk back along the road and came across three people by the road; a teenage girl, a man who could have been her father and an elderly man who was possibly the grandfather. The girl was wearing a yellow patterned dress and both men wore a sarong and shirt, none of them wore any thing on their feet. I asked if I could take their photograph and with out any hesitation they all posed for me. As I focused the camera it struck me they had posed in order of age with out any prompting. The girl posed with her arms behind her back holding the metal pale. The father stood with his feet apart and hands by his side and the elderly man was standing to attention with his feet together and hands by his side. Waving and saying thank you, they smiled and waved as I walked off with the intention of getting back to my hut before it got dark. When I arrived back at the path that joined the gravel road the sun was starting to set. I stopped and watched it sink slowly casting a long bright yellow finger directly at me across the lake. The sky went bright yellow just as the sun slid behind the trees on the horizon, a fitting end to an interesting day.

By the time I arrived back at my hut it was dark and was reminded about the lecture I had, 'not to out after dark with out torch' and thought I should buy my self one. The woman asked if I wanted something to eat, "definitely" I replied and sat out side in the light of the lantern as insects hovered around it and was given a large bowl of rice which I scooped up with my fingers and drank tea. The air was filled with the smell of burning wood from the fire, something that had become familiar since I had arrived in India especially when I had camped out at the Periyar Animal Sanctuary. I spent some time talking to the woman about my day and telling her about where I lived, she listened intently and seemed to reflect on the difference between our lives, her rustic one here in Sri Lanka and mine back in Britain with cars, shops every where and doctors not too far away. Eventually I said good night and settled down in my hut with a mosquito coil burning and my large towel pulled up over me.

The next morning I had a wash from the well, ate a quick breakfast and set off to catch the bus for Batticaloa after saying good bye to my hosts.

There was a long queue waiting for a bus, far too many to get on one bus, fortunately a bus for Anuradhapura pulled up and many of those waiting got on. Sometime later the bus for Batticaloa arrived with enough seats for everyone. I had calculated that the journey would take about two hours to cover the sixty odd miles. The country side changed from paddy fields either side of the road to palm trees and scrub land, the side of the road had a dusting of sand as we got closer to the coast. Feeling excited about being on the coast I was looking forward to swimming amongst the coral. The bus stopped for some passengers standing by the road, two young white women got on which took me by surprise having not seen any white people on the buses so far. They came towards the back where I was sitting, almost straight away we were talked excitedly, I did not have to ask where Jill and Sarah were from, it was obviously the London area. They had been in Sri Lanka a few weeks and spent most of their time by the beach. They explained where they were staying there was miles of sandy beach and the guest house was friendly. They asked where I had been so far and told them about each place in turn and that I was going to Batticaloa. They both suggested I should get off where they are staying, Kalkudha. The bus drove through a small plantation of palm trees, made a sharp turn and was next to the sea. We are getting off here Jill said, being so close to the beach and the sea it looked idyllic and got off as well. I asked Jill and Sarah where they were staying but said there were no spare rooms. I felt a tug at my arm, and a small girl said "you can stay at our house.

"There you are you have a place to stay" Jill commented. As they went to walk away said "I'll see you around", "yes maybe" they replied.

The girl told me to follow her and pointed, "this is my house". The tall green house was constructed of palm leaves. It was fenced off with high up right posts and palm leaves strung between them forming a screen. An arched entrance covered with palm leaves lead in to a small court yard with a well and plastic garden furniture. A middle aged man came out to greet us wearing a pair of grey trousers and white shirt. He was stout and had a friendly face, holding out his hand he said "My name is Thomas", shaking hands,

"I'm Peter".

"Do you need some where to stay?"

Saying I did Thomas replied "I have a spare room at the far end of the house" and held out his hand to invite me in. Inside I could see the palm leaves were lashed to a sturdy wooden frame. There were large windows with platted palm leaf flaps and a bench by one of the windows. The bed room was about the same size as my hut at Polonnaruwa, with a wooden framed bed and canvas stretched over it, a thick reed mat covered the floor. I asked how much the room was, "ten rupees" replied Thomas.

"I'll take the room".

As an after thought Thomas mentioned at night there will be some rustling in the roof, "this is okay it is only rats". "That's okay as long as they are friendly ones" l replied to which Thomas laughed. Thomas told me that if I

wanted a wash I can use the well, Smiling I replied
"okay" thinking that this was becoming the norm.
"If you want some thing to eat ask my wife and she will
cook some extra food, you will be eating the same as the
family".
"I would like to have some thing to eat later", Thomas
told me his wife was cooking rice and crab mixed with
coconut. This sounded so good and told Thomas I could
not wait.
I asked about the coral reef and Thomas said " there
wasn't any coral, the cyclone came through Kalkudah
and destroyed the coral reef and our homes, that is why
we are living in this temporary one. Thomas then excused
his self because he had to get ready for work.
Even though there was not any coral I still wanted to have
a swim, putting my swimming things on and grabbing my
snorkel and mask I set off for the beach across the road. I
stepped on to the soft white sand and walked under the
tall palm trees that lined the road. The sea was fairly
calm, ideal for snorkelling but I just could not believe the
beach, the strip of sand stretched out in to the far distance
for several miles with palm trees as a back drop and the
blue sea gently washing up on to the sand; amazingly the
beach was almost deserted. I strolled down to the sea and
plunged in to the warm water. With my mask pulled over
my face I submerged under the water which was clear and
was able to see for ten or fifteen feet. Swimming out from
the shore I could see that Thomas was right the coral was
dead, ghostly white coral branches pointed up towards the
surface as if reaching for help. The coral must have been

162

amazing before the cyclone; if it had done this under the water it must have been devastating on land. I swam around in a hope to find some coral that had survived but there was no sign of life in the coral or any fish. It was so disappointing; maybe this was why the beach was deserted. I did not let this spoil my swim, it felt good to be able to bob along floating on the surface. Loosing track of how long I had been snorkelling but looking back at the shore I had swum out a few hundred yards. Slowly heading back I carried on looking for any sign of life but there wasn't anything, not even bottom feeding fish.
I sat down on the sand to be dried off by the sun. Admiring the spectacular view wished I had my paints and a sketch book too record this memorable moment. Once dry I walked back to the guest house to get dressed. There was something about Kalkudah that made me feel at home, the sort of place where I felt comfortable and Thomas's guest house was the ideal place to stay.
Once dressed I decided to catch up on my letter writing and let everyone know about this perfect beach. I had been writing for a few hours when I was asked if I wanted something to eat. It felt like the ideal time and said yes. A large plate was brought out full of rice with shredded crab meat and grated coconut, I had been looking forward to this all afternoon it sounded as though it would taste nice and on my first mouth full it definitely was. The taste was indescribable with the flavours of the rice, crab and coconut all mixed together. Even though I felt hungry I took my time and savoured each mouthful. Thomas's wife asked if I liked the meal, wondering if she thought there

163

was something wrong I assured her it was a very good; "its the best meal I've had so far in India and Sri Lanka". Having eaten I went back to my letter writing whilst drinking tea. I wanted to get all of the letters written so I could have the next day exploring, swimming or lounging on the beach; or maybe bump in to Jill and Sarah. Having finished my letters there was still some light left so I walked out on to the beach. The evening sea breeze felt cool and a relief from the warmer air in land, the waves lapping on to the beach sounded soothing, yes I was sure this was the perfect beach; no high rise hotels or noisy tourists. Walking back under the palm trees it was darker than it appeared, foliage covering the ground making it difficult to see if a snake was about. I took my time treading carefully thinking I should have a long stick to prod anything that remotely look like a snake but made it back to the road without coming to any grief.

Back at the house I found Thomas sitting outside, saying hello he invited me to sit down with him. I told him about my swim and what a nice place Kalkudah was. Thomas agreed "I would not like to live any where else". I told Thomas how much I enjoyed the meal and that it was the best I had eaten in India and Sri Lanka. Asking Thomas about his job, he explained that he did shift work at a local hotel sometimes having to do night shifts and work on the reception. Tongue in cheek I commented that it sounded like hard work to which Thomas said "no it is not too hard". The girl who met me from the bus came out to say good night, Thomas told me that Melinda was his favourite daughter because she works so hard and helps

164

everyone, "not that I don't love my other children but Melinda is my favourite". Thomas said good night and she went back in to the house.

We talked for a bit longer and then Thomas said he had to get up early in the morning for work. Saying good night he went inside. Feeling tired myself I went off to bed, just as I was settling down in the dark there was a rustling sound coming from the roof which became quite vigorous, ignoring it I drifted off to sleep.

I woke the next morning, the palm leaf screen filtered the sun. Out side I hauled up a bucket of water from the well, As I washed Thomas's family gathered out side to watch me, there was obviously some entertainment value in me washing. Especially when I poured the bucket of cold water over my self which made every one laugh and applaud; making sure I was clean I threw another bucket of water over my head which caused even louder laughter. Having dried myself off and got dressed it was time for breakfast which I had been told was hoppers. Hoppers turned out to be plain tasting small pan cakes with a fried egg, ideal for starting the day. Having eaten I set off to explore Kalkudah. Following the road I passed a few temporary homes as well as a hotel but there was not much else to see. I found a post office much to my delight and posted my letters from the previous day and bought some post cards. Writing a quick message on the back of each one I posted these as well and made my way back to the guest house. Getting changed in to my swimming things I headed for the virtually empty beach. I spent the rest of the morning in the sea diving down in to the deeper

165

water beyond the dead coral hoping to see some fish but there was nothing here either, not even a curious shark. My rumbling tummy signalled I had done enough swimming and went back to the guest house. Lunch was a plate of rice with some spice which I felt was enough to see me through to the evening.

In the afternoon I walked some considerable distance along the virtually deserted beach taking in the idyllic picture post card view. By the time I had arrived back at the guest house the sun was setting and could not resist watching the sky change colour as the clouds turned from yellow to pink and then purple.

The evening meal was rice and meat in a coconut sauce. Just as I finished eating Thomas came home from work, we sat outside in the balmy evening air talking. I mentioned about going on to Kandy in the morning, Thomas told me how pleasant it was. Thomas was very curious about what it was like in Britain, he had heard so much and wanted to visit Britain, especially London. I described London as best as I could and also the surrounding counties. Thomas felt he would like London because it sounded exciting. Thomas mentioned how much he admired Winston Churchill and wanted to read about him; then asked me to send him a book about Winston Churchill,

"I will try and find one for you when I got back home". Our conversation lasted in to the late hours when it became obvious we were both tired. Settling down on my bed and once the lights were out the familiar rustle in the roof started as the rats scurried around in the rafters.

166

My wash from the well the next morning entertained Thomas's family as I poured the cold water over myself. After a quick breakfast I was ready to move on and said fare well to Thomas and his family. To remember my time in Kalkudah I asked if I could take a photograph of everyone together. Thomas thought this was a good idea and called everyone outside and gathered them around him, each one taking up their own pose, a family photo which Thomas would have been proud of. My stay with Thomas and his family was a memorable one I have never forgotten.

Soon after saying good bye the bus for Batticaloa arrived ready to whisk me off on the next leg of my journey in to the Sri Lankan Central Highlands.

Meeting friends of a friend

The bus terminal in Batticaloa was busy but fortunately not many people seemed to be going to Kandy and had three seats to myself, once all of the passengers were on board the bus pulled away leaving the coast behind and headed inland. I hoped to be in Kandy by late afternoon. The country side changed from coastal low vegetation that looked parched to more lush green foliage. Crossing over rivers as the bus started to climb through a forest where it had just stopped raining. Large heavy wet leaves drooped down from the branches. The bus drove on under a threatening grey sky, passing houses by the side of the road and through towns. Around mid-afternoon the bus stopped in a town called Mahiyangana at a cross roads. Before the passengers got off the bus driver announced we were stopping for an hour, then added "you must be back here, I will not wait"
I wondered how much further it is to Kandy, it looked as though we were heading towards some grey mountains beyond Mahiyangana, maybe it was not too long before we arrived in Kandy. I walked across the road to a tea shop and became the centre of attention, attracting a crowd who wanted to know about me and asked the usual questions. Whilst eating some rice and drinking tea I explained where I was from, where I had been and where I was going. When I asked how far it was to Kandy they all agreed that it was not much further.

There was a large poster of Buddha pinned up on the wall, a white line drawing on a black back ground. I asked if it was possible to borrow the picture and copy it, "I'll send it back after I had finished". The tea shop owner was reluctant to do this but the others in the tea shop persuaded him to let me have it, after being given the address to send the picture I noticed the time and rushed to catch my bus. The bus was completely full, even the central aisle was jam packed with standing passengers. Managing to squeeze on right at the front I sat on a ledge next to the window screen. The bus looked over crowded but not being far to Kandy the bus driver must have felt it would be okay for the short distance we had to travel. The bus drove out of Mahiyangana in the direction of the grey mountains and threatening grey clouds. The bus was lively with excited Sinhalese chatter. I was equally excited, being right at the front of the bus with a grand stand view of the road ahead. A man next to me started talking to the driver, every now and then the driver turned his head to look at him. This conversation seemed to become quite lively which made the driver turn his head even more which was quite perturbing. As the road started to climb in to the mountains the light gradually faded until the only light available was from the head lights. Either side of the bus and beyond the head lights it was pitch black, the driver continued speaking to the man next to me. Suddenly out of the shadows appeared a sharp bend in the road, whilst still talking and looking at the man, the driver deftly spun the steering wheel, the bus turned away from the edge of the road and the dark precipice. Feeling

169

that we had been lucky with that bend I hoped the driver would pay more attention as we climbed higher up the mountain road.

Another sharp bend appeared in the buses head lights, the driver was still talking to the man next to me, as the bus approached the bend he looked away and seemed to steer closer to the edge, so close it looked as though the front wheel was right on the edge of the road which was a bit worrying to say the least. At the next bend the driver was looking where he was going but the bus still seemed to be closer to the edge than it needed to be.

As the bus climbed higher it turned sharply around several tight bends that suddenly appeared out of the pitch dark whilst the driver carried on his conversation. I clung on in anticipation that the bus might suddenly fly off the road, not that it would help in any way. The road straightened out and levelled off much to my relief which was to be short lived as the road descended steeply, when the driver seemed to slip the gears in to neutral and free wheel down the mountain which was even more hair raising.

As the bus approached a bend the driver applied the brakes just enough to slew around the corner. Still the driver was talking to the man next to me. I was now convinced we would not make it to Kandy.

Then out of the darkness as the bus turned a corner there was a brightly lit hut beside the road. The bus pulled up in front of it and everyone got off.

I grabbed my rucksack with the intention of not travelling any further by bus; I wanted to arrive in Kandy alive. The bus driver went to stop me, "you cannot stay here, there are no rooms",

"I wasn't going to stay here but walk the rest of the way to Kandy".

The driver looked surprised, especially when I told him he was not paying enough attention to the road and the bus had come very close to edge. The driver's friend interjected and told me that the driver knows the road very well.

Looking at him I retorted "he might know the road very well but I would feel safer walking".

The driver quickly replied "you cannot walk, the tigers will get you".

Smiling at him I replied "there are no tigers in Sri Lanka"; instantly correcting himself added "Leopards will get you".

In response I told them "I would sooner face a Leopard than get back on the bus".

The driver sternly looked at me "I cannot leave unless everyone gets back on the bus". With a brief pause suggested he would make room at the back of the bus for me. I could not help thinking that if the bus suddenly goes over the side of the cliff it does not matter where I sit. Briefly reflecting that maybe my protest would make the driver be more cautious I agreed. The conversation had attracted a large crowd of unhappy passengers who wanted to get going. Reluctantly I got back on the bus and was given a seat towards the back. There was an air of excitement in the bus, I crossed my fingers trying to convince myself that this will help. The bus pulled away

171

and seemed to be travelling at a more sensible speed, or maybe it was my imagination.

The rest of the journey was on a relatively flat road then started to steadily climb for about half an hour until the bus arrived in a town square. The bus driver called out "Kandy" and everyone got off and went their own way. As I went to get off the bus the driver asked me if the driving was good,

smiling I replied "it was good" which brought a wide smile to his face.

Before I could get my rucksack on my back a man asked me if I needed some where to stay, wearily looking at him and thinking it was too late to try and find a guest house myself replied "yes".

"Follow me I know where you can stay".

I was lead along the main high street to an alley where there was a set of steps. The man pointed and said "up there". I took out a bank note from my pocket and gave it to the man for his help. Climbing the stairs I was met at the top by a man. "You want somewhere to stay"? Not waiting for me to reply he added "I have a room here". Opening a door he told me I could sleep tonight and pay in the morning, saying thank you I put my rucksack down and just crashed out on the bed and almost instantly fell asleep. Waking the next morning in the small room I was eager to get out and start exploring Kandy, a place that I had heard so much about from George and others. The botanical gardens, the gem stone museum, George's friend with his shop, the Temple of Buddha's Tooth and so much more. First I needed to wash or shower which turned out to be cold as usual, then went to look for some where to eat. I did not have to walk far to find a tea shop and ordered an omelette. Having eaten I set off for the Temple of Buddha's Tooth which I was curious about, why a Temple for Buddha's tooth?

The Temple was close to the town centre not far from where I was eating. The approaching path led straight to the entrance, next to a lake. The temple had a similar appearance to an old Chinese building with a red curved roof and a white exterior wall. A Bridge crossed a moat, leading under an arch and in to a court yard. Inside the temple it was cool, the room with Buddha's Tooth was decorated with a gold relief design and had a statue of Lord Buddha behind a golden fence preventing any one getting too close. Buddhist monks in their yellow cloaks stood next to the gate as well. Looking around the room I admired the art worked and stared in wonder at the decor. Visitors put their hands together and bowed in silence, I contemplated doing the same but decided to just stand in silence. Eventually leaving the room, outside the temple was an information board which said that the Temple of Buddha's Tooth was an extremely sacred Buddhist Temple. The Temple houses one of Buddha's teeth under several gold domes which was brought to Sri Lanka by Princess Hemamali. The atmosphere in and around the temple was serene with everyone talking quietly. Just outside the temple door were some zoological specimens and one of them was a Russels Viper. Looking closely at it the pattern on the snake was very similar to that of dried leaves and would be difficult to see hidden on the forest floor amongst the dried foliage, this brought home the advice I was given in Anuradhapura.

After visiting the temple and the grounds I walked around the lake, it was some 400 yards across. Towards the centre of the lake was a small island with several palm trees towering above the island. The lake itself was edged with palm trees and behind the temple and old palace was a forest of tall mature trees which came down to the lakes edge dipping their branches in the water. In the distance was a series of forest covered hills. The lake portrayed the tranquillity of the scene in the reflected image of the temple and trees. A road climbed up a small hill, at the top was a panoramic view of the lake, temple and surrounding hills. The view looked spectacularly picturesque with a building so well preserved since the sixteenth century, and still standing. Sitting down on a bench I took in the scenery and noticed that the island was in fact perfectly square and was obviously man made, an idyllic retreat for the Sinhalese monarchs for a private picnic. It all looked ideal for a Hollywood film set where explorers would discover a lost city.

Remembering that I wanted to visit the gemmology museum and botanical gardens, I needed a map of Kandy to find my way around and found one in a book stall. There were several for sale from the basic black and white printed map to the more luxurious full colour touristy type with pictures of several places of interest. Opting for a cheap basic one, it showed the botanical gardens were some distance away. It also had the Gemmology museum and college marked which was on the way to the botanical gardens.

The gemmology college was a small building and the museum was adjacent up a set of wooden steps that lead to a small room. Displayed around the edge of the room were several glass cabinets with various gems, both precious and semi-precious that included Sapphires, Rubies, Emeralds and Diamonds. The semi-precious gems include Garnets, Peridots, Moonstones, Tigers eyes, Topaz, Turquoise, Opals and many more. Above each one was an information sheet describing the gem stone and where it could be found around the world. Not all of the Gem stones originated from Sri Lanka, but Sri Lanka was described as one of the main centres for Sapphires. Marvelling at the many different gem stones on display I wondered if it was possible to study gemmology; it looked as if it would be exciting and extremely interesting. There was an information leaflet about the courses which started in September and lasted three years, not having the finance or the time I was disappointed. Prising myself away from the gem museum I set off to the Botanical Gardens, not knowing what to expect but felt it would be interesting with an array of brightly coloured tropical plants.

The Botanical Gardens proved to be further than anticipated, a few buses drove past but the walk was pleasant looking at the various colourful homes high up on a bank beside the road. The entrance to the Botanical Gardens was a wooden arch, branches from trees either side of the wooden arch hung down, with a red brick wall surrounding the gardens. Through the entrance I could see

175

a wide avenue leading around the gardens bordered by brightly coloured flower beds and trees, some with broad trunks. Walking under the arch the full height of the trees became apparent, they were some hundred metres or so tall, just seeing these trees made it worth the effort getting here, the tropical flower beds either side of the wide avenues were an amazing riot of colours.

Some of the trees had commemorative plaques stating when they were planted and why they were planted, such as the palm tree planted in 1901 to commemorate the visit by George V. Though not botanically adept I marvelled at the huge palms, firs and brightly coloured tropical flowers. The wide avenue led me around the garden past various flower beds and borders in a loop until I found myself back at the entrance without surprisingly seeing another person.

Remembering the craft shop George suggested visiting was close to the entrance to the botanical gardens, finding it I climbed the steps up to Chamalee Jewellers & Arts & Crafts, a shop with a blue façade, large pane glass windows and a glass panel door. Inside a man sat at a large wooden desk, opening the door a bell chimed and the man looked up and said hello. Holding out my hand "hello I am Peter, George said I should come to visit you and ask about the Batik designs you have". The man smiled "my names Simon, I have been expecting you" and invited me to take a seat, "George wrote and told me so much about you". I told Simon that I had met some Dutch people in Anuranapura who were studying Sri Lankan Batiks, their work inspired me to find out more.

176

"George told me about your shop and I should visit you". Mentioning the gemmology course Simon told me to beware if I intend buying any gem stones, "some cut glass looks similar to the genuine article until you study them closer. There is one simple test any one can do when checking if a gemstone is real or just cut glass". Simon opened up a draw and took out two blue shiny multi-faceted gems, "which one is real?" Not knowing I just pointed to one of them. "no! That is glass, see how easy it is to be duped in to buying a fake stone". Simon then told me that a genuine gem stone feels cooler than cut glass. This did not seem possible as any object would be the same temperature as that of the ambient air around. Simon asked me to hold my hand out with my palm facing down, then placed one of the gem stones on the back of my hand, waited than replaced it with the other gemstone and asked if noticed any difference in the temperatures. The gem stones where relatively small, about half an inch across but thought I could feel a slight difference between the two. Simon told me to try again and placed each gem stone on the back of my hand again. This time I noticed a difference and said the first one was the real gem stone. Simon smile "yes that's right"

He asked if I was going to visit Ratnapura, Not having planned too but now he mentioned it I thought why not and said yes. "In Ratnapura there is gem stone market, some of the dealers will sell you some thing but you cannot verify what it is especially if it is uncut. Do not buy from these people. A bright red Garnet can look just like a Ruby to the untrained eye". Simon then added

177

"there are reputable shops in Ratnapura who will give you a warranty to guarantee what you are buying".

Thanking Simon for the advice he suggested looking at the batiks., excitedly I said yes. "We need to go next door and around the back to the work shop".

The workshop was a lean to shelter with four large tanks full of water and large benches with fabrics laid out on them. There were several women working. Some were working on the fabrics using small brass cups which had small down ward pointing spout on a stick whilst some other women appeared to be washing the fabric. Simon explained that they were applying the wax to the area's that don't need to be dyed. Once the wax has hardened the cloth is dipped in to a tank of dye and left to dry. Once dry the wax is boiled out which also sets the dye. Once dry another colour can be added by repeating the process until we have the finished design. It looked so easy but time consuming, also a lot of space was needed to dye and wash out the wax. Watching the women made the dying and washing process look elegantly easy.

Having watched the women working skilfully for some time we went back to Simons shop after thanking every one for letting me watch them work. Back in the shop Simon said "I need to give you some thing to remember our meeting". He took out a small blue crystal about quarter of an inch across from his draw. Simon explained that it was an uncut Sapphire. I asked Simon how much he wanted for it but to my surprise he did not want anything, "it is too small to cut and the wrong shade of blue", even though to me it was a distinct blue; obviously

I had a lot to learn about gems. He also gave me a small booklet about the Kandy Esala Perahera Festival. Simon explained that the festival was held in July and August with processions around Kandy led by decorated elephants. The processions sounded amazing but I planned to return to India and would not be in Sri Lanka for the festival. I thanked Simon for the Sapphire and booklet and after saying good bye made my way back to Kandy ensuring that I had the Sapphire tucked away safely.

By the time I arrived back in Kandy it was mid-afternoon and needed something to eat. Popping in to one of the many tea shops I ate a large rice meal and drank several teas whilst reading the booklet which described in detail the history of the ceremony and processions. I wanted to see the festival but life moves on and thought I would return to see it another time.

I pondered over my map and wondered what to do next having seen most of Kandy, and got to meet Simon. Eventually I came to the conclusion that I should move on to Nuwara Eliya which I had been told many times that it was just like England where the old rich colonials tried to create their English idyll home from home up in the Sri Lankan Highlands. I was curious what the 19th century's rich and aristocracy' idyllic England would look like, nothing like the real England I would imagine.

After my meal I paid the Temple of the Tooth another visit to see what it was like at night and walk by the lake. It was just turning dusk, lights draped over the roofs, individual buildings and the exterior battlement walls illuminating the whole structure, befitting a building devoted to a relic of Buddha. The view was spellbinding during the day but at night it was mysterious. There were a number Sinhalese people walking around the grounds but not any westerners which seemed strange. Outside I sat on a bench in the balmy evening air soaking up the Buddhist ambiance, looked out over the sparkling lake reflecting the temple lights. Reluctantly pulling myself from a perfect evening I slowly made my way back to the main part of town where there was still some night life and sat in a tea shop until it was dark and the stars shone overhead. Determined to catch the earliest bus possible to Nuwara Eliya but unsure when it was.

 Back at the guest house. The owner was standing on the veranda, paying for the two night's stay and told him I will be leaving in the morning. Asking where I was going, when I told him he said the bus does not leave until mid-day. This would give me plenty of time to walk around Kandy and visit the shops. The days walking had worn me out, that night I slept like a log.

Waking refreshed the next morning I packed my things up after a shower and booked out. I managed to find a tea shop where I could sit outside, as I drank my tea an air conditioned bus pulled up. There was a pregnant pause before the doors opened and disgorged its passengers. Straight away several were fanning themselves in an effort to cool themselves down, others were more concerned with their camera's, after checking them over they dutifully followed their guide towards the temple who strode off pointing in the direction they should all be walking. It almost looked comical as the tourists struggled to keep up burdened by their photographic equipment hanging around their necks and silver cases housing their lenses whilst others frantically fanned themselves.

Having finished breakfast I ambled along the road and almost literally bumped in to Rolf, we shook hands and tried to catch up on each other's journey. Rolf introduced me to Helga who he met after arriving in Sri Lanka. They told me about a concert by Ravi Shankar in Kandy and had come to see it. Rolf asked if I was going to watch it, exciting though it sounded I felt like moving on and wondered who Ravi Shankar was. Helga announced he was the best Sitar player in the world. I briefly thought whether I should stay for the concert but decided to catch the bus. We chatted for a while then said good bye.

I came across a book shop where I spent ages hunting along the shelves for one to read, most were second hand science fiction by a variety of authors. Eventually finding two that took my fancy I decided to have a proper meal before catching the bus. Whilst eating and reading an English voice asked if it was okay to sit down at my table and said it was okay. The person looked just like the archetypal back packer with scraggly hair, and wearing a mish mash of clothes of various Indian styles. My names Eric, I stopped eating and reading and said my name was Peter, "good to meet you Peter". Eric ordered a tea and tried to engage me in a conversation about where I had been and where I was going. I just paraphrased my journey through India and around Sri Lanka and said I will be going back to India. Trying to eat quickly and avoid talking which most probably appeared rude but I was more concerned about catching the bus on time. Eric told me about his experience of his trip in India and what he had planned, as Eric talk I nodded every now and then to make it appear I was listening. Finishing my meal I got up grabbed my rucksack held out my hand and said "it was nice meeting you Eric but I have a bus to catch". Eric gingerly held out his hand after a brief hand shake I walked away.

Soon the familiar red single decker bus arrived, finding myself a seat half way down the bus I settled down hoping it would not be as hair raising as my journey to Kandy and arrive in reasonable time. The bus slowly pulled out of Kandy following the road up the hill. The road undulated with the occasional steep incline, weaving as the road hugged the sidings of the hills. The journey felt sedate, maybe because it was day light and I could see how close the bus was to the edge of the road. The hilly scenic view of tea plantations seemed to stretch as far as the eye could see; on the other side of the bus the tea plant covered hill side climbed away from the road, this was Ceylon tea country. Occasionally we passed people with wicker baskets on their back picking the tea leaves from the bushes. They all appeared to be women dressed in their bright saris and short tops. The tea bushes were jam packed together, it did not look as if there was enough space between them to walk through the vegetation. Driving at a reassuring speed the bus wound its way along the hill side road in to the afternoon until the light faded turning an inky black. Eventually the road levelled off and buildings appeared either side of the road, they had wooden fronts and carved balconies which reminded me more of the Swiss design than one you would find in England.

The bus stopped in a square surrounded by several wooden two storey buildings, none had any light. The street was deserted; the only sound was from the passengers getting off the bus. Climbing down in to the cool night air a young lad came up to me and asked if I wanted a place to stay. Initially surprised someone was up this time of night then drearily said yes, "follow him". We stopped at a wide oak porch above a door with a large brass knocker. The lad knocked on the door with a thud that would wake any one up, after a brief pause the door was opened by the slim man. Both spoke in Sinhalese and the man nodded, the boy confirmed that there was a room available.

Saying thank you I gave the boy a rupee note and stepped in to the dark house. The interior was decorated with wooden panelling that reminded me of the house from the Adams Family TV series rather than an old English house. It was quite chilly, only wearing shorts and a T shirt it was not surprising. I was shown to a room with a large old wooden bed and several blankets on it and thick curtains at the windows. The man said I could pay in the morning and closed the door behind him. Climbing in to the bed tiredness took over and was soon in deep sleep. I woke but the room was still dark and decided to go back to sleep, then I noticed a slim strip of light on the wall. Looking at the curtain there was a slight gap letting the day light in. Throwing back the blankets I instantly felt the sudden chill of the room. Quickly washing in the basin I got dressed and went to enquire about breakfast; with so much hype about how English Nuwara Eliya was I expected a fully cooked breakfast. Just along a wood panelled corridor there was a room with a large dining table with two people sitting at it. They both looked at me as I walked in, a blonde woman dressed in a printed loose top greeted me with "G'd day", the man distinctly and very English said "good morning". Introducing themselves as Sarah and John I sat down on the opulently cushioned chairs and told them my name. Sarah had a large pineapple and offered me some saying she had enough and could not eat it all, taking a slice I jokingly wondered if a cooked breakfast was on the menu.

A Sinhalese man came in to the room and asked if I wanted anything to eat. Asking for a boiled egg he left without any further comment, I wondered if the boiled egg would be the same as those in India, hard. The three of us talked for about our trips around Sri Lanka. Sarah had travelled from Australia, across Indonesia via Bali which most Australians seemed to have done, then on to Sri Lanka. John looked quite well dressed for a back packer wearing a shirt and pressed trousers and had flown straight to Sri Lanka. My boiled egg arrived, we all took a keen interest in whether it was hard boiled, cracking open the shell it became obvious it was hard, we all laughed at the absurd interest at the state of an egg had created. A pot of tea was brought out which tasted absolutely marvellous, maybe the best tea I have drunk. During our conversation I mentioned about going up to the top of the hill over looking Nuwara Eliya. Sarah pointed out that there were several hills overlooking Nuwara Eliya, flippantly replying with a smile I said "the tallest one" which Sarah commented was the highest point in Sri Lanka.

Not thinking about the altitude I was at and only wearing a T shirt, shorts, sandals with my rucksack slung over my shoulder I set off. Maybe not the ideal dress for hill walking, but snow wasn't anticipated, as far as I knew. The climb was quite steady at first; looking up the hill top was partially shrouded by cloud but felt it would be burnt off by the sun later.

A worn path lead under some low trees and bushes. Higher up the hill I looked back at Nuwara Eliya, there was a panoramic view of the lake and surrounding countryside partially masked by the misty cloud. After a few hours the gradient became steeper but the path was still well defined as it weaved back and forth. The trees gave way to tall bushes which could easily harbour a Leopard which would make the walk very exciting. Looking back it felt as though I was looking directly down on Nuwara Eliya. The bush gradually petered out until there was just long grass, cloud swirled around the hill top giving the occasional glimpse of the surrounding hills and the valleys. The individual buildings in Nuwara Eliya were hardly distinguishable. At the top it looked very Spartan with scrubby grass and some short stubby bushes, the opposite side of the ridge dipped away in to short dense scrub. Stopping to take some photographs I could feel the chilly moist air.

Admiring what I could see of the scenery between the gaps in the cloud I heard some voices; looking around a man and a woman came over the brow of the hill, saying hello they stopped close to me on the summit. We introduced our selves, Laura and Richard looked about twentyish and had travelled through Africa over land from Cairo to Dar Es Salam.

They described their journey from Cairo on a large barge with numerous passengers. It meandered down the Nile stopping at various villages and towns allowing people to get on and off. Many of the passengers were families who had their supplies for the journey and cooked the meals on board.

There was no timetable and all of the passengers were at the mercy of the captain's whim. They excitedly explained the hilarious moment when the barge took an unscheduled stop in an Egyptian town where the men on the boat were challenged to a football match. Something they could not refuse so they all jumped on to a bus and went off play this match, the barge football team returned victorious three days later. The town where they played the football match turned out to be a day's drive away, then they played the match, had a victory celebration afterwards, then travelled back.

Disembarking from the barge Laura and Richard travelled across country to Kenya where they went on safari. At the Tanzanian border they encountered a very over zealous customs officials. Wanting to cross the border and travel on to Dar es Salam. The customs official asked to see their entry visa but Laura and Richard did not have one. The customs official explained they could not enter Tanzania without a visa, Laura and Richard asked how they could get a visa. The official told them they could get one in Dar es Salam and expected to get their passports stamped and be allowed to travel to Dar es Salam. The official still refused them entry because they did not have a visa. Laura and Richard pointed out that he had said they could get a visa in Dar es Salam where they can show the authorities their entry stamp. The Customs Official explained in a way only customs officials can under stand the logic told them that they can only go to Dar es Salam to get an entry visa if they had an entry visa that allow them in to Tanzania. They were totally dumbfounded and bemused by this catch 22 logic. Laura and Richard suggested they should have an entry stamp that allowed limited access with enough time to travel to Dar es Salam where they could get the visa. After some reflection by the customs official he agreed to this suggestion and stamped their passports. Their story sounded farcical and hilarious; after the event. Laura mentioned that I did not look like the usual back packer travelling around India or Sri Lanka wearing beige shorts and plain T shirt, it was more suited for the African bush and asked if I had been to Africa.

Replying that I had been to Kenya with the British Army Richard asked where I was posted, "Gibraltar, Ireland and Belize" I replied. Laura and Richard said it sounded as though I was in the same regiment as their friend and asked who I was with, "Three Queens!" They told me their friends name "do you know him? There was a pregnant pause of disbelief then excitedly replied "yes I do".

It was hard to believe that we were quarter way around the world on top of a hill and accidently met each other and found we knew the same person, we laughed at the irony. I asked how he was and they explained he was well but not sure where he was at present partly because they had been travelling. At one point Laura wondered how high we were, I pulled out my Bartholemews map and even though the superimposed map of Sri Lanka was relatively small the contour colours indicated the different heights quite distinctly.

After some scrutinising, negotiating and guesstimating we came to the conclusion it must have been about five thousand feet.

Richard and Laura quizzed me in depth about Belize then said they will have to visit Belize when they travel through South America on their homeward leg of their trip. Telling them they should and was sure they would enjoy the country, being a small it's easy to get around and you should be able to hitch a lift. On the main road we walked the short distance in to Newara Eliya which looked deserted and warmer down from the cloudy hill top. Saying good bye I went to find myself a place to eat and to write a letter bringing my family up to date with my unbelievable encounter.

I spent the afternoon drinking tea whilst writing a lengthy letter about my morning hike which felt surreal; it just showed what a small world it really was. You can be out in the wilds somewhere and meet someone and find you have something in common. Finishing my letter and posting it I returned to my guest house and decided to catch the bus to Ratnapura in the morning; maybe even buy some gems. With the evening drawing in it felt cooler and decided to turn in early after having some thing too eat.

The next morning I managed to find the showers which were warm and refreshing. Richard was already having breakfast; apparently Sarah had caught the bus the previous day. Opting for an egg breakfast, I paid my bill then went to catch the bus. Having to wait an hour, which felt like an eternity I killed the time drinking tea and admiring the various buildings, none were half timbered as you might expect in an old English village but the wooden fronted houses added to the quirkiness of Nuwara Eliya.

The bus arrived in the quiet square. Choosing a seat half way down the bus, I had found this the best place to sit on the buses in India and Sri Lanka, the pot holes did not feel so bumpy.

Adams Peak, steps leading into the clouds

Only a few passengers got on the bus which allowed me to stretch my legs out across the seats whilst taking in the countryside. Leaving the last house behind, ahead of us were the bright green hills and valleys. Tea plantations hugged the hills sides with tea pickers tucked between the tea bushes filling their baskets with their fresh crop of leaves to be sent around the world for the early morning life saver or kick start of the day.

The road weaved its way down the hill sides as the bus navigated the bends at a sensible speed, unlike the free wheeling adventure a week earlier. As the journey progressed I found that instead of looking down on the countryside from the top of a hill I was looking up at the peaks which gave a sense of perspective and how high Newara Eliya was.

The hilly tea plantation country side gave way to a flat landscape filled with rice paddies, streams and tall trees. It occurred to me after passing several small villages that no one had asked for baksheesh, something I had become accustomed to in India and at times expected to be asked, but at no time was there a hint of any begging in Sri Lanka.

The roads straightened out and the bus picked up speed. Tall palm trees stood either side of the road and a river that opened in to a lake. The increase in the speed of the bus built up the anticipation that we might be reaching

Ratnapura soon. Alas this was not the case and the journey took another hour or so.

The climate definitely changed from the cooler climes of the hills to the more hospitable temperature appropriate for shorts and T shirts. Palm leaf and wooden buildings started to line the road and very soon the bus came to a halt at what was the bus terminus which consisted of a few bus stops in a market square. A large number of people stood near the bus terminus, getting off the bus I realised they were all men and seemed to be talking in a discreet way, at times quite urgently. On one side of the wide open market square were several shops, far over to the other side of this wide open area were some houses on stilts made of palm leaves. Amongst the crowds were some westerners watching the Sinhalese men talking over something that was in their hands, now and then one of the men pointed forcefully at what the other person was holding, and looked confrontational.

I made my way around the crowd towards one of the palm buildings in a hope it might be a guest house. I climbed up a set of wide steps to a platform where there were several pairs of shoes and called out through the open door.

A middle aged Sinhalese woman appeared and beckoned me in. Obligingly I took my sandals off and left them by the door. Seeing my large rucksack the woman second guessed that I was going to ask and said intuitively "you need some where to sleep, you can sleep here; how many nights"? Not having thought too much about how long I wanted to stay in Ratnapura I told her two nights. "That is okay, I have a space over here for you, I do not give meals you can only sleep here". This sounded like a reasonable arrangement, confident there would be somewhere to eat in Ratnapura. I was shown my space on the palm leaf floor in a corner of a large room which several other backpackers shared who already had their belongings laid on the floor. There was no floor covering but luckily I had my reed mat which I felt would be sufficient. The woman instructed me not to spread all of my things about, "you must keep them tidy. Smiling at this instruction, it brought back memories of living in a barrack room.

Putting my large rucksack down I got myself organised then set off to explore Ratnapura, especially the jewellery shops and find somewhere to eat. The men haggling in the market square looked entertaining with their gesturing and stern expressions, there was a lot of head shaking and hand waggling, then with out any warning hand shakes and smiles. Unsure what they were haggling over but I had a good idea; gemstones! I watched them until my stomach told me that I needed to be somewhere else and soon found a tea shop with tables outside. Sitting down I called for a tea and some rice.

Whilst eating I watched the people busily walking by and was surprised how many backpackers were in Ratnapura. Having eaten it was time to browse the jewellery shops which were close by and soon found myself gazing through the windows at displays of large Rubies and Sapphires laid out on black velvet.

Many of the shops had the names in Sinhalese and

English. Some windows had displays full of rings, necklaces, ear rings and bracelets, mainly in gold. The carat of the gold was not displayed but felt it must be similar to the standard in India, 18 or 22 carat. Many of the designs had a gem stone in lays such Garnets, cut Rubies, Star Rubies, Moon Stones and of course cut and star Sapphires of the richest pure blue imaginable. Gem stones could be bought separately which were laid out on black velvet, the prices looked very expensive but when converted to sterling they were relatively cheap. I was the tempted to buy some to help pay for my trip around Sri Lanka but it would have been a large part of my travel budget and decided it would be best to err on the side of caution.

Browsing around the shops I came across one with a wide selection of post cards. Most I had seen before and sent home but one in particular grabbed my attention, it showed a finger shaped mountain that towered above the surrounding hills topped with buildings at its summit. There were several different images of this peak, at sun rise, on a clear day and sunset taken from different angles. On the back it read "Sri Pada (Adams Peak) mountain shrine venerated by Buddhists, Hindus and Moslems, Height 2233 metres". From my own calculation 2233 metres was just over seven thousand feet, but where was Adams Peak? It looked as though it was one of those places I should climb, especially being such a high point in Sri Lanka. I asked the vendor of the shop where Adams Peak was, "it is not far, but it will take you all day to climb to the top". All day to climb to the top, this sounded like a challenge and wondered if I could climb to the top and be back down in time for tea; as they say in all good adventure books. Enquiring how to get to Adams Peak, the vendor told me to catch a bus from the market; at Adams Peak there were steps all the way to monastery at the top. It sounded straight forward and decided to climb Adams Peak the next day, the view from the monastery at the top of Adams Peak looked exciting.

As the light faded the shops owners lit their lanterns or turned on their lights which gave the shop facades a welcome glow. I bought myself another read mat just to ensure that I was comfortable enough sleeping on the floor and headed back to the guest house for an earlyish night to ensure I did not miss the bus for Adams Peak. At the guest house several backpackers were sitting in small groups talking. One group seemed to be have a heated debate and arguing amongst themselves and thought it not to intrude. Another group were having a quiet conversation, they looked up and said "Hi!" saying "Hi!" back I asked if they had just arrived. One of the group said "yeh!" then carried on with the conversation. Whilst no one was using the washing facilities I took the opportunity to clean myself up, as expected the water was cold, maybe the lack of mod cons was the reason for the serious conversation. Feeling clean I tried to get some sleep, the serious conversation was still in full flow, someone mention that they had to sleep on the ground. The palm leaf floor was not a bad surface to lay on, it felt springy and creaked but was comfortable enough. Laying down on my reed mats and pulling my towel over my head I managed to eventually doze off despite the whispered complaints.

I was woken the next morning by somebody walking about, the palm leaf floor creaked as they paced about. Getting up I rolled up my mats and large towel. Had a quick wash and left for the bus terminus. The market square was already busy with the gem traders, haggling over the price for their precious merchandise. At times the haggling was so strident it seemed that the traders would come to blows and then there would be the shaking of the head from side to side and the price was agreed with a shaking of hands. I browsed around the market whilst waiting. A number of vendors had plastic sheets laid out on the ground covered with vegetables and fruit. There were small pineapples the size of a large potato which looked tempting, deciding to buy one of these for later and several small bananas, which I ate whilst waiting for the bus. Just several people boarded the bus for Adams Peak and got a seat of my choice, none of the passengers were westerners. After a short wait the bus left Ratnapura following the palm tree lined road, passing individual homes and rice paddies stretching out in to the distance then turned in the direction of the distant hills. The bus steadily climbed up in to the hills passing tea plantations. After a few hours the bus turned right in to a large gravel bus and coach terminus. Several coaches were parked up to one side with a number of Sinhalese people standing by them dressed in trousers, some women wore saris and a few men wore sarongs. Some carried a rucksack slung over their back or a bag which gave me the impression

195

that the climb to the top of Adams Peak would be relatively easy. A sign pointed at the start of the climb where there were large stone steps of irregular height, grass grew between them forcing the individual steps to lean forward. Each step had been eroded smooth marking where the pilgrims had stepped over the many years or even centuries. Taking the first few steps I wondered how many had used the steps before me. Initially the irregular height of the steps made it difficult to get in to some sort of rhythm but after climbing the first few hundred the spacing became more even and managed to adjust my stride to a steady pace. The path weaved its way up as it skirted around large boulders and under trees which restricted the view of the route ahead. The angle of the climb at Adams Peak varied from forty degrees to a steeper gradient. After the first hour my stride became accustomed and was able to walk along quite quickly. I passed groups of pilgrims who were walking at a more leisurely pace, now and then I slowed down which gave me an opportunity to talk to some of the people which broke the monotony. Branches hung over the lower part of the path giving much needed shade but they thinned out as the path climbed.

After climbing for about two hours I came to a small shelter constructed of wooden poles and a large sheet. This was a tea shop that also dispensed cold drinks and some food; I opted for a tea, a welcomed refreshment. Talking to the vendor I asked how he got everything up to his tea shop which felt like a silly question, he looked at me with a perplexed expression, "I have to carry it up", we talked for a short while but felt if I stopped too long it would be difficult to get my legs going again. Now and then there was an opportunity to see the distant summit, if I craned my neck; the view looked daunting. Each time I stopped to see how I was doing the summit seemed just as far away as had done previously, it was like a dangling carrot tempting me to carry on and reach the elusive summit. Along a wide stretch of the path I slowed down to talk to a family who were ambling along as if they were walking in the park, one of the group mentioned they were on a family pilgrimage. They all seemed surprised to see me, I was the only white person they had seen on their walk and was bit of a novelty. A man with the group asked if I was going to the top, saying I was he wished me a safe journey and hoped to see me at the top. Saying good bye I dashed off, stopping occasionally to see how much further it was to the summit. In a clearing I could make out a queue of people trailing up some steep steps, it was reassuring that I did not have much further to go. The path broke through the cover of the trees and I could see the surrounding countryside with other hills spread out in to the far distance, some of them were lower than where I was standing which gave some perspective of how high Adams Peak was. A large stupa was beside the path that did not look as if it had been constructed from the surrounding rock, obviously every thing was brought up the hill. The wide path met some very steep concrete steps with a hand rail, it climbed in to the clouds that had now formed around the summit. The last four hundred yards or so were almost vertical. Towards the top my legs started to feel the strain with each step, similar to a walk I did up Pen-y-Fan in Wales. Finally climbing through the swirling mist I stepped up between two buildings and arrived at the monastery. Looking about there was very little to see, the cloud blocked the view but there was an occasional break that revealed the distant hill tops. If the stupa further down was amazing at that altitude nothing could have prepared me for the buildings standing at the summit. There were several small stone buildings standing on the flat tiny area, a narrow path circumnavigated the summit, pilgrims slowly followed it around back to the stairs.

It felt very cool standing in the cloud now that I had stopped walking and trying to catch a glimpse of the hills below. The damp chill persuaded me to start making my way back down. Descending the first few steep steps was painful, my thighs strained to stop me from toppling down the stairs. If my legs gave way now there would be no way of stopping my self-falling down the almost vertical steps and bumping in to people climbing up. Having taken a few steps my muscles eased as they took the strain and my legs got in to a rhythmic skip down each step as I held on to the railings. Reaching the bottom step where it levelled off I was able to trot along with the downward momentum. Meeting the family I had spoken to earlier the man asked if I had been to the top yet, saying I had he smiled, "you must have had some divine assistance". We all laughed, it was ironic when I was not a Buddhist, Hindu or a Muslim. Caring on with my descent, egged on by the thought that I could be back in Ratnapura before dark was an encouraging incentive. The bottom uneven steps made it difficult to drop down each one, unable to keep up a rhythm and had to take each step with strained effort. Coming to the last few steps with great relief I stepped on to flat ground and looked forward to getting on to the bus and sitting down and rest my weary legs.

The journey back to Ratnapura took a bit longer than I thought but we arrived in good time, stepping off the bus I felt my muscles and tendons straining with each step as I headed for a tea shop and something to eat.

Whilst eating a well earned meal I mulled over where to go next. Ratnapura was so close to Colombo, the capital of Sri Lanka but reflected on George's suggestion that I should visit Kutchchaveli which was on the opposite side of the island and a lot further away. George had painted such an idyllic picture of the beach, but I also wanted to visit the Diyaluma Falls were not too far from Ratnapura. I had found out that though the Diyaluma Falls was not the highest waterfall in Sri Lanka at seven hundred and twenty feet it was high enough to warrant a visit. The thought of seeing the water cascading from such a height was too exciting to miss. I just had to find where the falls were and how to get there. I felt a book shop would be the best place to ask and might have a tourist guide. Checking at several places that sold books only a few sold tourist guides then I stumbled on one that seemed to specialise in tourist information. First I asked if the owner had any information about the Diyaluma Falls. Rummaging through several publications he came up with one small booklet. It had small maps indicating where places of interest were. It had a short paragraph about the Diyaluma Falls but the guide was more aimed at the wealthier tourist rather than the back packer.

Asking if I could catch a bus from Ratnapura the shop owner pointed and said the bus leaves from there; "what time?", "I am not sure" came his reply. It sounded I needed to be up early to catch the bus. My main concern was how to get to Kutchchaveli from The Diyaluma Falls. It was dark and the shops were lit up, even after my excursion I was in the mood for some window shopping, especially at the jewellery shops just to look at the Rubies and Sapphires. The shop windows kept me transfixed with the amazing array of colours in the gem stones which was reflected by the gold silver. After a late tea I wandered back to my guest house, several people had moved in and were trying to make excursion plans. A woman asked me if I had been to Adams Peak. Explaining that I had there in the morning and was worth the effort climbing to the top. They were deliberating over whether they should climb it during the day or at night and catch the sun rise having been told it was very spectacular when the sun rose casting a huge finger like shadow across the forest below. I mentioned that the summit had been shrouded in cloud and prevented a good view. My advice did not seem to help much and took myself off to get some sleep.

Getting to sleep proved difficult whilst the others talked about their trip the next day, they seemed to talk for ages about the best time of day and having to walk up in the dark which was countered with the brilliant sunrise they would see. I was so glad I did not have to negotiate everything I did; it would be so tedious. Eventually at some time their conversation just faded away only to be woken by creaking of the palm leaf floor as someone walked about, wishing they would go to bed but realised it was morning. Getting up I rushed about to get myself organised for the journey to Diyaluma Falls. Quickly washing and putting on clean clothes I dashed off hoping I had not missed the bus.

Managing to grab several bananas from the market I ate breakfast and bought a tea and poured it in to my metal mug.

Once everyone was on the bus it set off along what was now a familiar route edged with palm trees that lazily drooped as they gently waved in the tropical breeze, colourful improvised houses and friendly faces. The bus made steady progress, even with the occasional stop to pick up passengers, passing many rice paddies where farmers worked with their oxen pulling a plough. In the distance were the familiar central highlands. About midday the bus started climbing up a winding road giving a panoramic view of the relatively flat chequered countryside of paddy fields and woodland. After an hour or so the road flattened out and the bus came to a halt on a deserted stretch of road with foliage either side. The driver called out "Diyaluma Falls!" Getting off I spotted a yellow sign saying "Diyaluma Falls", it pointed in to the bush by the roadside. Throwing my rucksack on to my back I followed a path that dropped down amongst the trees and bushes. After a short distance I heard somebody walking up behind me, looking around there was a white man with black hair. He almost caught up with me then said "hello my names Sean".

Sean had a southern English accent which was reassuring to hear. I told Sean my name but we refrained from asking each other where we were from. It became obvious we were as mystified as each other where the water fall was as we followed the path over the relatively smooth rocks to meet a small stream. Wondering where it went we followed gurgling trickle to a wide flat area of smooth white rock surrounded by grass, small bushes and short trees. The stream ran down a gully in the rock and vanished over a cliff, we both realised this was the top of the water fall.

Putting my rucksack down I walked up to the edge where the water vanished over the cliff by a short sturdy tree that leaned out over the cliff. Walking up to the edge I put one hand on the tree to support my self and looked down, from where I was standing it was a sheer drop straight to the bottom which I estimated to be about 300 or maybe 500 feet to a rock pool and next to that was the road where a bus was parked; it looked minute.

The view was exciting and kept me transfixed as I stared down at the vertical drop and felt the urge to take a photograph. Moving away from the edge I got my camera out and noticed Sean was standing some distance from the edge, I told him about the fantastic view but Sean said he would take my word for it and wondered what I was doing, explaining that I was going to take a photograph he asked if was wise; "of course it is, I can lean against the tree, it's sturdy enough. Making sure I had film in my camera I positioned myself by looping my arm around a branch in a way so I could hold on to my camera with two hands and used my knee as a support against the tree trunk. Once in a comfortable position I focused the camera and adjusting the f stop to get both the top of waterfall and the road below in focus. Satisfied with the camera settings I pressed the shutter button, click! Moving away from the edge to wind the camera film on as I considered taking another photo, to my amazement I had attracted a small silent audience intently watching me. Smiling at them I packed my camera away, having seen the waterfall but not quite as intended I headed back to the road with Sean. It was getting late in the afternoon and needed to find some where to stay. Sean said he was staying at a hostel at Haputale and suggested I might be able to stay there for the night. We waited at the road side and before long a bus arrived which took us the short distance past tea bush cover hills. In Haputale we walked the short distance to the hostel, it had a homely busy atmosphere about it, the evening meal was being cleared away by the guests who were supervised by the hostel owner.

All of the guests were of various nationalities. Introducing my self to the hostel owner I asked if a bed was available. The hostel owner shook his head from side to side then said he believed there was one and asked me to follow him. We entered a long dormitory with about ten beds either side reminding me of a barrack room. Standing at the dormitory door the hostel owner said "I have this one here if you want it". The bed looked clean and not having much choice I said it would be fine, asking if there was any food the owner shook his head and said matter of factly "all finished". It was disappointing but I was not starving; all I really wanted was a shower or wash. The showers could only be used in the morning so I had to be satisfied with a wash. Joining the others in the lounge there was a mix of Germans, Australians, New Zealanders, English and some Americans. The conversations were mainly about every ones experiences and where they planned to go next. When asked about my plans I mentioned about going to Kuchchaveli, several backpackers asked where it was and could only say it was near Trincomolee. "What's it like?" some one asked. "I don't know except it has a good beach".

Some of the other backpackers gave me a quizzical look then some one asked "is that all?" When asked about accommodation I admitted I wasn't sure if there is any, then flippantly added "if it comes to the worst I have my tent".

When someone mentioned this sounded risky, smiling I replied "there s nothing like a bit of adventure". I felt that not many back packers or even Sinhalese had been to Kuchchaveli and it was an opportunity to see a place that not many others had visited.

Eventually the conversation died out and I decided to write a letter home about the days events before I had forgotten what happened. This took longer than anticipated, by the time I was getting towards the end of the letter the last few backpackers drifted in to the dormitory and got in to bed and felt I should do the same. Almost as soon as my large towel was draped over me I was sleep.

Kuchchaveli, a beach like no other

Waking early the next morning several backpackers were already busy packing their rucksacks. After a quick cold shower and a welcome breakfast of porridge I made my way to the bus stop; it was about an hour for the next bus towards. To kill time wandered around the shops and admired the view across the hills covered in vivid green tea bushes which contrasted with the clear azure sky. One shop sold small wooden boxes of different teas with the familiar Sri Lankan Lion holding a flag. Deliberating what tea to buy I opted for a box of Dunhinda Tea feeling it would revive fond memories of my time in Sri Lanka. The half full bus arrived, asking for Trincomolee the bus conductor replied "you must change buses, "I will let you know when the bus has arrived at the connecting terminus".

The road passed tea plantations with tea pickers filling their baskets. As the bus descended we left the tea plantations behind to follow a road lined with trees and the occasional house. As the landscape levelled out palm trees dotted the landscape with the chequered pattern of rice paddies. The descent from the Central Highlands to the lower plains brought on a noticeable rise in the temperature and the prospect of warmer evenings. Occasionally the bus picked up passengers at ad hoc stops. After some distance the bus pulled in to a bus terminal surrounded by trees, bushes and parched grass.

The bus conductor called out that this was my connecting terminal for Trincomolee.

The bus terminal consisted of three long concrete islands with four bus stops on each. Each bus stop had a long queue of passengers waiting patiently in the now hot sun. Finding the bus stop for Trincomolee I put my rucksack down hoping the bus would arrive soon. There was very little shade on the hot, stark white concrete which reflected the bright sun light. A man with a wooden crutch and one leg was making his way along the queues of passengers; every now and then he would stop then raise his amputated leg and hold out his hand begging. This was the first person I had seen in Sri Lanka begging but as he moved along he did not seem to get much sympathy or money from any one. Eventually arriving to where I was standing, fixing his eyes on me he raised his amputated leg and I pretended to ignore him. He persisted and stood there silently resting on his crutch waving his stump and holding out his hand. Doing my best to ignore him, it proved difficult and eventually relented and gave him 2 rupees. He moved on along the queue of waiting passengers, it was then I noticed across the far side of the bus terminus a large crowd had gathered.

Wondering what had attracted the attention of all of these people I lifted my rucksack on to my back and walked over to find out what was so interesting. Joining the back of the crowd I caught a glimpse of a woman sitting on the ground. Weaving myself through the crowd for a better view a middle aged woman was dispensing small phials or bottles which she was filling up with a brown liquid from a metal tray that appeared to have twigs in it, but realised they were not twigs but chicken legs and bones. There was an air of excitement as customers in the crowd bought the small bottles of this strange concoction. I could not resist taking a photograph to remember this impromptu scene, I was totally intrigued why anyone would want to buy this brown liquid. Returning to my bus stop I ask someone what the woman was selling, "medicine!" came the reply. The brown liquid did not look suitable for medicinal use or liable to invigorate a healthy recovery from any ailment, the taste of the brown liquid would most likely have a similar effect as the medieval universal remedy for general ailments; slug soup.

The bus was a welcome sight, it had been difficult waiting in the scorching midday sun without any shade but now I was able to squeeze on to the bus. Pulling out on to the road the bus headed for Trincomolee. The countryside looked parched compared to the greenery of the Central Highlands and its tea plantations, Sri Lanka was a country of geographical contrasts with the beaches, plains, hilly high country and mountains that made Sri Lanka so interesting.

Feeling excited about Kuchchavelli and what it might look like, besides being a good beach, was there any coral to dive on or any forests to explore? The bus stopped frequently for passengers to get on and off and gradually filled up. It was late afternoon now and wondered if I would arrive in Kuchchaveli before dark. Houses started to fill the road side which I took as a good sign that we were getting closer to Trincomalee. Without any formal sign of where we were the bus stopped in a wide open dry dusty patch next to a narrow lagoon, the bus conductor call out "Trincomalee".

Dotted around the dusty patch of land were several bus stops, one of the bus stops was for Kutchchavelli but which one. Asking a driver he told me I needed to catch the bus for Jaffna. After asking several people the bus for Jaffna I soon found the one I needed, but no one knew what time the bus was liable to arrive, I obviously had to be patient. Sitting down on the ground I watched the other passengers going about their business, it seemed that some had just finishing work, others had just been to the market and were laden with their shopping. Unlike India there was no barging, pushing or queue jumping.

A bus pulled up and after confirming it was for Kutchchaveli there was a feeling of relief that I was on the last leg of my journey. Passing the out skirts of Trincomolee the bus followed a perfectly straight road with trees either side then on the right they thinned out and I caught my first glimpse of the blue sea that contrasted with golden yellow sand. On the left was lush green vegetation but very few houses. The straight road crossed several bridges whilst I stared out at the inviting Tropical Indian Ocean.

Before long the bus pulled up by a hut, the conductor called out "Kuchchaveli" and found I was the only person getting off. The hut turned out to be a tea shop which was directly opposite the beach, under several palm trees were some boats. Close to these was a small hut with a palm leaf roof. No body seemed to be about except for those in the tea shop. Inside the tea shop I asked if there was a place to stay and as an after thought ordered a tea and rice.

The vendor pointed at the small hut by the palm trees, "you can stay there".

Asking who owned it the vendor replied "he will be here soon" and he sent a boy off with a wave of his hand. After about five minutes a young tallish Sinhalese man arrived and introduced his self as Charles. When he asked if I wanted somewhere to stay I assumed he was going to let me stay at his house but Charles mentioned I could stay in the hut for a small fee of ten rupees per night. He asked how long I wanted to stay, after some thought replied three nights and felt I could always extend my stay in Kuchchaveli, if needed. Handing over thirty rupees Charles gave me a key.

After finishing my rice we walked over to the hut and unlocked the wooden door. There were two windows, a concrete block with a mattress for a bed and a bed side cabinet on which was small bottle filled with oil and a wick. Charles explained this was a lamp and all I had to do was light the wick, "if the wick burns down just pull it up". Even though the room was very Spartan it felt secure having my own key. Charles explained I should give the key to the owner of the tea shop when I leave. Charles added he would come around in the morning to make sure everything was okay. Thanking Charles he said good bye and walked off across the beach. Whilst there was some light I wandered off along the beach which stretched for some 500 yards in each direction in sweeping in a shallow sweeping curve. At one end a cluster of rocks jutted out in to the sea with waves breaking on them.

Set back from the beach on the other side of the road were some low scrubby bushes. It felt so good be able to walk on warm soft sand again. The sea was almost perfectly flat, small waves gently rolled on to the beach making a slopping sound as the wave tipped over and a faint hush as the water crept up on to the sand. The light was fading as dusk started to draw its veil across the sky. There were no obvious lights along this part of the coast, not even from any houses that might be tucked in to the foliage. The only sound was from the sea and the palm trees gently swaying in the evening breeze, George said it was a good beach and he was not wrong. The last glimmer of light vanished, I decided to get some sleep even though it was still quite early, it had been a long day but I wanted to be up early the next morning. Back in the hut I lit the lantern which gave off a warm flickering glow casting large eerie shadows on to the wall, the mattress was firm but comfortable. Once I was settled down with my large towel over me it was difficult to resist dozing off and was soon asleep.

Suddenly waking in the dark room and unable to get back to sleep I went outside to be greeted by a faint glow of dawn stretching along the horizon above the indigo sea. The faint glow gradually grew brighter until the sun made its grand appearance rising above the distant waves bathing the beach and sea with its warm rays. The quiet morning air was broken with faint distant voices that gradually grew louder. I could make out the silhouettes of several men walking towards the boats. There was a wooden clunking sound as they got the boats ready, having checked the boats the crews started to heave them down towards the water. One of them saw me, called and waved, waving back this triggered a reaction from all of the others with a chorus in Sinhalese which I took for good morning.

The boat crews pushed the boat across the sand, then a subdued thud as a wave hit the wooden bow and slid in to the sea. Once in to the water the boat rocked up and down on the small waves. One of the crew held on to the boat as the others jumped in, once the last fisherman boarded the boat they paddled towards the rising sun silhouetted against the yellow sky which bathed the whole beach with its warm light.

Voices came from the direction of the tea shop, it was time for a tea and some breakfast before a swim. The tea earn was steaming and the vendor was frying what looked like hoppers. They were ideal and asked for three plus a tea. Sitting in the opening of tea shop I took in the perfect tropical view whilst sipping my tea. The hoppers were surprisingly filling and could not resist ordering another two. My appetite sated it was time to get in to the brilliant blue sea. Grabbing my diving mask and snorkel dashed to the inviting sea, pulling my mask over my face and placing my snorkel in my mouth I submerged in to the lukewarm water. Excitedly swimming out from the shore coral covered rocks sat on the sea bed with small brightly coloured fish flitting in and out of the crevices and hiding

212

holes. Swimming parallel to the beach I occasionally dived down for a closer look at the small fish, I noticed what looked like a coral branch; it moved and I realised this was a sea snake. I decided to avoid getting too close and watched it swim off, at the same time looked for any others that might be about.

I spent some considerable time snorkelling up and down the beach some thirty or fifty yards off the shore, it was so much fun and exciting that I lost track of time. The stinging on my back told me I had been out in the sun too long and needed to get out of the water and sit in the shade. I headed for the tea shop for a rice meal and refreshing tea. I noticed that the fisher men's boats were back on the beach and apart from the few people in the tea shop the beach and road was deserted; the only sound was the low tone of Sinhalese spoken by the men in the tea shop.

After the meal and a second tea I walked along the beach to the far end of the crescent and saw Charles, "hello! I was coming to see you, we shook hands and he asked how my day has been. Explaining I had been swimming all morning. Charles mentioned he swims out on the coral to catch the fish so he can sell them to collectors. Almost saying that I disagreed but reflected that it most probably helped him pay the bills. Out of the blue Charles asked me to meet his family and pointed to the foliage that lined the beach, "my house is just over here".

Walking between the bushes for about thirty yards there was a small wooden hut, a pretty young woman who looked about twenty and wearing a red saree laboured over a large metal pot on a fire. Charles said something in Sinhalese and she smiled, smiling back I said hello. Charles asked if I wanted something to eat but replied I had just eaten, Charles said he had lots of rice and it would be okay for me to stay, to this he took the lid off a large galvanised metal bin and I could see it was almost full but again declined. We talked for some time mainly with Charles asking me about where I was from, what it was like and my family, excitedly I told him about everyone, including my aunts, uncles and cousins.

Out of the blue he asked if they sold spear guns in Britain, when I said they did he asked if I could buy one and send it to him, then suggested next time I visit Sri Lanka I could stay in his house. I asked what the spear gun was for and Charles said it was to catch fish so he did not have to buy them from the fishermen. Because it was to help Charles support his family I agreed to send him a spear gun once I get home and liked the idea of being able to stay with Charles and his family on a return visit. Charles got very excited and spoke to his wife in Sinhalese which bought a smile to her face; putting her hands together she bowed. I bowed back which made both of them laugh. Making an excuse that I wanted to walk to the end of the beach I said good bye.

Also walking along the beach were two boys carrying a net and a pot but other than them there was no one else about. Just making it in time for the tea shop before it closed, bought some cold rice and ate on the beach by the hut, the evening was peaceful with the sound of the sea lapping at the sand. A gentle breeze picked up as the last light vanished leaving every thing in various shades of indigo. It crossed my mind that I should write home but with the light gone I did not want to use the dim light of the small lantern and decided to turn in for the night.

It was still dark when I woke and decided to go out on to the beach to watch the sun rise. There was not a hint of sun light but I did not feel tired so walked along the beach with the cool night air coming off the sea, a stark contrast to the heat of the day. I ambled along the beach until the sun started to tint the horizon with a pale yellow glow and faint audible stirrings could be heard coming from the tea shop as the vendor prepared his self for the day. Making my way over to the tea shop I asked for a tea and some hoppers then waited until the vendor had some hot water. Watching the sun rise made me think of my time at Cape Comorin and having to watch the sun rise for my keep. The fishermen readied their boat and set sail for another day's fishing. Having eaten I went down to the sea with my mask and snorkel then swam out to explore amongst the coral and rocks. Some locals were also swimming and I swam over to them. They had some small hand nets, asking what they were doing they showed me they were trying to catch the small fish. I floated on top of the water watching them swim down and net the small fish, they were then put in to small plastic bag. This did not seem right reflecting on what used to happen with the gold fish you could win at the fun fair. Besides the fish catchers I had the whole beach to my self , it felt so luxurious having so much space to myself without the intrusion of the modern world, except for the daily bus to and from

Trincomolee.

The tell tale sign of my back getting sun burnt made me realise it was time to get out of the sea. Back at the hut the fishermen had returned and were watching another up in one of the palm trees. As I approached them they waved, waving back I watched the man in the tree holding a jug attached to a rope. The other fishermen said something in Sinhalese and indicated that I should have a drink. Changing in to my shorts and T shirt I joined them. The jug was full of liquid which was poured in to several small clay pots. One was offered me one, asking what it was a fisherman replied "toddy" and added "coconut drink" then rolled his eyes and pretended to wobble which made the others laughed. I realised that this toddy was a homemade alcoholic drink made from the water collected in the jug that was tied up in the palm tree. Taking a gulp it had a pleasant coconut flavour and distinct kick. I indicated my approval of the taste and took my time finishing my cup. Once finished they offered me some more but declined, though it was pleasant I did not want to get drunk and maybe have my things stolen and feigned being drunk which made them all laugh. Waving good bye I headed for the tea shop.

Taking my time over the tea and some coconut biscuits I realised that I needed to write some letters. Retrieving my writing pad from the hut I sat down in the tea shop and wrote about Kuchchaveli describing the beach, swimming in the perfect blue sea and relaxing in such peaceful surroundings. Words did not seem to be able to do justice to such a perfectly tranquil friendly idyllic place. I was sure the letters would make every one envious of me lounging about whilst they worked back in chilly Britain but there was no guilt. The evening was closed in; Kuchchaveli seemed quieter than ever an ideal time to walk north along the road in the cool evening air to see what it was like further on. The road curved around the beach to the spit of land at the far end and then turned slightly in land. Low trees and bushes were on the left with the sea curving round on the right. A few houses lay back from the road with their lights glowing like stars. The road climbed slightly to the small spit of land from where I could see two small bays with the road running beside them, then the road turned left over a bridge which crossed a small lagoon. Several houses sat by the water's edge in the peaceful setting. There did not seem to be much point in walking any further and turned back. Pondering about the next day I decided to move on even though I felt reluctant to leave Kuchchaveli. The intention was to catch the bus back to Anuradapura, stay there for a few days then catch the ferry back to India.

I woke the next morning with the sun already up and not wanting to miss the bus I quickly washed, packed my things and went over to the tea shop. Several people were sitting in there, asking what time the bus was to Trincomolee they said it would be soon which I took as being some time in the morning. Ordering a tea and an omelette I took in my last view of Kuchchaveli and gave the key to the vendor as instructed by Charles.

Soon after I had finished my breakfast the bus arrived and reluctantly boarded it, leaving Kuchchaveli felt a shame

217

but I was starting to miss the lively hustle and bustle of India. Before long we were in Trincomolee at the dusty bus terminal, the queue for the Anuradapura bus was quite long. After about an hour or so the bus arrived, every one squeezed on, standing passengers packed the centre aisle. There just was not any more room and was sure the bus would not make any impromptu stops along the way and arrive in Anuradapura at a reasonable time.

How wrong I was, the driver was very obliging and stopped when ever someone flagged him down. The bus became absolutely packed with no way to get off quickly even if I wanted to. The country side rolled bye with dry beige grass, and short trees which changed to a familiar patch work of rice paddies at different stages of cultivation. Tall palm trees with long drooping branches waved good bye as we drove past. The driver still persisted on stopping even though there just was not any more room but everyone seemed to take the crammed bus in a light hearted way and jovially chatted.

With the regular stops for the road side passengers the bus journey took longer than anticipated and eventually arrived by the late afternoon, much to my relief. I headed to the guest house where I stayed previously and looked forward to sleeping on the soft bed and having a shower. Letting my self in I said hello to the staff who seemed a bit evasive, I asked if they had a spare room and was told I could not stay in the guest house, "the guest house is government property" came a reply. I asked if there was any where else I could stay and was given directions for a local hotel which was past the site of the ancient city and the shops in the city centre.

The hotel had a wrought iron gated entrance surrounded by a whitewashed wall. There was a water feature in the middle of the small court yard with a palm tree growing out of it. The hotel was whitewashed with white net curtains at the windows. The main doors lead in to a small foyer with a wooden desk and a man standing at it wearing a pressed white shirt. Once booked in I was shown to my room along a carpeted corridor.

The room was large with a double bed draped with a mosquito net. It looked extremely plush and luxurious compared to what I had stayed in over the past few weeks, most of all it had what I really wanted; a shower and could not resist testing the water to see if it was hot, it was. Stripping off I stood under the hot water, it felt luxurious washing myself with the hotels fragrant soap. I spent some considerable time under the shower, almost obsessively scrubbing myself down with the flannels and washing the sea salt out of my hair then dried myself off with fluffy soft white towels.

Feeling cleansed it was time to eat and wondered what might be on the menu, anything would do as long as it was not rice. I was not disappointed; there were potatoes and vegetables with chicken or beef. The choice was too much to bear, finding it difficult deciding what to eat I was tempted to order everything. In the end I ordered the beef and a tea. Bone china tea pot arrived with bone china cup and saucer, it felt so decadent. Not having the energy to walk anywhere I relaxed and soaked up the opulence, it might be the last chance I would get to experience such surroundings once I return to India. The meal was just perfect and felt strange having eaten so many rice meals. There were some Sri Lankan news papers in English which allowed me to catch up on some of the international news. Britain was having the usual winter of cold wet weather and fog which made me glad I was lounging in the Sri Lankan tropical heat.

By the time I had finished reading the papers it was dark, my eyes were feeling heavy and the thought of a soft mattress and pillows was too much to resist. Once in bed I sank in to the world of slumber drifting off weightlessly and slept through the night to wake with a start the next morning wondering where I was, it felt too comfortable. Recovering my senses and remembering I was in a hotel and not dreaming, also the indulgent comfort was temporary and I needed to catch the train for the ferry back to India. The comfortable bed and hot shower was making it difficult to leave but I was determined to catch the train. The Breakfast choices made it even harder for me rush and I felt like languishing around the hotel for the day or travel over to the Sri Lankan West coast and visit Colombo instead of catching the ferry. Breakfast was an omelette, toast and a pot of tea, the height of luxury. Having eaten I packed my rucksack, paid my bill and went to leave. At the main door one of the hotel staff told me not to go outside, two other hotel staff were franticly rushing around the water feature in the court yard with a stick. The man who stopped me leaving said that there was a snake eating the fish in the pool which struck me as a trivial reason to ask me not to leave. After several minutes of watching the hectic snake chasing and thrashing which involved the occasional frantic shouting I left for the train station. The platform was quiet; nobody else seemed to be catching the train and very few people were on the train.

The journey to the ferry terminal was brief, I watched the palm trees and homes beside the railway line as they sedately drifted past. Tthe train started to gradually slow down until it came to a gentle and almost polite halt at a platform. Getting off I stepped on to a long single platform with a booking office at one end. No staff were about to ask for advice but there was a large notice board giving the ferry times in Hindi, Sinhalese and English, the ferry was not until 7pm but no time was given when to buy a ferry ticket and imagined it was the same as Rameswaram, the tickets would not be available until an hour or so before the ferry sailed which meant having to spend the rest of the day waiting.

I crossed over the railway line to a make shift tea room with a tar paling cover, inside were wooden benches and tables with a sandy floor. Flies flitted about, a stark contrast to the hotel a few hours earlier. Ordering a tea I sat down and decided to write a letter not knowing when I would get the next opportunity back in India on my journey north. Having written a paragraph a white guy walked in dressed in a loose T shirt and baggy trousers sporting a moustache. He sat at my table, "hello my names Jean" it was obvious from his accent he was French.

We talked about where we had been in Sri Lanka which

221

was interesting because there had been a few places each of us had not been to. Jean was very interested in Kuchchaveli and talked about it for some time. Jean asked me if my trip to India was going to be my first and explained that I had travelled down the west coast from Bombay to Cape Comorin then to Rameswaram for the ferry. Jean had flown straight to Bangladesh and then after a short visit crossed over the border to Calcutta. Asking how crowded Calcutta was Jean replied it was not as busy as Bangladesh. Jean explained he travelled down the East Coast to Rameswaram. Mentioning I was thinking about travelling to Calcutta but Jean said that the trains are stopped at night by bandits who got on the trains and robbed the passengers. This did not sound like the India I had experienced so far which gave me second thoughts about where I should go. I told Jean about the Kashmiri's I met in Bombay and how friendly they were, their description of the Kashmir Valley sounded idyllic with Srinagar and Dal Lake surrounded by mountains. As we talked about our travels another white guy came in who was dressed as an archetypal Jesus Christ. All he wore was a white sarong and had long curly blonde hair. Looking at Jeans expression I could see he thought the same as me, he looked very peculiar and out of place. Having bought a tea he came over to our table and introduced his self. Michael did not wait to be asked where he was from, "I am from Germany!" he exclaimed. This struck me as strange but it got that question out of the way without asking. Michael said he had spent some time in Sri Lanka and was looking forward to go to India, "it is not clean here and Sri Lanka was over crowded". We mentioned that India was the same but Michael was adamant it was not. Almost laughing at Michael's naivety I thought he will have a big surprise when he gets off the ferry at Rameswaram, and wondered if he would last for any length of time in India. We all ate together but Michael kept complaining about the flies which I or for that fact Jean had not really paid much attention to, maybe I had become accustomed to the flies whilst travelling through India. Michael made it very apparent he was not happy at all with Sri Lanka with his string of complaints which became monotonous after a while. Having finished eating Michael went outside which was a huge relief, I was not in the mood to listen to his grievances. I told Jean that Michael was going to have a lot of problems travelling through India; Jean laughed and said "I think you are right". Realising it was going to be boring waiting for the ferry to arrive I asked Jean if he wanted to play a game of chess. Jeans eyes lit up and said he would like to. Taking the small round travel chess set out of my rucksack Jean admired the craftsmanship, I explained that it was made from Ebony and Sandlewood and how much I liked the smell of the Sandlewood. We had several games over numerous cups of tea with both of us winning and eventually concluded it was a draw. A train pulled in to the station and thought that if it was going to get busy I would have something to eat before boarding the ferry; Jean decided the same because it could be some time the next day before wc might get to eat again . Finishing our meals we went outside to see if we could buy a ferry ticket but the ticket office was still closed. On the platform some Sinhalese or Tamils were sitting at a small table playing dominoes and behind them was Michael leaning against the wall nonchalantly watching them. He looked so strange with the Sinhalese dressed in shirts and trousers and him standing there in his sarong looking very pale considering the length of time he had spent in Sri Lanka.

Another train pulled in to the station and disgorged a large number of loud passengers. Some went over to the tea shops whilst others started to form a queue even though it seemed a bit premature. Some passengers asked me and Jean about the times for the ferry but we could only repeat what was on the notice board and struck up a conversation with several other back packers. Sarah had not been to India yet and asked what it was like, those of us who had been did our best to describe what it was like without trying to make it sound too scary. Sarah turned out to be from New Zealand and the two others from different European countries, we made a merry international troupe. Just as it was turning dusk there was the anticipated distant sound of the ferry horn, but it was a while before the ferry could be seen. Another horn blast from the ferry prompted some passengers to form a queue. Our small group carried on talking and decided to wait until the queue was shorter. The ticket office opened its metal grills which triggered a manic rush with a lot of the passengers pushing in at the front and waving their passports. We all looked at each other in disbelief at how frantic it had become, Michael suddenly appeared and

Jean asked if he was going to queue but Michael just said he already had his ticket. This annoyed Jean who felt that Michael should have taken our passports and bought all of them in one go; I was surprised he got his ticket so soon considering the amount of passengers jostling at the kiosk. We joined the queue but we were not getting anywhere with the amount of people pushing in at the front of the queue.

As we waited patiently a constant stream of people barged in to the front. Susan commented about this and I suggested we should do the same but nobody else in our group were keen to. Having resisted this similar behaviour whilst travelling through India now was a time to do the same. I asked everyone for their passports and their fares then explained I was going to get in at the front and asked them to look after my large rucksack. I weaved my way through the throng of people at the ticket kiosk and made it to the front of the queue; leaning forward I held out the passports and shouted "five tickets" as loudly as possible without a hint of being heard. Shouting even louder in my best parade ground voice I barked "five tickets", but there was still no response. My arm was knocked out of the way and I was pushed back by the force of those either side of me. Lifting my arm up again I noticed the French Passport was on top. In a moment of inspiration I swapped Jeans French passport for my larger British black and gold leaf one. Stepping forward with my elbow jutting in front of me I squeezed in to a slim gap, leant forward with my arm out stretched. Without any hesitation the passports were snatched from my hand.

225

Standing akimbo to brace myself on the spot, my elbows slightly jutting out to the side I was asked how many tickets, holding up five fingers and shouted at the top of my voice "five" and handed over the cash. Each passport was checked, the money counted and the tickets were slipped inside each one. Once the passports were handed back I firmly clutched on to them as I slipped back past everyone standing behind me. Once out of the crowd I gave everyone their passports and tickets, much too their delight. Some one asked how I had managed to get the tickets with so many jostling to get served, "I put my British passport on top", everyone laughed as we headed for the waiting ferry.

Once on board it felt like an anti-climax as it dawned on me that this was the end of my Sri Lankan journey. Once the gang plank was hauled up and the ropes untied the ferry blasted its horn and set sail for India. We chatted until the early hours. Feeling drowsy I found a space on deck, using my large rucksack as a pillow and clutching my smaller one I laid down for a restless sleep in anticipation of arriving in Rameswaram for any mail waiting for me.

Part Three
A long journey to Srinagar

Mahablipuram, a brief excursion to the coast

The ferry arrived at Rameswaram about midmorning on a
perfectly calm sea and anchored some five hundred yards
off shore. The excited passengers disembarked on to the
tug drawn barges that had pulled up alongside, it then
transported the passengers to the quay and waiting
customs officers under the large tin roofed building.
Disembarking at the quay the Indian immigration officers
checked everyone's passport and immigration papers;
occasionally a passenger was questioned. As the front of
the queue slowly but surely got closer I felt the
excitement of returning to India. A woman in front turned
to me, "I hope my family are waiting for me" and
explained she was meeting her family outside and then
travelling north. She asked me my name and then said
hers was Barbara. Barbara was pretty and looked about
20, she did not look Indian or Sinhalese, more African.
During our conversation Barbara said she was from South
Africa and explained that her mum was Indian, "she is
already here with relatives".
Eventually arriving at the front of the queue I handed over
my passport to the Customs Officer and without any
formal questions or inspection my passport was stamped

227

with a visa; so different from the extremely officious passport check at Bombay Airport. Walking out of the shady customs shed in to the hot sun the light was dazzling. Barbara was with her family and introduced me to her mum, aunt and two cousins. Having said hello Barbara's mum said they had to leave and we unfortunately said good bye.

Remembering some mail might be waiting for me at the palm leaf guest house I turned and saw the guesthouse owner standing at the entrance, "you have a letter" he called out. I was over taken by a wave of excitement having not expected anything to arrive at such an obscure address. Whilst signing in the visitor's book an English voice behind me asked if I was Peter, turning around a guy about 20 was standing there. I was apprehensive, why would somebody I have never met before ask if I was Peter? Tentatively I said "yes";

"my names Roger", then to my utter amazement he said "I am from Harlow". I was absolutely speechless, here I was a quarter of the way around the world at the unlikeliest location in Southern India under a make shift structure and I bump into somebody from my home town. Quizzically I asked Roger where he lived in Harlow, still not sure whether to believe him.

"Hookfield!" he exclaimed; this was just too bizarre; we lived less than a mile from each other. What's more some of my school friends lived in Hookfield and could not resist asking if he knew any of them? As I told him the names Roger said he knew all of them, now I wanted to pinch myself; was this real. Asking Roger what school he attended, to my utter amazement he replied Latton Bush, the same school as me. Roger had seen my friends recently and I quizzed him about them. It all felt strange catching up on them here in India. With all of this excitement I had forgotten about my letter from home and pointed out I needed to read it. Quickly opening the envelope I found four pages written by my mum saying how things were at home and how everyone was. It felt so good to read everyone was well and wished they were here as well.

Having read the letter I joined the other back packers and the owner. It was a mixed crowd. A Norwegian in a cheque shirt and trousers, an American who was wearing a black turban, short black embroidered waist coat and sporting a trimmed beard, Roger, myself and Tom from Manchester. We talked excitedly about our experiences in India. Saying I was travelling north the American asked me if I was going to Calcutta or Delhi, "I don't have any definite plans yet but I was considering going to Kashmir or Nepal". The American said if I travel up to Kashmir I should also visit Amritsar, the religious centre for Sikh's around the world with its magnificent temple decorated in gold. It sounded amazing and a place I needed to visit. Sharing our antidotes; each one sounding funnier and more amazing than the last. The American told us about an Austrian he had met. Every time he told some body he was from Austria they replied "yes Australia I know where that is".

He tried to correct them saying "no Austria" which tended to confuse some Indians and they replied "Australia?"

After this happened several times he resorted to telling everyone he was from Disneyland which everyone had heard of. Tom told us a more sombre story about the buses that travel to Kathmandu, every now and then a bus falls off the mountain road, and recounted that some back packers travelling on top of a bus that slid off the road managed to jump clear. We all agreed this was a good reason to travel on top of a bus.

This prompted me to explain about my hair raising journey to Kandy. Noticing it was getting late and having to catch the train to Madras for an Indrail ticket I said farewell to everyone and hurried too Rameswaram train station. Buying a second class ticket I boarded a carriage full of back packers and luckily found a seat. The atmosphere was lively and hot; everyone seemed to be talking at the same time filling the air with different accents and languages. As the evening wore on the conversations died down to a low murmur. The train pulled in to several stations, as passengers got off the train there was more space on the seats, eventually there was enough space for me to lie down and try and get some sleep using my T shirt as a pillow. The train journey seemed to be quicker than previous ones I had been on and arrived the next morning at Madras station. It was not as busy as Bombay's Victoria Station, it had a calm silence about it. Finding the ticket office I bought my Indrail ticket without having to negotiate queues or crowded platforms. Leaving the station with the intention to stay a few days in Madras I walked out from the cool shade of the station in to the hot bright sunlight.

Overcome by a feeling of reluctance to look for some where to stay in a large city I impulsively went back in to the station and caught a train for Mahabalipuram. I had been told about the ancient temples on the beach a number of times, and was advised to visit Mahablipuram early in the morning to watch the sun rise. Being only a short distance down the coast it made sense to go there next. Getting to Mahablipuram required me to travel in land, change trains, then catch the next train to Mahablipuram; a straight forward journey.

The train gently pulled out of Madras and rumbled along the track at a steady pace through the East Indian countryside, it looked extremely green with a patch work of paddy fields and other crops. Having stopped at several stations it felt the journey was taking longer than anticipated, checking my map I discovered the train had gone past the connecting station, luckily the next station was not much further.

The station was almost deserted, and lacked any facilities, not even a waiting room or a tea stall. Being a quiet station I wondered how long I might have to wait for the next train back towards Madras and asked the station attendant. All he told me was "soon".

Soon could be an hour or the next day so I asked "how soon".

With a smile and a shake of the hand he said "very soon". Resolved that the train will arrive when it arrives I sat down in the shade of the platform awning. After about two hours a train pulled in to the station and stopping with a gush of steam. It was a relief not to wait over night, being sure there was not a hotel or guest house available. The train travelled back towards Madras with out any sense of urgency at a nonchalant pace. By now it was late afternoon and I was feeling a bit hungry. Eventually arriving at my connecting station which was just as quiet as the previous one, but it did have a tea stall on the platform. I asked a man dressed in the familiar beige uniform worn by all station staff, or any one in a position of authority when the next train to Mahablipuram would be arriving. With a sideways shake of the head and a wave of the hand told me "not now".

With a patient smile I asked "when?"

"Tomorrow morning" was the reply.

Asking the pertinent question, "When tomorrow morning".

The man nonchalantly replied "early".

I was beginning to feel that this questioning and answering was a bit of a game for this genial gentleman that helped pass the time away working on such a quiet mundane station.

Trying to construct the question to get an answer I wanted, "what time is early?"

"Very early" was the reply.

Trying to be a bit more cunning with my next question and asked "was the train after 3 o'clock".

The man looked as if he did not understand me and I quickly said "after 3 o'clock tomorrow morning".

His face lit up and he said "no, before 3 o'clock.

"Is it after 1 o'clock".

He then became quite animated with a big smile and said

"yes after 1 o'clock. I paused briefly pondering if my next question should be a more specific but reflected that between 1 and 3 am was good enough, smiling I said thank you.

The sun was now setting and I needed a tea before the vendor closed up his stall. I fished out my metal mug and asked if he could fill it up. He looked at me with a rather bemused expression and shook his head and indicated it was too big. Realising that the mug was larger than two glasses of tea I asked for three tea's which made the vendor smile. He also had a primus stove with various trays laid out on his stall containing rice, chopped onions, garlic, peas and other vegetables. I asked for a plate of rice at the same time pointing to emphasis what I wanted thinking that the man might not understand English. He pointed to the other trays and spoke in Hindi obviously asking what I wanted. Choosing the onions and peas they were all fried up together, the aromatic smell intensified my hunger. After a few minutes I had a cooked meal for a few rupees. Having eaten the welcome meal I could not resist another one, the vendor smiled and joyfully hummed as he cooked another meal. The station assistant came over and talked to the vendor in Hindi and laughed then told me that the vendor said I was a good customer. I smiled and said that he makes nice tea and cooks a nice meal. The station assistant spoke to the vendor, he looked at me smiled and bowed with his hands together.

Eating the meal and drinking tea whilst talking to the vendor and station attendant helped pass the time. The prospect of having to wait for the train on such a quiet

233

station was a daunting prospect. Anticipating that the vendor might be leaving soon I bought another three teas and poured them in to my mug. Having sold me the tea's the vendor bowed again and wheeled his barrow off the platform. There was a small waiting room with a bench at one end of the platform and sat down to read to help alleviate the boredom, at the same time consciously thought I must not fall asleep and miss the train.

As it grew dark the large domed waiting room light came on, it was just bright enough to allow me to read. At the same time the light attracted a number of moths that flitted around the illuminated globe making regular audible taps as they hit the sphere. At the same time crickets chirped in the foliage beside the platform adding to the tropical evening chorus. The crickets eventually grew silent, the only sound was the tap, tap of the numerous moths on the light. The time dragged on in to the early hours, by now the light in the waiting room had attracted hundreds of moths which were fascinating. Each had its own distinct patterned wings and of various sizes, an entomologist's heaven. As I was getting to the point of just barely staying awake the sound of a distant train broke the silence. Its head light shone like a star in the pitch black and gradually grew in size and brightness as it approached the station illuminating the foliage either side of the track. Getting myself ready in hope it was the train I wanted the station attendant appeared from nowhere and called out that this was my train to Mahablipuram. The train slowly approached the station with its bright blinding head light illuminating the platform, it seemed to take an exorbitantly long time to come to a halt, then stopped with a billowing gust of illuminated steam. The journey to Mahablipuram was slow. After a few hours the train came to a halt at a completely deserted, dimly lit station. Carriage doors opened followed by subdued voices of the other passengers. Getting myself ready and expecting to walk to the beach I stepped out in to the early morning chilly air; a contrast to the temperature further in land. Walking along the dimly lit platform and down the road I following the others unsure where they were going. After a short distance we arrived at a bus station. I asked one of the group if they were going to the beach and quietly said "yes, this is the bus". Every one waited in silence which gave the visit to the ancient temples an air of reverence.

It was still dark when the driver arrived, we all climbed aboard and the early morning silence was broken as the engine roared in to life. Slowly driving along the dark empty road it felt like the silent moment before the dramatic part in a film. Before long the bus came to a halt, once the engine was turned off I could hear the surf. Excitedly getting out of the bus I felt the chilly sea breeze and wished I had a jumper to wear but was reassured by the faint yellow horizon against contrasting with the dark blue sea.

Walking along the beach of soft sand I could make out one of the old temples that had been on the shores for over a thousand years. The temples had intricate carvings decorating the spire and had carved pillars around the outside. I completely forgot about the chilly breeze as I

235

marvelled at the majestic work that had gone in to the carvings and how they had lasted for so long with very little weathering from the elements. Looking closely and touching the fantastic ancient structures I imagined the sort of people who had carved them so long ago which now stood on the beach, some washed by the surf rolling up on to the beach. The sun rose in to the sky and more people arrived, women elegantly dressed in the brightly coloured saris and the men wearing sarongs and white shirts.

Sitting down I felt the warmth of the sun on the soft sand and suddenly felt drowsy and wanted to sleep. Resisting the temptation, I decided to catch the bus back to the station to start my journey north. At the station a train was waiting bound for Bangalore. Not keen on going back there but thought it would be good to revisit Mysore for a few days. Boarding the train I found an empty compartment, laying down felt my eyes slowly closing. A whistle sounded distant which was followed the shunt the train as it pulled out of Mahablipuram on its way towards Bangalore.

I dozed, occasionally waking and looking out of the window at the countryside, noticing the changes from the lush green to the parched beige. At one point I abruptly woke to find a smartly dressed man in the compartment. Not knowing how long he had been there I sat up and said hello, all I got in return was a nod and resigned myself to looking out of the window. The ground looked dry except for patches of farmed land and people working on their plots. I asked the man what time it was, he told me it was

236

three o'clock. I was now feeling very hungry and wondered how long it was before the next station. After an hour or so the train slowed down and stopped at a platform. Children crowded the carriage window trying to sell their goods; one had small pineapples and a mango. Buying everything he had brought a huge smile to his face and instantly became the centre of attention of the other children. After several minutes at the station the train puffed and panted blowing out smoke and ash in to the air as the engine tugged the carriages and slowly gained momentum. Smoke bellowed out of the engine and wafted back in to the carriage with traces of ash and cinder as the train careered on across the Indian plain. Getting my knife out of my rucksack I sliced the succulent pineapples, they tasted glorious.

Wondering how far we were from Bangalore I asked the man, "not far" came his reply. Thinking not far could be any distance, I would just have to be patient. The train travelled through the night and in the early hours arrived at Bangalore station, it was busy with passengers and porters rushing to get where they had to go. Finding the right platform for the Mysore, I boarded the waiting train. It was more packed than the one from Mahablipuram, maybe the passengers were going to Mysore for their holiday.

The journey did not take long passing though the lush countryside and arrived at the busy station; it felt good to be back in Mysore, a familiar place. Walking out of the station I made my way down the main road hoping to find a hotel or guest house that had a vacant room. The first few I tried were full, then I saw a large building down a side road with a large brown door with a sign above it in Hindi. It looked like a hotel and thought there was no harm enquiring. I opened the door and walked in to a small dark foyer with an equally small reception desk, it looked like a hotel reception. Asking if there was a spare room the man behind the reception desk checked the register and said there was one. Having signed in the visitor's book I was given a key and told the room was on the third floor.

The narrow corridors were difficult to navigate with my rucksacks. The doors to each room were close together giving the impression they might be small. Finding my room, as expected it was small but clean and had a comfortable bed with a large wardrobe. A sign indicated the bathroom was along the corridor and not having had a proper shower for a few days, except on the train with lukewarm rusty water I definitely needed one before going any where.

The bathroom was a shower cubical not much bigger than a broom cupboard but it was a shower. Turning the tap the anticipated cold water gushed out, then surprisingly started to warm up. Presuming the water was from a tank on the roof that had been warmed by the sun, but to my amazement the water became scorching hot filling the small cubicle with steam; at last a hot shower. It felt relaxing washing off the grime of the last week and took advantage of this luxury. In case it was a one off I stayed in the shower for some considerable time; heaven. Feeling refreshed I went to find somewhere to eat and came across a small busy tea shop with a large number of westerners. Picking a palm leaf I washed it and sat at a table with several others. Almost as soon as I had sat down a large pile of rice was served up with several poppadum's, along with three small spice dishes. I crumpled up the poppadum's and sprinkled the crumbs on the rice. Tea followed quickly as did the introductions to the other people sitting at the table. We exchanged anecdotes of our travels, to an outsider the stories would have sounded as if we were all trying to outdo each other. We also talked about where we intended to go next. Explaining I was either going to Nepal or Kashmir, two of the guys said they had been to Nepal and a lot of back packers contract hepatitis from the water and were ill for a week, looking jaundice with a yellow tinge. This did not sound appealing in the least and thought Kashmir was the best option. The conversations lead to food, someone mentioned the food they missed the most. Admitting the food I missed was breakfast cereals such as cornflakes, everyone laugh. Simon said he missed doughnuts which made us laugh even louder; it was the simple foods we all missed, not the extravagant meals. Somebody mentioned that two Germans had made doughnuts for themselves but soon started making them for other backpackers and were making a lot of money out of it.

The conversation went on for some time until eventually I said good bye. Wandering down a road I came across a street I did not remember from my previous visit to Mysore; Silver Street. The street was about three hundred yards long and on either side were Jewellers. Each window had silver and gold jewellery of every description; rings, necklaces, earrings, bracelets, ankle bangles, silver and gold coins, women's ornamental chains for attaching to the nose and ear; and ingots. A lot of the jewellery was inlayed with gem stones which could also be bought individually. As I passed each shop the owners tried to beckon me but resisted going in. The prices were far more expensive than those in Sri Lanka which made me wary of buying anything. Loosing track of time whilst gazed at the vast array jewellery and eventually succumbed to being invited in to some shops, especially when offered a tea. By the time I finished browsing the shops along Silver Street it was dark. Returning to the hotel I wearily climbed the stairs, got in to my room and flopped out on the bed.

The next thing I knew it was morning and still dressed. After Indulging in a luxurious hot shower which felt so extravagant, had breakfast at a tea stall then set off for Mysore Palace. On the way I came across a life size drawing of a Hindu god in the road by the Maharaja of Mysore roundabout. The drawing was very intricate and had obviously taken a long time, passing pedestrians were throwing money on to the drawing to show their appreciation of the art work. Soon I arrived at the Palace; the grounds were peaceful and quiet. Deciding to go inside the palace the splendour and opulence was obvious. Large golden pillars supported the ceiling also decorated in gold. The golden decoration on the ceiling and pillars reflected in the polished marble floor making the rooms glow. It looked just like something from a fairy tale and spent some time taking it all in; It was hard to believe that somebody lived in such luxury when millions of people in India struggled from day to day to feed themselves.

After wandering through the palace I walked back in to Mysore, around the back streets I came across a grey stone church with a double spire either side of the large arch edged with carved stone. Each spire had its own arched door way, also of carved stone. This was the first time I had seen a church in India which looked sublime with its Gothic architecture that would not be out of place in any European city. I could not resist going inside and discovered this was St. Philomena's Church. Quite a few people were sat in the pews and walked around. The interior was cool, maybe a good reason why so many people were in the church. The walls and ceiling were painted white and light flooded in through glazed windows, the high arched ceiling was supported by tall arching pillars. Sitting down on one of the pews to admire the architecture, the atmosphere was serene, people talked in a subdued tone very similar to the Hindu and Buddhist temples, it had a therapeutic and calming effect.

After spending some time in the cool church I went to buy some jewellery from one of the shops in Silver Street and browsed the shop windows again in case I might have missed something the previous evening. Entering a shop with jewellery I spotted previously the owner said hello with a wide smile. Waving me in he asked if I wanted a tea, how could I refuse? He asked where I was from and various other questions which I did not mind. I found that

241

by socialising with vendors it helped when haggling down the price. The owner eventually asked me what I was interested in,

"the silver pendant with a window and a pendant hanging set with a large bright red garnet" I replied. "You also have a pendant with a large amethyst set in it".

"I know the ones you are talking about" and got the black velvet trays from the window. He told me about the work that had gone in to the two pieces of jewellery and how much the gem stones weighed, both were about 7 carats. The shop owner told me the price; pausing I offered a lower price,

"no, no that is too cheap" but gave me lower price than his original one.

Feigning that I was thinking about this price offered a price for both. After some thought about this the owner smiled and suggested his new price and added "they are very good pieces" as if to remind me.

I paused then shook my head side to side, smiled and said "okay". The shop owner held out his hand to close the deal. We talked whilst drinking tea, and decided to buy a third pendent. Looking carefully at each one in turn in a glass cabinet I opted for a bright green Peridot and offered a price just below the one on the label, the shop owner instantly agreed.

Having bought some presents for home I felt it was time to leave Mysore and head north. Whilst eating in one of the tea shops I studied my map of India and after some deliberation I decided Hyderabad would be my next destination. Having been told about its museum with

242

displays of art work and antiques it sounded like the ideal place to visit. Hyderabad did not look too far away, maybe an overnight train journey. Unfortunately the next train was not until the following day. After booking a seat I walked around aimlessly soaking up the Mysore atmosphere for the last time, a place I had come to really enjoy and where I felt at home. Eventually finding myself back to my hotel I called it a night, had a hot shower to make the most of this rare treat and settled for the night.

A hair-raising moment in Hyderabad

The next morning, after possibly my last hot shower for some time I made my way to the station where I had breakfast. Asking for a soft boiled egg caused some amusement as I tried explaining how to cook a soft boiled egg by boiling it for three minutes. The person working in the tea shop had an attentive look with a wide smile and a side ways shake of the head. Could I get a soft boiled egg? I waited in anticipation. It was some time before the egg arrived, cracking it open as expected it was hard boiled. The person working in the tea shop asked if the egg was okay, smiling I said it was and thought worse things could happen.

The train arrived about 10am, having found my first class compartment. Now on my way north to Kashmir I felt excited about this part of my journey that was to take me through central India, in to Rajasthan and the Punjab. With the first class compartment to myself and sitting by the window I had an uninterrupted view of the countryside.

When the train gathered speed a shower of hot cinders from the steam engine blew in to the compartment. Changing my seat to the opposite side I watched the parched countryside vanish in to the distance. The sun bleached grass looked very different to Tamil Nadu and Kerala. Every now and then there were small groups of huts in the distance next to ploughed patches of brown

244

earth. I found that the Indian countryside mesmerising, a stark contrast to Britain. I decided to write a letter home whilst events of the last few days were fresh in my mind. As the journey wore on in to the evening the landscape turned a light purplish grey which gradually grew darker as the sun went down. As the light faded a murky veil was drawn across the landscape.

The train passed through several stations, each time children of various ages crowded the window trying to sell food and water in small clay pots, when drunk these were discarded on to the railway track making a distinct cracking noise as they shattered. This seemed such a waste and could have been used again. Fruit was offered along with samosas and what looked like onion bargees. Some children asked for baksheesh and paisa and felt if they wanted to make some money they should try and sell some thing

A man got on at one of the stations, stowed his luggage and sat crossed legged then asked the usual questions. Not having much else to do I obligingly talked about Britain and in particular England in some considerable detail. Then he asked how I was finding India, replying I was enjoying my journey he told me that I must have been too India before.

Confused by this comment said I hadn't.

The man pointed out to me as if it was a well known fact "you could have been to India in a previous life."

I could not help but smile and found myself shaking my head side to side in agreement, "maybe you are right".

Knowing how much people in India believed in

reincarnation it was interesting that they also considered non-Hindu's could be reincarnated.

"You do not seem to be very religious" he said in an enquiry way.

"I consider myself to be a Christian but don't usually go to church".

"Maybe you are agnostic?"

Something I had never really thought about and agreed, "yes maybe I am".

Out of the blue he said "we don't like Western Christians trying to convert us".

Inquisitively asking "do many Christians try to convert Indians?"

He sternly replied "they do".

"Does that included Mother Teresa",

"she is different because she does a lot of good work in India".

Having been curious about the cast system I asked if it was connected to religion or class. The man looked at me, smiled and shook his head side to side and said "it is complicated but both are connected". He explained that you can be an Indian in an important job but you can still be in a lower caste than the next person doing the same job. Also an Indian can have a lesser important job but might be of a higher caste. I asked if class was different to caste. The man said it was, that is your social standing with in your caste and society. Agreeing it sounded complicated and maybe I would never understand. He advised me not to concern myself about the caste system, it makes life much easier.

246

We talked for some time until it felt late and decided it was time to get some sleep; pulling down a bunk and putting my large rucksack at one end, climbing up on to it I quickly fell asleep with my arms wrapped through the straps of my small rucksack.

The next morning I woke early, the train steadily making its way towards Hyderabad with the refreshing cool morning air wafting in to the carriage. The earth looked even more arid, a distinct contrast to the green fertile soil in the South with the tall bright green trees. I hoped we would soon arrive in Hyderabad so I could have a long day looking around; at about 9am the train pulled in to a very busy Hyderabad station. Passengers were waiting for their train or making their way to another platform, porters carried luggage and tea stalls were crowded with customers buying their breakfast. I weaved my way along the busy platform to left luggage. Enquiring about the train times I was told there was one that evening or the next day. Once free of my large rucksack it felt easier to squeeze through the crowded station and made my way to the main entrance where motor rickshaws waited ready to whisk passengers away.

Jumping in to one I asked to go to the museum. The driver sped off as if he was the only person on the road, swerving around pedestrians, carts and cows down the narrow streets which seemed narrower than anywhere else I have been so far. We arrived at the museum, much to my relief. I picked up a guide leaflet which explained the history of the museum, 'it was the Palace of Salar Jung III, the ancestral home of his family. The collection of art and artefacts was collected by Nawab Mir Yousof Ali Khan. Ali Khan had assistants travel the world buying up works of art for his personal collection. Ali Khan was considered to be the richest man in the world at the time when he put together his collection'. The museum included paintings, bronzes, clocks, antiques and his own large personal toy collection; thousands of old Briton lead figurines in mint condition; the sort I remembered playing with when younger which my Dad passed on to me and my brothers. Wandering through the museum I took my time in each room studying each painting, sculpture, bronze, suite of armour, furniture, ornate clock; I was especially fascinated by the small radiant Moghul paintings. The museum was busy but quiet with an air of serenity, similar to what you find in most museums and art galleries around the world.

After visiting the last room I decided to get something to eat and walked out in to an extremely busy street, it was just like Madurai but not as noisy. After having something to eat in a crowded tea shop where everyone sat at a bench eating with their fingers I walked through the narrow streets, intending to make my way to the station. Coming across a small post office tucked between taller buildings I remembered the letters I wrote on the train. The post office was about the size of a large bedroom divided across the middle by a desk with a metal grill. I asked to post my letters to the UK.

Inquisitively I was asked "where were the letters going?" Correcting myself "The United Kingdom"

The post clerk took out a large book and flicked through

the pages; stopped and looked up" I cannot find the United Kingdom".

"It might be listed as, G.B. or Great Britain" I suggested, after another flick through the pages there was a shake of the head, we don't have Great Britain in our book. Remembering the problem I had posting my parcel in Cochin asked "is England was in the book?"

The clerk calmly thumbed through the directory with a flick of each page, suddenly smiled, "yes you can post to England". Having stuck down the stamps with the glue provided I noticed the time on post office clock; it was late and thought I might miss the evening train. Outside in the narrow street I was not sure the way to the station, stopping a motorised rickshaw I asked for the station. The driver sped off showing little concern for pedestrians, cows, other traffic or his own personal safety let alone mine. Pedestrians seemed to be oblivious to the rickshaw racing along the narrow street but both managed to avoid each other as if by instinct.

The rickshaw came to a sudden halt and the driver announced "the station". But it was not the station I had arrived at earlier. Describing what the station looked like and emphasising the time my train was leaving.

The drivers face lit up, "yes I know that station!" he exclaimed. Slipping the rickshaw in to gear we raced off down the narrow streets faster than any sensible person could safely navigate between the pedestrians. The rickshaw swerved and weaved, somehow avoiding any type of obstacle that stepped out in front. Suddenly we were confronted by two carts moving towards each other, the gap between the two carts looked far too narrow for even a small rickshaw and expected the driver to slow down. To my astonishment he accelerated, racing along the middle of the road. I sat right back in the seat forcing myself hard against the cushion; putting my arms out on either side and tensed my leg and arm muscles, bracing myself for the inevitable collision between the rickshaw and one of the carts, or even both. The gap was far too narrow but the driver did not slow down, he careered on relentlessly past the pedestrians either side. Just at the moment of the inevitable impact I instinctively shut my eyes, clenched harder to the side of the rickshaw whilst gritting my teeth waiting for the violent jolt of the collision.

Suddenly I heard "Don't worry I will get you to the station", opening my eyes I was speechless. Somehow as if by a fete of magic the rickshaw had squeezed through the gap that did not appear to be there. I could not understand how, but we had made it. Letting out a huge sigh of relief my arms and leg muscles relaxed. Looking behind there was a scene of oblivious normality. After what seemed like a miraculous escape the rest of the hair raising journey to the station felt sedate.

At the station I paid the driver and gave a tip for getting me to the station on time, and uninjured. Squeezing through the pedestrian traffic in the station I collected my luggage and went to find the correct platform which was not so straight forward. Asking a platform attendant I was directed through what seemed a wall of people. Passengers were sitting on the concourse with their luggage piled up as they waited for their train to arrive. Porters were helping to carry luggage to and from the trains, some had large baggage trunks on their heads and parents herded their children, prompting them to stay close as they negotiated the crowded station. Platform attendants called out to passengers and the service engineers shouted above the noise as they checked the carriage couplings.

Navigating my way through the crowded station was difficult with my rucksack but eventually made it to the correct platform and train. Once in a first class compartment it felt sanity had descended in my small oasis. Sitting by the window I watched the general chaos on the platform through the grilled window as if watching a movie on a small screen TV. A platform attendant armed with his red flag walked past, blew his whistle and waved the flag signalling the driver to start. The trains whistle blasted in reply and with a sudden jolt the train lurched forward. Slowly gathering speed the train pulled out of Hyderabad of station on its way to Aurangabad my next destination. The train rumbled along through the now dark countryside as I wondered how the rickshaw had made it through the gap. Even today I cannot understand how it had navigated between the two carts and avoided the pedestrians without having a calamitous accident.

A Surreal Musical Ensemble

The train rumbled through the evening stopping at several stations. Each station had its own individual character and design. Some stations had a sense of urgency about them with the platforms full of passengers, station staff, people selling food at the carriage window or individuals asking for baksheesh or paisa, whilst other stations were calm and tranquil. Several had brightly painted wooden fret work that edged the awnings whilst others were plain white. The lighting varied, some stations were brightly lit whilst others were distinctly subdued.

As the evening wore on the stations became quieter but children were still on the platforms selling food and water in the familiar small clay pots to the passengers through the grilled windows. Whichever station the train pulled in to it stayed for about five minutes which allowed passengers to get off, buy some food and get back on again just as the whistle was blown. Between stations the train trundled through what seemed like a barren nocturnal landscape, devoid of any visible lights or habitation. The faint undulating horizon meeting the indigo star lit sky gave the illusion that it was peaceful and quiet out on the plains. Eventually overcome by tiredness I settled down to sleep in one of the bunks. The train arrived at Aurangabad about 9am the next morning by which time it was already hot. Aurangabad station had a light airy atmosphere about it and a lively buzz, but not over crowded. Leaving my rucksack at left luggage with the intention to find a guest house or hotel I left the station to be confronted by a bus terminal directly out side with several parked buses. One of the buses had a large sign advertising a guided tour of Aurangabad, an ideal opportunity to become familiar with Aurangabad. Joining the end of a small queue of western tourists, some one behind said "hi", turning around the guy introduced his self;

"I'm Richard". He sounded American but turned out to be Canadian. He was wearing a pressed cheque shirt, pressed trousers and smart shoes. Richard had a friendly temperament and we chatted about the usual things of where we had been and shared stories and antidotes of our travels. The conversation for some reason changed to the Monty Python film 'The Life of Brian' and our favourite parts from the film; it was obvious we had a similar sense of humour.

Among others in the queue was a stocky black man about five feet six tall, Richard said "hello" but he did not reply. He appeared angry and intimidating, it seemed best not to talk to him.

Richard said "hello again". Getting no reply Richard asked me if he had said any thing wrong.

Shrugging my shoulders replied "I don't think so".

Eventually the driver opened the doors to the bus and everyone got on board. The Black man sat by his self which made him conspicuous whilst everyone else talked, mostly in English. The guide climbed on to the bus, introduced his self and described the tour around

Aurangabad, "the first stop will be at the fort and then we will visit the Bibi Ka Maqbara". Having finished the introduction the driver started the engine and drove the short distance to the fort past loaded carts pulled by bullocks and followed over-loaded lorries that created a dust cloud which wafted in to the bus through the open windows.

Arriving at the fort the guide asked us to stand by the entrance once we were off the bus. The fort was made of grey stone with a wall some thirty feet high; a bridge crossed a 50 foot deep moat that lead up to a large arch lined with decorative carving. Once the tour group had congregated at the arch our guide explained how old the fort was, who owned it and that in its hay day the moat was filled with snakes and crocodiles. A precarious obstacle for any would be attacker let alone trying to scale the high walls. We walked under the arch in to a double portcullis gate way. The walls on either side had slits and narrow slews', the second archway lead in to the fort. It was explained that the second archway would have had a strong latticed gate.

Anybody who made it this far had boiling oil poured on them from the slews' whilst arrows were fired at them through the gaps in the latticed gate and the slits in the walls; at the same time barbed caltrops were dropped down impaling the attackers feet, this description drew comments of shock from several tourists.

We entered the fort grounds and were surrounded by the high walls topped with battlements. The tour lasted for about an hour where we could walk around the fort at our leisure.The Black man walked off by his self which seemed best but Richard insisted on trying to talk to him even though he did not reply. Thinking Richard would eventually get the message and give up but he persisted on getting a reply. It was apparent Richard was not getting the message. The next stop was the Bibi Ka Magbara, we were all surprised to see the Taj Mahal or what looked like the Taj Mahal. Our guide talked about the building and said this was a scaled down copy of the Taj Mahal and constructed at a later date and was not entirely made of marble. Even so it still looked magnificent and wondered if I needed to visit the Taj Mahal it self now I had seen the Bibi Ka Magbara. We visited a few more tourist sites around Aurangabad, one spot in particular was peaceful, set in amongst some trees were large stones with ancient Sanskrit carvings. Sitting down on a large carved stone for a short break Richard seemed perturbed about not getting a reply from the black man. "What do you think is wrong with him?"

"I don't know, maybe he's upset about something".

The Black man was sat opposite, suddenly standing up he walked towards us with a serious and stern expression. I wondered why he would be walking towards us considering he had ignored Richard so far. He stopped directly in front of us, bent down and stared directly at Richard just inches away from his face. Even though I was sitting next to Richard he ignored me as if I was not there.

The Black man paused then spokc to Richard in a quiet but menacing tone with an strong American accent of a southern state. "I have left your world, I do not want to be part of your world and I do not want to talk to you or you to talk to me". He paused, stood up right and then went back to where he had been sitting. Being so close to this brief conversation it felt as if I was watching a close up of a movie as the unexpected tense scene unravelled. Thinking that just about said it all but Richard surprisingly asked "what have I done?"

It was obvious Richard would never know or understand so I just shrugged my shoulders and said "don't know". Soon after the brief but direct encounter we all got back on to the bus. Richard did not say much and appeared worried about what the black man said to him; feeling that I would most probably never see him again it was not worth worrying about.

As the bus made its way back to the station I realised that we had not seen any Hindu Temples or cows; it seemed strange not to see any having become accustomed to the tall temple spires. Back at the bus station the guide announced that there will be a guided tour of the Ajanta Caves the next day with the bus leaving from the same place. He explained that the Ajanta Caves were Jain temples carved in to the rock out in the desert. This sounded interesting and decided that I had to go on the tour. Richard said he was unable to go because he was catching the evening train. After saying good bye I went to find somewhere to eat; walking along the road and looking for a tea shop I saw a group of women who looked familiar. Then I realised it was Barbara and her mum from Rameswaram. Barbara came up to me and we

256

hugged each other, it was so good to see a familiar face. We were both surprised to see each other, especially in Aurangabad. We talked quickly at the same time trying to find out what the other was doing. Barbara said she was in Aurangabad for a few hours and had to leave soon. After talking for about ten minutes Barbara said she had to go and left with her family. It was so disappointing seeing her leave.

I found a small busy tea shop and decided that as it was so popular it must be a good place to eat. Sitting at a table where a youngish looking Indian man was already sitting and said hello. He was wearing a slightly grubby white shirt and had red bloodshot eyes. The man had a different accent from the Indians I had met so far in the South, he sounded slightly English. Mentioning that he did not sound as though he was local or from Southern India. He explained that he lived in the north up in the hills where he owned a hotel; his family had sent him south to recover. I looked at him quizzically and my expression prompted him to tell me that he was making a lot of money and started smoking Marijuana which was easy to come by, eventually becoming addicted his work was affected so his family sent him south. I asked if it had worked, "it is hard to find any Marijuana in Rajasthan. Do you smoke Marijuana or hashish?"

"No".

"Do not to smoke it, it is not good for you".

After talking about other things I asked if there were any hotels in Aurangabad, "there are no good hotels in Aurangabad, I would not stay in them". I teased the man and said he was biased because he owned a hotel which made him smile. After eating and drinking several glasses of tea I decided that instead of walking around Aurangabad to find some where to stay I would sleep in the stations waiting room for the night, ensuring I would be up early for the bus to The Ajanta Caves.

Saying good bye and wishing the man the best of luck I walked around the shops which mostly sold every day items such as cooking pots, sauce pans, electrical goods and food but none sold camera film. Convinced I would need some film for the trip to The Ajanta Caves and would be disappointed if I did not have any.

Aurangabad was an interesting experience, the atmosphere was different compared to that of the south, there weren't any rickshaws and the shop venders did not seem to go out of their way to get you to come in to their shops or pressure you to buy their goods. The evening wore on and not knowing the time I made my way back to the station firstly to check the train times the next day, one went to Udaipur in the evening. Collecting my rucksack from left luggage I made my way along the now busy platform to the waiting room for a long over due shower. The refreshing cold water washed off the dust, what looked like a dark suntan on my feet and legs faded with the water. Even though the station was busy it was not excessively noisy, sitting on the platform I watched the passengers and station workers busily go to and throe as I drank tea out of my mug. It felt as though I was watching TV; detached from what was going on around me with out any one paying attention to me. The station gradually became quieter and I eventually went in to the waiting room and settled down for a night's sleep.

Covered with my large towel and using my large rucksack as a pillow I dozed off on a wooden bench.

The chorus of the station activity woke me the next morning. I started my day with my mug full of tea and some samosas. After having a shower and a change of clothes I handed my rucksack in to left luggage and joined the queue for the trip out to The Ajanta Caves.

There weren't any tourists from the previous day's trip, or as many which allowed me to have a window seat to watch the country side. The tour guide boarded the bus and introduced his self as he did the previous day then explained the journey to The Ajanta Caves would take some time with out any stopping, we were not told any specific time of arrival but as with all journeys in India anything could happen. The sun felt extremely hot, all of the windows were open to help create a breeze through the bus. It was not long before the bus had left the outskirts of Aurangabad and was travelling along the dusty tarmacked road. Vehicles in front created a dust cloud and sand blew in through the open windows, it was a choice of having a breeze and the dust blowing in or suffering the greenhouse conditions of a closed dust free bus.

The country side was more barren and arid than what I had seen so far. Flat beige parched earth baked dry by the hot sun stretched off to the horizon. There was the occasional isolated patch of green adding a splash of colour on the landscape. Now and then the bus passed a

259

small community of temporary huts built by the road where the children would run by the bus shouting out Paisa or Baksheesh.

After about two hours the bus pulled up in front of a wooden barrier. The tour guide announced "when you get off the bus do not go beyond the barrier". Once off the bus it was obvious why, on the other side there was a sheer drop of several hundred feet in to a large crater. Below was a semi-circle of granite cliffs topped with foliage. The tour guide explained how difficult it was to find the caves and the reason they had remained hidden for so long. "The caves below were abandoned for over a thousand years until a British Officer, John Smith chased a tiger and stumbled across the caves in 1819". We got back on the bus and descended in to the crater via a spiralling road and parked under some trees.

Getting off the bus we followed our guide along a path that led up towards the line of caves. The guide stopped us at the first cave and explained that they are small and we had to wait until there was enough room for us all to go inside. Once in the cave the guide pointed at the art work on the wall and even though it was slightly faded and flaking in places you could make out the design quite easily, a large mural of a partly dressed couple, the man was wearing a crown. The mural was possibly done before Christ and it had lasted well considering the weather conditions in the area of hot and maybe at times cold air. It reminded me of the paintings at Sigiriya.

We left the cave and entered the next one with the guide describing what we could see ourselves. Deciding to leave the group I looked at the other caves at my own pace. I could not help marvel at the intricate art work for the period. Getting around all of the caves before the rest of the group had finished I went to look at the stalls I had noticed earlier. Some sold crafts of various types but most of the stalls had crystals of different sizes and types clustered together; one was about two feet across. There was purple Amethyst, clear and rose Quartz, Topaz and many more. There were also large pebbles, asking what they were the vendor told me it was a Geode, picking one up he held it in both hands and pulled it apart to reveal sparkling crystals in side. The join between the two halves were a perfect fit and indiscernible when joined together. Limited by the space in my rucksack, plus the weight I was able to carry my choice was restricted. My eyes kept getting drawn to the large cluster of Amethyst crystals, picking it up it must have weighed at least ten kilo's. Browsing the stalls to find the best crystals and geodes; I was excited each time I opened a geode anticipating what was inside. Some had modest tiny crystals whilst other geodes had large angular ones. At one stall the vendor asked where I was from, when I said England he excitedly asked me if I had anything from England. Explaining that I didn't have much with me, he replied it can be anything. I rummaged through my small rucksack taking out pens and other items. By now a small group had gathered around me, when they saw the pens someone asked if they could have them and offered me some geodes and crystals in exchange. At first I was reluctant as I needed a pen to write my letters and did not feel it was a fair swap,

261

considering the time and effort they must have spent finding them. They insisted and eventually I relented and gave them the pens, in response I was told to take something in exchange. They were all so persistent and eventually I relented. Pointing out one of the pens did not work but they were not worried, they just wanted something from England. Finding a few more things I handed them out trying to compensate the stall owner's generosity. I decided to choose a few geodes, being enclosed there was less chance of them getting damaged, and being hollow they would be lighter than a solid crystal or rock. I wanted to pay for some of geodes but the vendors refused the money which left me so over whelmed. I had something that would remind me of this moment and my trip to The Ajanta Caves.

Other vendors asked me if I had anything they could swap. Rifling through my rucksack again I found some British coins which they got very excited over. There was about two pounds in various denominations. Again I was overawed by their generosity as the vendors exchanged the coins for more geodes. I was curious about how they found a geode, they looked just like any other rock. A vendor explained they had to go out and look for possible rocks, by tapping each one with a small hammer, a geode sounded hollow. This made me realise the real value of the Geodes was far more than what I had given them considering the effort that went in to finding just one out in the heat testing likely stones or rocks.

The tour guide called to the group that we were leaving soon. Saying good bye to the benevolent friendly stall holders I walked back to the bus. As I boarded it a young boy stood in the door way, he asked what I could give him for a stone he held out in his hand. I suggested he could sell it for several Rupees to another tourist. He asked me my name and told him it was Peter, "My name is Afrique Jaffa";

"I am glad to meet you Afrique". I rummaged through my rucksack and pulled out the letter I received from home. Giving Afrique the letter I explained it was from my mum, also giving him five rupees a huge grin stretched across Afriques face as he gave me the uncut gem stone. The other passengers were still haggling with the stall holders as the guide got on to the bus. He asked why I left the group,

"I needed a drink!", not want to tell him his talk about the paintings sounded boring and meeting the stall vendors was much more interesting.

The bus journey back to Aurangabad along the dusty road seemed to take longer than going to the caves. Giving me a chance to marvel at the fascinating dry landscape and wonder how the people we passed managed to survive here. I also reflected about my memorable day talking to such fantastically generous friendly people. We arrived back at Aurangabad in time for me to catch my train to Udaipur.

Collecting my rucksack from left luggage I tried to find the platform for the train to Udaipur, this proved more difficult than anticipated and resorted to asking a station attendant.

"I will have to charge you for finding a seat" came his

263

reply.

Looking at him indignantly I asked to see some one in charge and went to walk away.

Straight away he touched my hand and said "no I will find a seat". As well as finding me a seat he personally escorted me to the train. Very soon the platform attendant blew his whistle, the train jolted as it took the strain of the carriages and gently rolled forward. Slowly gathering momentum the train left the urban landscape for the flat open plain. The parched earth was turned a golden yellow as the sun fell lower in the sky then eventually sank below the horizon; the ground turned to a light grey with the dark trees silhouetted against the evening sky. Everything gradually grew darker until it was pitch black. Unable to see anything out in the dark landscape I got in to a bunk and fell asleep clutching my small rucksack.

A resonating voice intruded in to my dream, then realised this conversation was directly outside the compartment and I wasn't dreaming. Feeling sure the loud voice would soon stop I did my best to ignore it. Suddenly the door to the compartment flew open and the light was turned on, a loud booming voice completely destroyed any thought of going back to sleep. Not in the mood for this rude interruption I rolled over to face the inconsiderate intrusion. Raising my voice so I could be heard abruptly said "why don't you go outside and have a conversation like any normal civilised person would". Instantly the arguing stopped, as I finished talking I found myself face to face with a tall broad shouldered, elderly grey bearded man wearing a turban, next to him was a shorter man in a

264

beige railway uniform and hat. Even with the hat he only came up to the bearded mans shoulder. Showing I was not intimidated I stared at turbaned man sternly. He silently stared at me for several seconds then left the compartment. The railway attendant turned off the light, once outside the argument started again in a more subdued tone. One of the other passengers in the compartment explained that the man was arguing because he had booked the compartment for him and his wife and they wanted the compartment just for themselves. Having said my piece I rolled over and went back to sleep.

The next morning after the bunks were put back up the tall bearded gentleman came in followed by a slight woman, they sat down with out saying a word. The other passengers fell silent. It was obvious they were Sikhs. He wore a black turban, had a trimmed beard and a moustache that curled at the ends. He was burly in stature and looked about fifty five years old. His wife was slim, looked about five feet tall and maybe forty five years old. She was wearing a beige rap that covered her head and loose dark red trousers with a gold floral design. From a thin leather belt around her waist hung a short curved dagger decorated with a carved white handle and sheath, both looked extremely serious. Nobody in the compartment spoke which felt strange, usually somebody would be talking. I tried to start a conversation and asked if anybody knew when the train would arrive at Udaipur. No body replied, maybe there was some reluctance to break the silence because there was a female in the compartment and the others were being polite. What ever reason it was obvious there was no point in trying to talk to anyone; especially the Sikh.

The carriage compartment gradually becoming stiflingly hot and the silence was excruciating, I was looking forward to getting off the train. Fortunately the wait was not too long; much to my relief after an hour the train arrived at Udaipur station. With its Victorian style of wooden fret work and facades. Once off the train I saw a sign for the station restaurant, this was the first time I had come across a station with a restaurant; an ideal place for breakfast. The restaurant had polished wooden floor boards and panelling around the room. Several wooden tables spread with chairs around, them. Each table was set with table clothes and a cruet set. Double doors lead out on to a veranda. Surprisingly I was the only person in the restaurant and perused the menu written on a board in chalk. I could not believe my eyes the menu listed cornflakes, porridge, toast, poached eggs plus regular Indian cuisine. I had never been so excited by the prospect of eating Cornflakes or porridge; it felt as though I had walked in to another world similar to going through the wardrobe to Narnia. Excitedly I ordered cornflakes with toast and marmalade plus tea. The tea arrived in a china teapot with a china cup and saucer. Soon followed by my bowl of cornflakes swimming in cold milk with the toast in a toast rack, it felt so indulgent. I could not help wondering how cornflakes found their way to Udaipur, putting a spoonful of cornflakes in to my mouth, they tasted better than any I had eaten before; or so it seemed. I took my time chewing making sure I savoured the flavour which seemed strange having eaten cornflakes so many times in the past, but these were special. Whilst eating my breakfast there was a strange sort of tuneful wailing noise which sounded familiar, but I could not place where I had heard before. After about ten minutes the noise stopped. Once I had finished the cornflakes I trowelled Marmalade on to the toast and again slowly ate each mouth full. The wailing noise started again and was definitely convinced I had heard this sound before but still could not visualise where, but was convinced it might have been in Britain. Either way I was getting to the point where my curiosity was getting the better of me and had to find out what the sound was; but only after I had finished my toast and the pot of tea.

The wailing noise started to grow on me as it stopped and started. Each time it stopped the tune changed but I still could not recall where I had heard it before. Having finished eating I went out on to a small veranda to see what the noise was that had been nagging me. Once on the veranda I was astounded; across the road in a fenced compound were several Indian men standing in a circle dressed in what appeared to military uniforms playing of all things "bagpipes!" It was one thing eating cornflakes in the middle of India but to hear and see Indians playing bagpipes was just unbelievably surreal. Having been in India and Sri Lanka for over two months there were obviously more surprises waiting for me. Standing on the veranda I listened to the ensemble playing their bagpipes until they finished then marched off.

Looking out from the veranda across the roof tops I could

see a large blue lake. In the middle of the lake was white building that looked like a palace. It looked very exotic set out on the large expanse of water, the type of palace you would imagine coming across in India. From the station a road invitingly lead down in to Udaipur. In the station foyer I bought a map and was ready to explore the narrow streets.

Following the road from the station the sun felt hot, once between the buildings I kept in the shade. Udaipur was definitely different to any place I had been so far. A lot of the men wore large wrapped red, yellow or white turbans. Women wore brightly coloured saris. It felt more peaceful and calmer than the towns and cities of the south. The tall white buildings reflected the sun light in the narrow streets making them bright. There was no pressure from the vendors to buy from their shops and nobody asked for Baksheesh. I weaved my way to through the streets to the edge of the lake for a closer look at the lone white palace. It had large windows topped with a domed roof and appeared to be floating on the water, bobbing up and down with the gentle ripples of the lake. The hills behind were a stark contrast with the pure white walls and the blue tinge of the water. It looked exotically Indian.

A group of women at the bottom of some steps washed their laundry with a dull thud as the clothes were beaten on the bottom step as they chatted to each other. Their jet black hair was tied back and the vivid saris contrasted with the blue grey of the water. I pulled myself from the tranquil scene of the women doing their washing and walked around the streets and by chance came across a tea shop that looked no different to any of the other buildings and just could not resist going inside. The cooler air was a relief from the hot sun, calling for a tea I sat at a table. Looking around the interior of the tea shop the white washed plastered walls had greyed with age. There was the sound of subdued conversation that did not sound like Hindi. Surprisingly nobody really paid any attention to me which made me feel comfortable and at ease. It seemed as if seeing a Westerner was an everyday event, if it was I had not seen any Westerners in Udaipur yet. Taking my time drinking the tea I reflected on how different it was in the north. The weather was definitely different it was dryer and felt warmer. Finishing the tea I stepped back out side to carry on exploring, in one of the narrow streets I came across a book stall with a wide assortment of titles, some were obviously second hand but even so it would be something to read on the train and relieve the boredom. After spending a while looking at what was available, all the time the vendor kept offering me various books that he thought I would be interested in, mostly Science Fiction written by Isaac Asimov. Not being a science fiction fan I feigned interest but turned these down saying I had read them. At random I picked up a book that looked as if it might be interesting and bought it just so the vendor could make a sale.

Turning a corner from a narrow street I came across a market square with mostly fruit and vegetables for sale. Each vendor had a canopy made from a wooden frame lashed together and a large cotton sheet draped across it to help protect the wares and the vendor from the hot sun.

269

Each vendor did their best to sell me something pointing at the mangoes, pineapples, limes, oranges, etc. I bought some oranges to carry in my rucksack and peel later. Remembering the advice when I served in the British Army, only eat fruit in tropical countries that can be peeled which always made sense. I attracted some attention, not just from the vendors but also children. Some were very enterprising and offered to be my tour guide. Others asked where I was staying and they could take me to a good hotel. I had not thought of stay in Udaipur and could not see any good reason to stay for any length of time. There were the palaces but other than that there was not much more to see. Having wandered around a good part of Udaipur hoping to buy a roll of camera film, something I thought would be relatively easy was proving elusive. Returning to the station I sat down over a glass of tea and looked at my map of India to see where I should visit next. The places in bold type jumped out but I felt that they would be large towns which might be disappointing. Not far from Udaipur written in small type was Chittorgarh which for some reason struck me as a typical North Indian town with its own character and personality. Having noticed this town on the map my eyes kept coming back to it, even though it was in small type it seemed to beckon me. The name it self was appealing and eventually deciding to visit Chittorgarh.

Asking about the next train to Chittorgarh I found it was not until midnight, reserving my seat I found somewhere to sit and read my book. Before long a westerner appeared on the platform; it seemed strange seeing a white face.

We said hello and it was obvious that Richard was from the London area. After the usual conversation Richard asked what had drawn me to India and explained I intended to travel around the world but was unable to decide how long to stay in India and opted to just visit India instead. I asked Richard the same question and explained he had come out of the British Army after serving with The Paras and worked with the Bahrain Army training their troops and was on an extended trip around the world. I asked how he got a job like that. Richard said you have to apply from Britain but if you have served in the Army or Marines you should get a job. We swapped stories about our time in the army until a train pulled in to the station and Richard boarded it.

As the evening wore on it became cooler, the station was quieter until it felt I was the only person about but every now and then I heard a faint voice or a noise letting me know there were others about. Eventually my train arrived, its head light beaming brightly out of the darkness. No lights were on in the carriages which gave the train a sinister appearance. The engine puffed as passengers suddenly appeared from nowhere, they climbed aboard followed by a slamming of the doors and then silence. I found my way to my first class compartment pulled down my bunk as quietly as possible with out disturbing the other passengers. Putting my large rucksack at the head of the bunk as a pillow I carefully climbed in to the bunk, wrapping my arms through the straps of my small rucksack and fell asleep.

271

Agra; a dream comes true

Even though Chittorgarh was not far from Udaipur it took the rest of the night to get there. Arriving early in the morning at a quiet station where passenger's waited patiently for their train, tea stalls served up early morning beverage and food for the passengers. Station porters waited to help passengers who needed their luggage carried. Just a few passengers got off the train which made me wonder if it had been a good idea to visit Chittorgarh. Before going anywhere I had a refreshing tea and freshly made spicy Samoa's, not your usual breakfast but it tasted nice. After a shower in the rest room I put my large rucksack in left luggage and walked out in to the already scorching hot sun, in the distance the ground was hazy from the heat of the sun. Outside the station were two horse drawn carriages waiting for passengers, this struck me as the idyllic way to see Chittorgah. Boarding a carriage the driver asked if I wanted to go to the fort, not knowing where or how far it was to the fort replied "yes". The carriage set off at a sedate pace with the horses hoofs clicking against the hot tarmac. Travelling along the quiet road the fort became apparent in the distance across the flat dry ground. Standing high up on a rocky hill the fort walls blended in with the terracotta red rock. The fort walls undulated along the ridge of the hill and a tower broke above the line of the fort wall.

As we got closer I could make out the battlements and the

272

monumental size of the fortress, it stretched the full length of the hill top for about a kilometre, the tower was more obvious and I could see that it was at least a few hundred feet tall. Glad to be travelling in the carriage with its canopy shielding me from the now harsh sun, with the fort being so far from the station it would not have been an easy walk. The fort looked more imposing as we got closer, sitting on top of its commanding view point. Eventually the carriage arrived in the cool shade at foot of the hill, looking up at the fort it was an almost vertical climb for some several hundred feet to the fort walls, an almost impossible route for any likely attack. Luckily there was an easier access via a steep walk way that lead up to the fort entrance where a man sold water underneath the shade of an arch. He indicated to me if I wanted a drink by using his hand with the thumb jutting out and pointing to his mouth. Paying for a small jug of water I watched the Indians drinking from the aluminium beakers which they held up above their head, tipped their head back and poured the water in to their mouth, something I had seen several times whilst travelling around southern India. I could not help staring at them as they did this without spilling a drop of water and tried doing the same myself. Even though it looked easy getting the right angle so the water poured in to my mouth, it proved slightly difficult and managed to give my face a rinse instead. Trying a second time I managed to get it right and drank the cool water.

Having quenched my thirst I stepped from the shaded archway in to the bright sunlight which made me squint.

Even though the fort was several hundred feet up on top of the rock there was not a whisper of a breeze, the forts walls trapped the hot air rising from the ground, it was sweltering. Looking around the grounds I was unable see the far end of the fort which made me realise its sheer scale. There were several buildings in various stages of disrepair, camels in the distance were transporting tourists around the grounds.

I decided to make my way over to the tall tower standing so prominently above the other buildings. Now that I was in the fort I could see that the red tower was more than a few hundred feet high. It had nine tiers with windows in each tier except the top one which had a balcony. The design of the tower appeared to have a Chinese influence about it with some ornate carving on each tier. Once at the foot of the tower I could make out the detail of the design with elephants, gods, tigers and geometric shapes. It was breath taking to think that a structure like this has lasted for so long, several hundred years if not longer. Whilst looking at the tower from each side I found a sign saying it was the Tower of Victory. It had a small entrance, climbing up on to the pedestal supporting the tower I leant down and crawled inside, it felt surprisingly cool, cramped and without anyway of climbing up inside. Sitting down on the cool paving slabs they sent a shiver through me as the sweat on my arms, legs and body cooled. The temptation to stay in the cool interior was almost too much and spent some time relaxing. Sufficiently cooled I was ready to explore the rest of the fort. Outside standing on the pedestal I could see the far end of the fort and followed a wide pathway. The interior walls of the fort were not very high but it was obvious they did not need to be, the climb up the hill would be difficult enough for any attacker. There were several large pools each filled with dingy coloured water. After walking some distance and still not at the far end of the fort I stopped at one of the water pools with several contented long horned buffalo's wallowing in it. They were tended by the turbaned herder who was sitting on one of them then climbed on to the back of another. The temptation to paddle in the water was irresistible and found the water was cool, the floor of the pond felt smooth. Feeling the cool water on my feet the temptation was too great to resist, taking my T shirt off I waded in to the murky water, any concern about the buffalos faded as I wadded up to my waist where it felt even cooler, then dunked down up to my shoulders. I wallowed in the water until my fingers became wrinkly but once out I was soon dry and feeling hot again.

Instead of walking about in the midday heat I decided to just sit down and look at the other buildings from afar. Some looked as though they were palaces and others appeared as though they might have been ancient temples, but were not as ornate as the temples in the south.

Having only seen a small part of the fort I felt the Tower of Victory said everything about Chittorgah Fort and its grandeur. The water seller was still at the entrance and drank a beaker of water before making my way down to the road to catch a carriage back to the station and managed to drink it all without drenching myself. Sitting

275

back in the shade of the carriage canopy I was suddenly overcome with hunger, but before eating I had to have a shower after wallowing with the buffalos.

After a refreshing cold shower in the waiting room I found a tea shop close by that made omelets which seemed like a perfect meal and ordered one. Very soon a large omelet arrived with green vegetables in it. Putting a large piece in my mouth I chewed, it tasted just right then suddenly I felt a burning sensation in my mouth. This intensified, my whole mouth felt as if it was being scolded by boiling water. The green pieces were chilies but not just any chilies; they were the hottest I had ever eaten. The owners of the tea shop who had been smiling as they watched brought over a glass of water but even this did not quash the sensation in my mouth. The owners were now laughing and asked if the chilies were too hot, all I could do was nod, my mouth and lips felt numb and I found it difficult to speak.

Recovering to some degree from my culinary experience I asked for an omelet without any chilies. They seemed surprised that I did not want any chilies in the omelette but one was made for me. For the rest of that evening I could still feel the sensation of the chilies in and around my mouth and resolutely promised myself I would never eat any more chilies in India.

Not in the mood to look for a guest house or hotel so late in the day, if there was one. I felt it would be best to catch the next train. Looking at my map it was hard to decide where I should go next, except for making my way to Agra to see the Taj Mahal. I opted to just catch the train

276

towards Agra and see where it was the next morning. There was a vacancy on the next train which was due to arrive in the next few hours, an improvement on the wait time I had at Udaipur. In the mean time I sat on the platform and watched the hustle and bustle of people going about their everyday life, it was amazing how much luggage some people had with them. Large trunks and suite cases which made me reflect on the small amount I had in comparison. A third of the space in my large rucksack was now taken up with trinkets and gifts. I had two pairs of shorts, several T shirts and a pair of trousers for when I get back to Britain, a few pairs of pants, a shirt and my sandals which I was wearing. The variety of dress in the north amazed me. Some people wore western style clothes or sarongs with a white shirt; women wearing brightly coloured saris whilst some women wore a long smock with loose baggy trousers and a scarf; the baggy trousers were also worn with saris. A lot more of the women were wearing jewelry in their nose and some had chains attached to their ears. I also noticed a number of women had a reddish floral design on their hands and feet which I found out to be henna; also there were a number of Sikhs.

The train eventually pulled in and every one on the platform picked up their luggage and tried boarding the train at the same time. It looked chaotic as everyone jostled in the door way, passengers tried to get on and off at the same time which meant nobody was going anywhere. This stand off lasted for several minutes when all of a sudden there seemed to be some compromise

277

where the passengers getting off made it on to the platform, the whole scenario looked a bit like a scene from an old Charlie Chaplin black silent movie. Once every one was on I climbed aboard. In the compartment I found I had company, it was a relief when the man said hello and introduced his self as Sahil and asked me my name, then replied "Peter is a good Hebrew name", smiling I said it was. Sahil looked about 40ish, slim and about five feet tall and sat cross legged. Sahil asked where I had been so far. I explained that I had arrived in Bombay then travelled south to Cape Comorin, to Madurai and on to Sri Lanka from Rameswaram. After Sri Lanka I traveled north to Hyderabad, Aurangabad and now I am in Rajasthan. He asked where I was travelling to. When I told Sahil Kashmir his face broke in to a broad smile.

"Kashmir is lovely this time of year with the blossom. The road should be repair by the time you travel over the mountains. It gets damaged by the winter weather and becomes dangerous". This sounded a bit disconcerting but hoped it was exaggerated. Sahil added, "you must visit Agra to see the Taj Mahal and stop at Amritsar to visit the Sikh Golden Temple, there was nothing like it in the world". Sahil suggested I should visit the fort in Jodhpur for the view and the blue buildings. I got my map of India out and asked where Jodhpur and Amritsar were; Sahil pointed out Jodhpur and then Amritsar saying it was north of Dehli close to Lahore in Pakistan.

Once we found it I noticed it was on the train line to Jammu where I needed to catch the bus for Srinagar. The

278

evening wore on as we chatted and then I decided it was time to settle down and thanked Sahil for his advice.
I woke the next morning with the noise of people talking out side the window, looking down from my bunk I saw several young faces peering through the bars. When they saw me their chatter became excited. Sahil waved his hand and shouted "jow"; 'go away in Hindi'. It was already hot outside but still early and felt it would get even warmer than the previous day. Three more men came in to the compartment and sat down. They all started to talk to Sahil, as he replied they looked at me. One of the new passengers asked me if I found it too hot in India.
Smiling with a composed expression, "the weather was ideal.
They all laughed and talked between themselves then one said to me "you must like the heat",
"yes I prefer it warm".
"How do you find Indian food" enquired another passenger.
After briefly reflecting replied "most of the food has been good but I have found some chilies extremely hot".
Everyone laughed, "we like these chilies, it means the food is always hot, even if it is cold..
The train travelled through the extremely parched countryside. It looked like a desert with no body in sight. Eventually the train arrived at Jodhpur. I said good bye to my fellow passengers and thanked them for their company. Stepping out on to the platform it struck me how quiet it was. There was a tea stall where I bought

some Samosas and three teas which I poured in to my metal mug. Leaving my large rucksack at left luggage I set off to find my way to the fort to admire the view. I made my way through the narrow streets which were more like alley ways. Many of the buildings were painted a sky blue which was easier on the eyes than stark white. Many of the men wore large yellow turbans.

Finding my way was not easy through the narrow streets, I could see the fort standing majestically high on the hill but weaving my way through the warren of narrow streets to the fort was like walking through a maze. I managed to get directions from some people who appeared to understand me and pointed in the general direction and eventually made it to the foot of the steep path that lead up to the fort. Climbing up to the top I saw over the flat roofs, slim minarets jutted above the roof tops pointing at the sky. The blue buildings made Jodhpur look like a surreal image of the sea with the odd white building looking like a breaking wave. The climb was not easy partly because of the sun was now high in the sky, sweat was running down my forehead and I could feel my back getting wet under my small rucksack. Making it to the top I looked over the battlements and could see the edge of Jodhpur with the distant hills on the horizon. As I caught my breath I admired the spectacular view and wished I had film in my camera but I still had not found a shop in Northern India which sold any.

Unfortunately the fort was closed and having seen the view across Jodhpur I made my way back down to the narrow streets and navigated my way to the station. The next train was later that evening which gave me a chance to explore Jodhpur some more and walked around the narrow streets. I had a mixed experience where some seemed to regard me with some suspicion whilst other were very interested to see me and asked the usual obligatory questions, what was my name and where I was from. My time in Jodhpur was relatively uneventful compared to some of the more lively places I had visited further south. Rajasthan felt peaceful, an ideal place to be and wondered if my next destination, Jaipur would be just as tranquil. I had been told about Jaipur several times by other back packers who mentioned I should see the palace and visit the bazaar which was a good place to buy gemstones.

The train arrived early the next morning in Jaipur to an already busy station, Jaipur was definitely not quiet. After having a much needed shower and putting my large rucksack in to left luggage; unsure if I was going to stay overnight set off for some breakfast away from the crowded station. Outside steps lead down from the station entrance to a wide forecourt with people walking to and from the station. There seemed to be people from all parts of India distinguishable by their different clothes and dress. Women wearing brightly coloured long tops and loose trousers. Most noticeable were the men with their different coloured turbans of red, yellow, off white or pure white and Sikhs with their black turbans. Standing out from the crowd was a Buddhist monk with a shaved head dressed in a red robe who did not look Indian, more Tibetan; what was most striking was his lack of luggage and just carrying an umbrella.

I was the only Westerner in the crowd milling about outside the station which I now took as the norm on my travels through northern India. Making my way down a wide busy road towards some buildings I could see Jaipur had a lively and vibrant atmosphere.

Walking along the wide pavement I passed a variety of business's selling various wares such as metal worked utensils, books and crafts. Noisy workshops could be heard with hammering and cutting. I found a tea shop that was not too busy, checking the menu the most appealing meal was the omelette but after my last experience with the added chillies I was reluctant to order it. When asked what I wanted I took a chance and asked for a plain omelette," no chillies!"

The man taking the order shook his head side to side and said "yes, no chilies".

When he came out with the omelette and put the plate down on the table I saw it was done perfectly but it had green pieces in it.

"Are there chillies in the omelette?" I enquired,

"they are only mild chilies, not hot ones".

Being hungry I decided to take a chance and tentatively ate some of the omelette. The chillies were not mild at all. The familiar burning sensation took effect immediately and my mouth felt it was being scorched. My discomfort seemed to entertain the men working in the tea shop. After guzzling several glasses of water the burning sensation abated, a little.

Reiterating I did not want chillies," just a plane omelette;

no chillies". With a smile they shook their heads and went off to cook a plain omelette. Arriving just as I wanted, it tasted perfect.

"The owners asked with a smile "was it a good omelette?"

"Yes it was" I replied, said goodbye and left to find the bazaar.

The architecture in Jaipur was different to what I had seen so far in Rajasthan or anywhere else in India. An earthy red wall with a white painted ornate design ran along the other side of the road. Some of the buildings were either the same earthy red or pink. The roads were bustling with cars, cycle rickshaws and auto rickshaws. Wheeled barrows loaded with fruit and vegetables were beside the road and bought some oranges to help me keep going through the day.

The earthy red wall stretched for some distance without an end in sight until I came across a triple-arch. A central arch for traffic and either side were smaller ones for pedestrians. Walking under the arch it felt I had stepped in to the old India with the bazaar full of stalls selling everything you could imagine. Material and cloth piled high of every colour and hue, spices, rugs, clothes, saris, rugs and crafts such as small soap stone dishes with semi precious stone inlays and mother of pearl, wood carvings, metal utensils and furniture with mother of pearl inlay. What particularly interested me were the hookahs with their different designs in copper or polished steel. It seemed that Jaipur was a hub for all manufacturers and craftsmen in India. As I walked past the vendors stalls they beckoned me over to look at their wares. Having all day I took up their invitations, especially when something caught my eye. Several vendors ordered tea as we talked and they tried to sell me their goods. Even though I explained that I only had a rucksack and what they were selling would not fit in it. They replied that it was okay they could post it on to my bank which sounded strange. Having wandered past numerous stalls I came to a junction, in one direction there were more similar stalls and in the other a wall with an arch. On the other side through the arch were more stalls and shops, but this was where the jewellers were. On display were white metal and gold rings, bracelets, ear rings, nose rings, necklace's and loose cut gem stones, it felt I had discovered Aladdin's cave . One vender had cut and polished semi-precious gems in small boxes on a table outside his shop, each gem stone was just a few rupees. There was a choice of Topaz, Garnets and Amethyst. Sifting through the boxes I picked out several cut stones, one was large and black which turned out to be a ten carat Smokey Topaz. There was no end of stalls to look at in the bazaar and was so glad I had found the one I wanted. I lost track of time wandering about the bazaar and decided to make my way back towards the station. I came across a large open wooden door, inquisitively looking inside saw four craftsmen working with some pieces of white material that looked like marble. Standing in the door way I felt the stifling heat inside. Asking if I could watch and with out any hesitation the craftsmen nodded and indicated for me to sit down. Sitting next to one of the men I could now see the detail of the carving in to what now looked like

284

Ivory, asking if it was ivory he replied that it was bone. He was carving an intricate chess piece of an elephant being ridden by a maharaja, this chess piece was the king. I marvelled at the skill and dexterity he used with his small manual drill boring away at the bone to achieve the detail carving of the elephant and the maharaja in his decorated carriage. I could have spent hours watching these men but needed to get back and find out the time for the next train to Agra. Not being far from Jaipur and looking forward seeing the Taj Mahal I was reluctant to spend any length of time in Jaipur. I said good bye to the craftsmen and thanked them for letting me watch, smiling they waved farewell.

Back at the station I was told the next train to Agra was at 1am. The thought of another long wait in to the wee hours for a train did not appeal to me but there was not much I could do. The station was busy so I went in to the waiting room where it was quieter, cooler and I could have a shower. After a cold shower I got some food from a tea stall on the platform and sat on a bench to eat. As the evening wore on I did my best to stay awake but eventually dozed off. When I woke the station was quiet and dark; wondering what time it was I asked a platform attendant busying his self the time, it was 2am. Asking about the train to Agra, "you have missed it" came his reply. He quizzically asked where I had been and explained that I had fallen asleep in the waiting room. He looked at me sternly and retorted, "the waiting rooms are not for sleeping". Right now this was not my chief concern, having missed my train and wanted so much to arrive early in Agra. Asking the time of the next train to Agra and hoped I would not have to wait too long, it was 9am the next morning. Being so disappointed having missed the train I ignoring the comment from the platform attendant and went back in to the waiting room to sleep. The next morning I was woken by a group of women opposite talking loudly. Looking at the large clock it was 7am, enough time for a tea and some food. Sitting up I felt a bit groggy, my stomach did not feel too good either, a tea and some food was needed. Standing up I felt even worse and did not feel like eating anything. Luckily just outside the waiting room was a tea stall. Armed with my metal mug I asked for it to be filled up,

Replying " not possible" and indicted that he only used glasses.

"Three glasses" and held up three fingers, poured them in to my mug and turned to walk back to the waiting room; suddenly without any warning I projectile vomited on to the platform followed by some violent retching. The people buying their breakfasts were totally nonchalant and ignored me. I had been lucky so far and not had any real illness whilst in India but now I was feeling clammy, hot and not in the least at all well. Returning back to the waiting room I sat down to drink my mug of tea which I managed not to spill whilst being sick. Luckily I kept it down; but food was definitely out of the question.

Finishing the tea I decided to cool my self down with a cold shower. I felt extremely hot and light headed; the last thing I wanted

Struggling to my feet I managed to shuffle the few steps

286

to the shower, shut the door and sat down in the large ceramic basin. There was an instant relief from the cold water. After several minutes and feeling slightly better I turned the shower off but sat motionless, the thought of standing up was too much to contemplate. Soon I felt hot again and turned the shower back on. Not wanting to stay in the shower all-day; I somehow had to get my self mobile; even if I did not feel like standing let alone walking any where. Making a concerted effort I stood up and got dressed.

Looking at my rucksack the thought of picking it up felt too daunting but with monumental effort lifted it and threw it on to my back with a hefty thump. I sluggishly shuffled out on to the platform with my head swimming and my legs wobbling. Slumping down on a bench tried to convince myself that I would be okay.

When the train arrived I barged past everyone and clambered on board, I was not in the mood to wait for every one to get off or on the train, I just wanted to flop down on a seat. Turning the fan on in the compartment to try and cool down only exasperated the situation by moving the hot air around and making it feel even warmer. All I could do was sit down and sweat which was pouring off me. Soon I dozed off; whenever the train stopped at a station I woke, finding it was not Agra dozed off again. Having slept for some time I noticed in my slumber the train was slowing down, but I wanted to stay where I was and hoped it was not Agra. The ticket collector opened the door to the compartment and called out "next stop Agra", exasperatingly I slowly sat up, then tried standing. I felt myself swaying and steadied myself whilst lifting my rucksacks.

Gingerly I made my way off the train and sat down on the platform to decide what I should do. The options were to book in to a hotel and wait until I was feeling better, go and visit the Taj Mahal and see how I got on or find a doctor. I was not in the mood for any food and just wanted to see the Taj Mahal.

Depositing my large rucksack in left luggage I shuffled outside; the road in front of the station was busy with traffic of every description; Ambassador Cabs, auto rickshaws, cycle rickshaws, buses and private cars arrived and left. Across the road with all of the traffic driving past was a stall laden with bright red sliced water melons. It was not the most hygienic place to sell food but thought water melon might be easier on my stomach, there was only one way to find out. Buying a large slice the watermelon tasted cool and soothing and surprisingly eased my stomach pain; at least there was something I could eat. Having finished eating at the road side I needed to somehow get to the Red Fort and Taj Mahal. Not being in a fit state to walk any distance or knew where to go a cycle rickshaw seemed like the ideal sedate mode of transport. Having not been on one yet it seemed the least exhilarating.

Lounging back in the seat the cyclist left the front of the station and without slowing drifted out in to the traffic. Vehicles of all descriptions swirled around us on either side; at times precariously close just missing the front wheel as they cut in. The cyclist seemed unperturbed and relentlessly careered on without slowing down for anyone or anything. It was not long before the rickshaw pulled up at a fort with large imposing battlements made of terracotta coloured stone, an arched entrance lead in to the fort with large towers over shadowing the entrance. The cyclist turned around and announced that we had arrived at the Red Fort.

Cautiously climbing off the seat I asked the rickshaw driver to wait and explained I wanted to go to the Taj Mahal afterwards, the rickshaw owner nodded and seemed happy with this request. Walking slowly I made my way through the arch, under the high wall and in to a large courtyard surrounded by the high battlements. Over looking the court yard was a high veranda topped with a domed roof supported by pillars. Climbing the stairs up to the veranda took a great deal of effort, at the top I stepped out to a magnificent view looking towards the Taj Mahal and the Yamuna River. My first glimpse of possibly the most famous iconic building in the world left me awestruck. It stood out above the tree tops with its four tall white minarets, the large white iconic dome and four smaller ones either side.

Seeing it from the terrace in Agra Fort made me realise that the copy of the Taj Mahal in Aurangabad did not compare to the real thing, even at a distance. Staring in amazement at what most people only get to see in photos or on television took away any thought of being ill as a sense of excitement took over. I did not want to spend any more time at the fort, I just wanted to see the Taj Mahal up close.

289

Walking back to the rickshaw with a more determined step I climbed in to the rickshaw. The cyclist pulled out in to the busy road peddling as fast as he could and seemed more concerned about getting to the Taj Mahal than the dangerous drivers who seemed totally oblivious to any other traffic on the road. The rickshaw turned on to the busy road slotting in between the other vehicles. At a round about we joined a long straight road, the rickshaw picked up speed as it travelled downhill which now felt precarious. Holding on to either side of the seat I tried to convince myself it was perfectly safe. A row of trees beside the road gave intermittent glimpses of the Taj Mahal between the branches and tree trunks as the rickshaw sped along.

The distance to the Taj Mahal was deceptive because it is so large, looking much closer than it really was. Finally we arrived outside the main entrance to the grounds in the most appropriate mode of transport for such an occasion. Outside the entrance lining the pavement stalls sold crafts of various kinds and of course tea. The main entrance was a large arch leading to an undercover reception, ticket kiosk and a tourist shop. Having paid the entry fee I walked in to the grounds with numerous people promenading about.

A long central avenue led directly to the dazzling white Taj Mahal, it almost glowed under the bright sun contrasting with the blue sky. Trees and short conifers lined the path ways either side of the long water feature. Walking down the path towards the Taj Mahal I staring in absolute wonder. The grounds extended out either side with well manicured lawns. About half way to the Taj Mahal was a raised podium where people were stopping to take photographs and pose with the Taj Mahal in the back ground.

One group of young Indian women and man posed, the photographer directed them for the best composition. They changed their pose several times until the photographer was happy then directed them to hold the pose with broad toothy smiles. The photographer was making some final camera adjustments when I noticed that the lens cap was still on, before I could say any thing the photograph was taken. The man being photographed also noticed the lens cover and pointed at the camera. The photographer looked at the camera lens; laughed. Quickly posing the group again he took a photograph and went their way.

I climbed up on to podium and sat on one of the marble seats to admire the view and have a rest; I was feeling light headed possibly from a lack of food. Whilst sitting down I suddenly remembered seeing a picture of the Taj Mahal when I was at Primary School, about 10 years old. It was a small picture but left an impression on me because I remembered thinking at the time I wanted to visit the Taj Mahal, fourteen years later here I was sitting in front of it. Looking around it struck me that I was the only Westerner which surprised me, if any western tourists were to be seen surely here would be the most likeliest place. Recovering sufficiently I climbed down from the podium and slowly walked towards the foot of the Taj Mahal. As I got closer I could make out intricate ornate decorations surrounding the Mausoleum and the podium it sat on. People were walking around the top of the podium but I could not see any obvious way to get up there. Noticing some people walking behind a screen that looked as if it was part of the podium and concealed steps leading up on to it.

Reaching the podium I studied the beautiful ornate decoration, the detail was so intricate. Running my hand over the smooth marble it felt perfectly flat. The floral design covered the whole wall with stems, leaves and flowers made of semi-precious stones flowing in every direction. At the bottom of the steps were a large number of sandals, everyone was expected to take their footwear off before climbing up to the podium and the Mausoleum. Taking off my heavy sandals made from old tyres, I was confident they would still be there when I got back. Climbing the white marble steps I thought about the hundreds of thousands of people who had done the same over the centuries. Mughals, Indians of various casts, the British at the height of the Empire and of course tourists. The floor of the podium was paved with polished marble that felt cool under my feet. Standing in front of the mausoleum I looked up at the white dome and marvelled at the grand scale of the structure. I thought the Gate Way to India in Bombay was magnificent but this was just awe inspiring, thinking about the skill needed to construct it and having lasted over 500 years, considering that few buildings can boast surviving a fraction of that time. Walking around to the entrance of the mausoleum I studied the intricate inlaid design closely; each piece

292

fitted perfectly and there appeared to be millions of them. Walking up the steps under the arch leading in to the shady interior, the cool air made me shiver, a welcome relief from the hot afternoon air. Visitors crowded into the walk way surrounding two cenotaphs in the centre. Marble panels with a delicate lattice design screened them. The interior wall around the inside had recessed arches rising some thirty feet with a marbled balcony all the way around. Alternate arches had a similar lattice design that allowed sun light in.

The cenotaphs were covered in an even more intricate floral design of inlayed semi-precious stones, it looked absolutely exquisite. One was smaller than the other but both were raised on a platform of the same size decorated with thousands of tiny flowers of semi precious stones. These stood on a floor with a thick black geometric inlay design.

Even though there was a large crowd moving around the interior it was peaceful and quiet, except for a faint whisper. I spent a considerable length of time admiring the intricate work unsure I would get a chance to visit the Taj Mahal ever again and wanted to make the most of my visit, and the cool interior.

Reluctantly leaving I walked out in to the late afternoon sun and slowly made my way back to the main entrance, stopping several times to rest and take a final look of this Wonder of the World. Outside of the grounds the noise and smell of food brought me back down to earth, there was a stall selling finger food such as samosa's and bargees, also tea and rice. I bought a small plate of rice and gingerly ate it which helped settle my stomach. Vendors on the craft stalls competed to attract the attention of every passing visitor, they called, waved and made a show of their stalls by holding out their hands and pointing down at their wares. The only stalls I was really interested in were those selling small sandstone dishes with the similar floral design on the Taj Mahal. I found one that was white, it had the similar lace work that was on the panels surrounding the tombs and a floral inlay design on the lid; a perfect memento of my visit to the Taj Mahal and bought this and two others. The cycle rickshaw had gone, the only other transport were some auto rickshaws, not in the mood to risk life and limb I made my own way back to the station.

The walk back to the train station felt long and arduous, stopping occasionally and sitting down I eventually made it to the station entrance and decided it was not a good idea to have walked back.

Having visited the Taj Mahal and the Red Fort I felt that anything else in Agra would be an anti-climax and decided to catch the next train to Amritsar. Having been told how spectacular the Golden Temple was and how it would leave me in awe, which made me wonder if it was more astounded than the Taj Mahal.

I bought another wedge of water melon and found that there was an overnight train to Amritsar in the next few hours. After retrieving my rucksack I came across four large bales of tightly packed cotton on the platform and sat on one, it was the most comfortable seat I had ever come across. Still feeling a bit groggy I was almost tempted to lay down but felt I would very likely doze off and miss the train. Sitting back on the cotton bale I watched the crowds of passengers and workers toing and froing with their luggage. Not being the centre of attention left me detached from what was going on around me, similarly to watching a TV and gave me an insight in to India first-hand. With a sense of relief the train arrived just when I was starting to flag and feel drowsy. Almost as soon as I sat down in the first class compartment I fell asleep clutching my small rucksack.

I was woken by the sound of distant voices which became clearer; opening my eyes I saw a crowd of children at the grilled window. At first I tried to ignore them but their constant chatter made it difficult, they were all trying to get me to buy whatever they had for sale or holding out their hands asked for baksheesh. One boy had a tray of clay pots filled with water, I bought two which seemed to make the rest even more frantic for me to buy from them but a whistle sounded and the train started to pull away from the station. Some of the boys ran along side the train until it left the end of the platform and sped off in to the night without me knowing which station we had just left. feeling it was time to pull down the bunk, I stood up and felt light headed but managed to put my large rucksack at one end pulled myself up and went back to sleep.

The next morning whilst half asleep I felt the reassuring rocking of the carriage. I could have stayed there for the rest of the day but knew this was not possible, the other passengers would need a seat at some time. Once fully awake I got down from the bunk and had a shower at the end of the carriage. Turning on the shower cold rusty water gushed out, regardless of the colour it felt refreshing and stayed under it for some time until there was a knock at the door and somebody called out in Hindi; once dressed I opened the door and was greeted by a queue of people waiting to use the toilet.

Back in my compartment the other passengers were sitting up. One of them said hello and asked how I was. Convinced they did not want to hear about a westerners ills said I was okay. Then was asked the usual questions, what was my name and where I was from? Another passenger asked where I had been in India and explained about my journey around Southern Indian and Sri Lanka and my journey north, so far. One passenger asked if I had been to Hampi. Saying I hadn't and admitted I had not seen it on my map, the passenger offered to show me where it was, tracing his finger over the central part of India he suddenly exclaimed Aha! As if it was a eureka moment. Hampi did not seem to be far from Bangalore and the gentleman explained Hampi was an ancient hill town, "You must go there!" he exclaimed.

Pointing that I was travelling north to Kashmir, he smiled and told me I was travelling a long way, "just like someone on a pilgrimage", which made us all laugh. The gentleman then asked if I liked India,

without hesitating I said it was exciting and very interesting.

"You must have been to India before."

"No I haven't".

"If you like it here in India then you must have been here

in a previous life".

Having been told this a second time made me feel any one was welcome. The train started to slow down and eventually pulled in to a station which consisted of just a platform. There was a large crowd of people waiting to get on with their luggage but standing out from the crowd was a young Sikh of about 25 with a moustache and short beard, carrying a shield and spear. On his waist he wore a sword and dagger. Tucked In his turban was some shiny metal crescents which I realised where smaller knives. The young man waited for the others to board the train then got on.

Many of those who had got off the train were filling up cups and jugs with water from a fountain, deciding this was a good idea and did the same. Fishing out my metal mug I jumped off the train, quickly filled up my metal mug to the brim and gulped it down, filled it again and got back on the train. I enquired when the train will be arriving in Amritsar, one of the other passengers held out his hand and waved it side to side and said "some time soon". Being accustomed too this type of explanation about time and distance I took it as being later that evening; but it could be sooner or even later, not being in a rush or feeling too well I decided it could take as long as it wanted. The whistle blew and the train pulled away from the lonely platform in the middle of what appeared to be the desert to continue its journey north. The countryside looked barren with no sign of any life or habitation, but the people who had been waiting at the station must have come from somewhere, it was one of those mysteries of India where things can just happen. The train travelled on through the hot, barren, arid landscape. After some time the train pulled in to a station with a few amenities including tea stalls. Before the train stopped I made my way to the carriage door where a rotund man with a large bass drum strapped to his front and carrying his luggage was standing. Amused that somebody would be wearing the drum on the train and how he was going to safely get down the steps. The train stopped and the people on the platform crowded the doorway, they had no intention of letting Mr Bass Drum off. He shouted at them but they were not giving way. Wanting to get off the train to buy some food I decided to assist him with a gently nudging. He lurched forward complaining loudly in Hindi but it worked and the passengers on the platform moved out of the way as the Bass Drum tottered towards them. Just as we exited the doorway on to the platform the passengers instantly filled the void jostling their way on to the carriage. Luckily Mr Bass Drum had landed on his feet and did not seem worse for wear. Having bought some Samosa's and a tea I got back on to the train just in time, relieved that I had managed to get something to eat.

The train careered on through the barren countryside. Every now and then small communities could be seen on the horizon but there was not any arable land. The morning drifted in to the afternoon as the carriage got warmer by the hour. I had several showers in a hope to cool myself down which proved impossible. As the day wore on the water in the roof tank heated up until it was lukewarm. As the evening faded in too night with the desert land scape turning pitch black there was the welcomed relief of the cooler air blowing in to compartment. The train occasionally pulled in to a station, most of them appeared to empty. Still not feeling well I had an early night to help the time pass more quickly and get a good night's sleep ready to explore Amritsar. Waking the next morning I felt better, obviously the food from the previous day had helped. Looking out of the window the landscape had not changed much, it was still the dry rocky earth. The passengers had changed and I was asked the usual questions. Hoping that the new passengers had an idea how much longer or further it was to Amritsar. Getting a reply that it would not be much longer, an improvement on the previous day and from experience this was a good sign, but it still could be a number of hours. About three hours later the train started to slow down, anticipating the train was about to arrive at Amritsar I got my things ready. The train slowed to a crawl passing a large number of anxious looking passengers, then eventually stopped at the extremely crowded station displaying a sign; "Amritsar". Grabbing my rucksacks and stepping out on to the platform I had at long last made it, but felt light headed.

Amritsar station was one of the busiest I had seen in Northern India, having to weave through the crowd packed shoulder to shoulder. On the wall a large picture of a regal man in what appeared to be Moghul style dress hung near the entrance. Without doubt this was a man of great importance but the poster did not say who he was.

299

Outside I found myself in an equally busy narrow street. Not knowing which direction the Golden Temple was I followed a large group all going in the same direction. I did not pay much attention to what was either side of the street as I was swept along, besides I was more interested in making my way to the Golden Temple. Winding my way through the narrow streets I found myself walking beside a high pure white wall, then arriving at a tall wide arch. Just inside were a large number of sandals and shoes which had been left as requested by a sign asking for all foot wear to be removed. Taking my thick soled sandals off I walked through a shallow foot bath and under a covered walk way of white marble supported by pillars extending either side. Looking through the arch I caught my first glimpse of the Golden Temple in a large courtyard set on a lagoon with a causeway leading out to it. The golden part covered the domed roof and half way down the sides. I could not take my eyes of this central structure which seemed to be floating on the water, the reflection in the water added to the spectacle. Walking out from under the covered walk way I stepped on to a wide path surrounding the lagoon.

There were a large number of people in a wide variety of colourful Indian dress walking around the lagoon; they stood out against the stark white structure that surrounded it. Considering the temple grounds were in the middle of Amritsar it was surprisingly quiet, apart from the faint murmuring of those visiting the temple. Walking around the lagoon I could see the Golden Temple was draped in golden metal on each side; topped with the large central dome and four small domed towers on each corner. Around the top of the sixteen metre building was a parapet and below this on each side were large windows. The golden metal ended some two or three metres from the base of the temple where it was pure white marble. After circumnavigating the lagoon I found myself at the wide causeway leading to the temple. Approaching the temple I felt a sense of excitement, similarly to my visit at the Taj Mahal, I felt privileged to be able to visit such an important building that was so sacred for Sikh's around the world. As I got closer to the temple the embossed ornate detail became clearer, there were panels either side of each window with a floral design, the upper part of the temple had a relief design. A path led around to the back of the temple where there was a panoramic view. Entering the temple through an arched entrance I found myself standing under a high domed roof with a golden interior and a small balcony with detailed intricate relief work; I could not help staring at the wonderful craftsman ship, it looked just as magnificent as the Taj Mahal. Eventually I reluctantly made my way out of the temple and walked around the lagoon again to make the most the days experience, Amritsar was definitely one of the high lights of my journey around India, never to be forgotten. As I went to leave the temple grounds under the covered walk way I noticed a number of plaques on the wall. Looking closer, inscribed in black was the name of a Sikh, underneath was a brief description of the military action he had died in plus the date. There were hundreds hung on the wall, impulsively I started reading them.

Each gave an account of the individual's bravery in battle. Many had died in World War 1, World War 2 and the Indo-Pakistan War winning medals for bravery, including the Victoria Cross. It was very humbling to read about so many Sikh's who had died in Europe, so far from home. Having read most of the memorial plaques I put on my sandals and made my way out in to the crowded street and headed back to the station, not wanting to stay in Amritsar after having seen the temple. I felt the urgency to catch the next train to Jammu, and the bus to Kashmir. The station was just as busy as it was earlier with passengers and porters going to and fro and the noise of the trains with their doors being slammed shut and the carriages shunting. Having retrieved my large rucksack I found there was an overnight train to Jammu which was due to arrive. Whilst waiting an Indian gentlemen came up to me and asked the usual questions such as my name, for some reason I was a bit suspicious but we struck up a conversation. He asked me if I was going to Lahore,
" where is Lahore?".
"Lahore is just across the border in Pakistan, it is a lovely place" came the reply.
I told him that it had not crossed my mind to visit Pakistan and felt it would be out of my way. The Gentleman told me I could catch the train to Lahore from Amritsar which surprised me; Pakistan was so close and would be so easy to visit. Reflecting on which way to go; Lahore or Kashmir but decided to head for Kashmir and wondered about visiting Pakistan on the way back. Some time later the gentleman's train arrived, saying good bye

he boarded it with a loud bang of the carriage door.
A few hours later my train arrived. As it pulled out of
Amritsar I watched the lit windows and buildings pass by
until we were out in the dark countryside. Reflecting that
it had been a long exciting day with wonderful memories,
also I felt better, just as I was heading to Kashmir.
Travelling whilst ill was not a pleasant experience and
hoped I would not have a similar experience again.

An unusually flavoured tea

No sooner had I fallen asleep I was rudely woken by a sudden jolt. The train had arrived at the most northern station on the Indian railway network, 'Jammu'. The temperature was cooler than that of the last few weeks, it felt more like a British summer's day. I gathered my things together and got off the train and stepped on to an almost empty platform. Jammu seemed to be almost deserted; there were very few people, and all I could see were several breeze block structures with tin roofs. Parked close to the station was a red single decker bus waiting for its passengers. The paint work on the bus had seen better days, just like many other buses in India. Climbing aboard I asked the driver if it was going to Srinagar, the drivers' response was a nod of his head and a wave of his hand to direct me towards the back of the bus. After sitting down I noticed that the females were sitting on the left and males on the right, there was obviously gender segregation. The passengers were all Indian of various ages, and wearing different styles of dress. Three young smartly dressed, loud and boisterous men got on the bus and sat in front of me. A woman boarded the bus with a wooden cage full of chickens which she put down in the luggage hold half way along the bus. The driver looked around the bus as if to check he had all of his passengers; turning back round in his seat and started the engine, the bus shook in to life, the window screen rattled which made me feel this the bus should not be on the road. When the bus pulled away the young men in front roared with delight.

After travelling a short distance through Jammu past several buildings with writing daubed on them the bus drove in to a large yard with several other buses at various stages of dismantlement or repair. Obviously somebody was going to fix the window screen or maybe we will get on to another bus, either way I felt reassured.

The driver got off the bus and called over to a man in a smartly pressed uniform who looked as if he was a foreman or manager; they both walked to the rear of the bus and looked under the wheel arch. Nobody else seemed that concerned or interested in what the pair were looking at but I found it a bit disconcerting. The driver talked excitedly then the foreman abruptly interrupted with a stern tone to his voice. There was a brief silence before the driver got back on to the bus and started the engine.

Driving out of the yard past several single storey buildings we were soon in the North Indian countryside heading towards some hills. My map of India showed only one road leading to Srinagar, it was relatively straight at first then wound its way in to the extended Himalayan range. The thought of travelling over part of the Himalaya's excited me especially when the contour colours indicated that we might climb up to about 11,000 feet. The road was relatively flat and mostly straight with the occasional bend. On either side of the road green meadows extended out for some distance with deciduous tree's. The air felt fresh and cool, a stark contrast to the 32°C plus in Rajasthan and the Punjab. The road had a gravel surface which made the bus judder and rattle with little benefit from the suspension but the window screen appeared to have stopped shaking.

As we progressed coniferous trees started to fill the landscape; the meadows gave way to hillsides. As the road climbed higher the hillsides became vertical rocky cliffs rising on the right with a equally steep drop on the left in to a canyon. The scenery looked spectacular and exhilarating as the road weaved its way 90° around a cliff face then back almost 180° on itself, this happened several times giving spectacular views of the now mountainous terrain.

After an hour or so along a straight stretch of road we met some military lorries coming in the opposite direction; there was no lay bye to pull in to and did not look as if there was enough room for two vehicles to pass each other. I thought that the lorry would reverse up but instead the two facing vehicles stopped, then gingerly approaching each other at a snails pace. The bus pulled over towards the cliff edge, it looked like the ideal moment for everyone to get off the bus as the two vehicles edged by each other. Now side by side I curiously looked out of the window; the rear wheel was literally on the edge of the road with a sheer drop of a few hundred feet. It seemed sensible for the bus to stop still at this point to let the lorry past but surprisingly the driver persisted on creeping forward. I became transfixed watching the wheel precariously rotate along the edge, dislodging small stones from the gravel road which fell down into the canyon.

Whilst staring at the wheel I was surprisingly calm with a surreal detachment from the precarious situation, it felt I was watching a dramatic moment in a film unfold. Looking briefly at the lorry it seemed as though the two vehicles were touching with barely a millimetre between them. The military lorry edged past at the same time the bus started to creep away from the edge towards the centre of the road; a feeling of relief come over me. Through out the encounter with the cliff edge the other passengers nonchalantly carried on talking as if this was an every day event and there was nothing to worry about. After the slightly hair raising moment the road climbed more steeply, the tops of snow-capped mountains could be seen in the distance, my first glimpse of the Himalayas held me captivated. As the bus steadily climbed the mountains closed in around us until eventually the bus came to a halt at a cliff face with a long single lane tunnel leading in to the mountain. The driver waited for several vehicles to make their way through the tunnel, it was then I felt the temperature was noticeably cooler; just wearing a T shirt and shorts did not help. The bus slowly entered the long tunnel hewed through the mountain; I wondered in anticipation what was at the other end; so far I could make out the sky. As the bus left the tunnel spread out below us was a wide valley, in the distance were snow-capped mountains. The road dropped down steeply which made my ears pop as we descended down in to the valley. The bus gathered speed travelling on a tarmac road edged by a drainage ditches. Either side were arable fields with young crops sprouting or brown after being freshly ploughed. It almost looked like the country side you would find in any part of Britain or Europe, except for the mountains as a back drop and bullock drawn carts slowly ambled along the road. Occasionally we passed a junction that lead off towards the mountains, people worked in the fields and small buildings could be seen in the distance. It was late after noon and it still did not look as if there was any end in sight. But after about an hour I noticed the bus was approaching some distant buildings which looked like a town. As we drew closer the other passengers became excited, it looked as though this was the end of our journey. The bus drove through the narrow streets passing two or three storey buildings made of brick and wood, then eventually came to a halt in a court yard. Once the engine was turned off the other passengers gathered their belongings.

At long last I was in Srinagar, it had taken me three months to get to Kashmir, now all I had to do was find some where to stay. Climbing down from the bus I was mobbed by a crowd of teenagers each telling me I should go with them for some where to stay, each one saying theirs was the best place. It had been a long day and I just wanted to sleep and followed one of the teenagers who led me away from the crowd at the bus terminal.

We walked around some narrow streets, down an alley and arrived at a canal lined with large boats. The teenager jumped on to one of them and told me to follow him. The temperature had dropped dramatically, it was distinctly chilly but as I went inside the boat it felt warm and cosy. A slim elderly woman about five feet tall asked me if I had eaten, saying that I hadn't she replied "I will cook some thing". The elderly woman told me how much she charged per night for the bed, 20 Rupees, just over £1 but at this point I didn't care if she charged 100 rupees.

The interior of the house boat was all pine and had a homely feel about it. A black metal stove stood in the corner with a kettle on it. After a rice meal and sweet insipid green tea in a china cup I was shown my bed room which looked inviting though cool. There was a large bed with several blankets and large plump pillows on it; after having spent the last three weeks sleeping on trains and in stations the bed was going to feel like absolute heaven. Putting down my rucksacks and having another tea I thanked the woman and said I wanted to sleep.

Covering myself up under the thick woollen blankets, the down pillows felt luxuriously soft and almost immediately fell asleep.

The next morning I woke, it was warm and comfortable under the blankets, looking out of the window next to my bed there was a thick dark, grey fog. The thought of staying in the bed until it lifted was appealing, but it crossed my mind that the fog might hang around for a few days and wondered if it would be best to catch the bus back; considering that I only had shorts and T shirts to wear and how chilly it was.

In the kitchen I could hear pots and pans being clunked about; braving the cold room I got dressed and went in to the kitchen which had been warmed by the stove. The elderly woman was cooking fried eggs and when she saw me poured out a cup of tea, heaped a spoonful of sugar and added some milk. Again the tea looked weak and insipid, but tasted refreshing even if it was different to any tea I had tasted so far in India or Sri Lanka. I ate the fried eggs with some flat oval bread that had a rim to it and hatching across the centre, it was firmer than the Naan bread I had eaten so far. It also tasted different Whilst eating I reluctantly explained that it was too cold for me in Kashmir and I was going back to Delhi, it felt a shame having travelled so far to get to Kashmir. The woman looked disappointed but seemed to resign herself to losing a guest.

Having packed my things I made my way back to the bus terminal which was already busy with some Kashmiri teenagers wearing woollen ponchos or blankets wrapped around their shoulders waiting for more tourists to arrive. When they saw me they all crowded around trying to persuade me to go with them to their boat house. Adamantly saying "I'm going back to Delhi".

But this did not deter them in any way and persisted on trying to persuade me to go with them. One of the teenagers said he remembered me arriving the previous day and asked why I was leaving so soon. I told him it was too cold for me and I wanted to be somewhere warmer. Smiling he said it will be okay the fog will go later and the weather will be hot all week; I could not help feeling sceptical. He asked me where I had stayed the previous night, when I told him he said those boats are always cold then added "my house boat is always warm and there is a very good view of Dal Lake".

He told me the bus for Jammu was not until later and suggested that I should look at his house boat, "if you did not like it you can leave", then added "if you come with me they will leave you alone. Reassured by his optimism I agreed to look at his house boat even if it was only to kill time before the bus for Jammu arrived. We walked out of the terminal in to the thick fog, crossed a road where the pavement followed a low stone wall beside a waters edge. The teenager told me his name was Amjad and asked me mine,

"its Peter" I replied.

Amjad suggested having a tea and walked over to a small shelter constructed of blankets about the size of a small garden shed, pulling back the blanket cover he beckoned me in. The structure had a wooden frame with the blankets draped across the top and down all four sides. Amjad spoke to the four men in what I took to be Kashmiri, looking at me they smiled and said hello. A stove kept the shelter warm and the tea hot. Amjad handed me a glass of green insipid liquid which tasted sweet, "this is Kashmiri tea, this is all we drink here in Kashmir" to which the others laughed. Amjad asked if I liked the tea and told him that it tasted good. Everyone in the shelter cheered at this comment. Once we had finished our teas Amjad said we should go to his house boat. Saying goodbye I reluctantly left the warm hovel and stepped out in to the chilly fog. We walked through the thick fog along the wall at the waters edge. Across the water I could just make out what looked like large pale

311

coloured huts, Amjad said his house boat was not far, "we just have to get a boat".

We passed a number of people on the pavement who appeared then disappeared in to the fog. Out on the water I could see small boats that looked like dugout canoes, some had a large pile on the bow. We arrived at a gap in the wall and Amjad walked down some steps on to a small wooden platform and deftly climbed aboard one of the moored up dugout canoes. Following down the steps I placed my large rucksack on the canoe and precariously stepped aboard. The canoe rocked, not wanting to fall in the water I quickly sat down which amuse everyone watching. The canoe was dug out of wood and some fifteen feet long and two feet wide with virtually no sides to it. The bow almost dipped down in to the water and didn't feel it should have three people sitting in it.

The owner of the boat pushed away from the small quay and with his single paddle gently propelled the boat out towards the now visible shapes which I could see were house boats. The canoe pulled up to a jetty between two large house boats. Precariously lifting my rucksack I got off the front which surprisingly did not sink in to the water. We were greeted by a middle aged man about five feet tall with a beard wearing a flowing cape, "welcome my name is Hajib", he then asked me if I wanted a tea, not wanting to offend Hajib I said yes. He poured me a glass of the clear sugary green tea, Hajib announced "Kashmiri tea is not like the others you get in India, it has a different flavour and it is better for you".

Hajib asked where I was from, when I said Britain Hajib

got excited and asked a stream of questions. We talked for some time and I answered Hajibs questions as best I could. Eventually he changed the subject and told me about his house boats which he was obviously proud of. "This one here is where my family live and this house boat is for guests and invited me to look inside. Walking the short gang plank I stepped in to a spacious room which was entirely pine and looked luxurious. There was a comfortable looking bed and windows on three sides, these gave a panoramic view of the shore and the mountains which I could now just see through the hazy mist. There was a rug and a small book case with several books. Hajib explained that they will cook breakfast when I am ready in the morning which is fried eggs and Kashmiri bread. I was getting the impression that everything in Kashmir was Kashmiri. I asked Hajib how much he charged and was surprised how cheap it was and decided to stay for three days.

Enquiring how to catch a canoe back to the shore, Hajib laughed, "they are not canoes; they are called Shikara". Hajib added,"you can call for one and it will come over for you"; it sounded just like a cab or taxi service. "There are a lot of Shikara's on the lake, if you need anything or want any help ask me. Don't ask anybody else because I can get you a good price".

I thanked Hajib for his help and after sorting out my things I hailed a Shikara to take me back to the shore. As predicted the fog had now lifted and I could see right across Dal Lake. At the far end, out in the middle of the water was a small island with a house on it and some trees. I asked the boat owner if it was possible to visit the island and he said it was and decided to visit it at some time. We reached the small quay; after paying the boat owner I precariously stood up and stepped off on to terra firma. It was warming up and was glad having not left earlier, if the weather stayed like this my time in Kashmir will be enjoyable.

Unsure where to go first I walked up a narrow lane between some shops constructed of wooden boarding. Each one had different things for sale; books, paint brushes, paper, vegetables gemstones, metal work and camera film; at last a shop that sold camera film. It was a shame that I had not managed to find any earlier in Rajasthan or Punjab. Now I could make up for lost time. I came across a tea shop that also sold coconut biscuits, it was too much to resist. Only Green Kashmiri Tea was available which I was now becoming accustomed to and enjoying.

Having finished the biscuits and tea I left the tea shop and followed a path that led up a hill behind the shops. Reaching the top I was greeted with a panoramic view of Dal Lake and the surrounding mountains. The island that I saw earlier looked so small from the scenic view. Across Dal Lake on top of a hill opposite was a large fort that over looked every thing below from its commanding position. To the left were a large number of buildings that lined the waters edge and a long road with what looked like a parade of shops. Dal Lake stretched round the back of the house boats where I was staying. The view was spectacular, sitting down on the grass I watched everyone below going about their daily lives along the roads and on the lake. Shikaras left a trail on the water as they made their way across the lake, but none of them went to the small island. Loading the camera film I shot off three photographs panning across to take in the panoramic view. What I really wanted though was some watercolour paint and paper, the view was idyllic for a painting. Even though the view was captivating I eventually descended the hill and walked along the lakes edge taking in the magnificent scenery and sensing the exotic Kashmiri atmosphere. Shop owners waved trying to beckon me inside to look at their wares. The pavement was busy with Indian tourists out for a walk, young couples, families and individuals. Lambretta scooters whizzed past ridden by couples with the woman on the back riding side saddle with her sari blowing in the breeze. There were families with the father steering, the mother sitting side saddle and children on the mothers lap. It looked impossible that so many people could be on a scooter; it also looked fool hardy because none were wearing a crash helmet.

Some of the Shikaras had a low canopy with curtains draped down the sides for privacy and the owner paddling at the back, others had the curtains tied up showing the comfortable reclining seats and cushions with their hulls painted in bright colours.

The less luxurious Shikara's were higher at the back with the front barely a few inches above the water. Some owner's squatted down on the bow as they paddled along which surprised me that they did not tip up and fall in the water. Most paddled at the back using a single paddle shaped like a Lilly Pad in a backward and outward motion that looked easy and elegant which sent the Shikara gliding through the water. Kashmiris of all ages young children to those who looked about 70 paddled their characteristic boats,

At the far end of the lake I could see the small island more clearly with the trees and the building and wondered if any body lived on it or used it for the idyllic holiday retreat, such as artists or novelists.

After walking the full length of the water front I turned back to find some where to eat. A small busy tea shop that served rice in a bowl looked ideal, and the tea was the clear green Kashmiri tea.

Having eaten I explored the small shops and found one that sold sable brushes and bought one of each size, from a size 0 to a size 10 which only cost about ten rupees. I needed to find some paper to paint on now. I hunted around the shops until the evening started to close in but could not find any.

Many Indians were now wearing jumpers and shawls and wondered where I could buy one. The water front was taking on a carnival atmosphere as more people promenaded along the esplanade. Lanterns hung from the canopied Shikaras reflected on the rippling water. Several house boats had lit their lanterns that reflected on the lake like long fingers reaching out to the shore.

The cool air persuaded me to go back to my house boat, the thought of the warm bed was too much to resist. A large number of Shikaras were by the quay waiting for passengers, I gingerly climbed on to one and quickly sat down as it wobbled, to the merriment of those watching. Telling the owner which house boat I wanted he effortlessly paddled the craft and felt it was just gliding over the water, voices on the shore faded as we approached the houseboat. The owner dipped the paddle in to the water to slow the shikara down, judging the approach just right we stopped at the jetty. As I climbed off Hajib appeared and asked if I had a good day. Replying I did and was glad I didn't leave in the morning but stayed on Dal Lake. Hajib smiled and said he was glad I did not leave Srinagar.

I asked about the island at the far end of the lake and if it was possible to visit it. Hajib said the island was called Char Chinar and any one can visit it; then Hajib suggested that he could arrange for me to be taken out on the lake in the morning,

"that would be good" I replied. Saying good night I decided to write some letters home about my day in Srinagar and have an early night, I was sure the next day would be busy and exciting.

Waking the next morning, sunlight flooded in to my room with a morning view of the mountains. I could hear a conversation in Kashmiri, footsteps on the jetty and the clinking of metal bowls and plates. Once up and dressed I stepped out on to the jetty and saw a woman in a long red top and trousers crouching by a type of kiln cooking. Saying hello she told me that my breakfast would be ready soon and then offered me a glass of Kashmiri Tea, a welcome start to the day. Breakfast as promised was

317

Kashmiri bread with a fried egg, it tasted marvellous and was surprisingly filling.

Hajib came out of his house boat and asked if I slept well and told me that somebody will arrive soon to take me out on the lake. "You can go any where on the lake, Hassan will take you there, but Hassan has to be back by midday so he can go to the mosque for prayers".

Soon after a wash with hot water in a bowl Hassan arrived, he looked about 13 but controlled his Shikara with adept skill as it nudged the jetty. The flat bottomed boat bobbed down in the water as I stepped on it, After sitting down Hassan pushed off with the Shakira gliding along in the warm sun, an idyllic day to be out on the lake. Stretching my legs out to catch the sun I dipped my hand in the cool water.

"Where do you want to go?" asked Hassan,

"I wanted to visit Char Chinar".

With that he pointed his vessel in the direction of the small island in the middle of Dal Lake. The distance was deceptive and took longer than I thought it would to arrive. As we got closer I could see there were four trees on the island, the building looked completely deserted. Hassan pulled alongside some wooden steps and moored up his boat. The island had a perfectly flat lawn, the bough's ladened with spring shoots spread out across the island covering it with gentle dappled shade. The building was similar to a large wooden summer house with large patio type windows, but the doors were unfortunately locked. Looking out from the Island there was a panoramic view of Dal Lake with the mountains

318

bordering the shore and the fort high up on the hill, an idyllic picturesque setting to paint.

A wooden diving board jutted out over the water, firmly anchored to the bank and hard to resist walking out to the end. Jumping up and down causing it flexed, the board had a good spring to it and on impulse I dived in to the cool clear water and swam out from the island. Having not swum since leaving Sri Lanka it felt good weightlessly wallowing in the deep water. Hassan dived in as well, obviously taking the opportunity to relax. After having a good soak and feeling a lot cleaner I got out of the water and we set off again in the Shikara.

Hassan suggested visiting the Shalimar Gardens pointing at the shore,

"yes lets go there" I replied, not knowing anything about the Shalimar Gardens.

Hassan paddled effortlessly across the lake towards where several other Shikara's were moored up. Skilfully pulling up by the other boats he moored up and told me to climb the steps to the gardens. As I got to the top step I saw a long water feature bordered by flower beds. Either side was a path leading to a pavilion and a perfectly cut lawn. The water feature stretched for some hundred metres with a row of small fountains along the centre. The pavilion had supporting pillars and beyond this were the mountains. A number of Indian tourists walked around the garden, the women's saris added colour to the early spring foliage.

Being conscious of Hassan having to get back for the mosque I returned to the jetty and asked where we could

319

go next, "we could go around the back of the lake" he replied.

I asked to paddle the Shakira and Hassan said it was okay; having canoed before and paddled a dugout canoe it would not take too long for me to get the hang of it again. Setting off I propelled the Shakira round in an unintentional circle. Hassan suggested I should push backwards in a straight line then flick the paddle outwards, it worked and I managed to keep the Shikara going in a relatively straight line. Looking around the shore as we travelled across the lake I had a closer look at the fort on the hill top above Dal Lake, I asked Hassan who lived there and he said it was a private fort but did not know who lived in it. Hassan directed me where to go across the lake," head for where the lake narrowed and the buildings on the waters edge". The buildings looked similar to those on the Venice canals. Some of the buildings were three stories high with timber frames others were constructed of just brick. Several had balconies and each window was different, they looked as if they had all been salvage and fitted in to the brick work ad hoc.

Sedately paddling past the buildings Hassan told me to steer to the left, as we turned the corner I could see we had arrived back at the house boats which gave me a chance to see them close up. They all looked spectacular with their wide birth; some had wide French style windows opening on to a covered balcony. As we approached the houseboat Hajib was waiting and looked extremely serious and spoke to Hassan in Kashmiri with a stern voice, once I was off the Shikara Hassan quickly paddled off. Hajib told me he had promised that Hassan would at the Mosque on time, but he was late.

"It was my fault because I asked to paddle" I replied. Hajib did not reply, he just turned and walked away.

After the mornings tour of Dal Lake and the paddling I was hungry and went over to the shore and found a cosy tea shop and wrote a letter describing my trip around Dal Lake. Having eaten and written my letter I went to post it. Meeting Amjad he asked me to help him talk to some German tourists he was trying to persuade to look at his house Boat. Not sure how I could help Amjad explained that being a tourist I could tell them that if they went with him they would not be chased by anyone else; if they did not like the house boat they could leave. Admiring Amjads intrepid persistence I asked where the Germans were.

We walked to the bus terminal and he pointed them out in the tea room. There were four sitting around a table drinking tea and not looking at all happy. I introduced myself and asked them if they were okay. They all said hello and spoke very good English which was a relief. They told me that they had been harassed by a lot of youngsters trying to get them to go to their house boats. Replying I had the same problem and almost went straight back to Dehli which they were seriously considering. I told them that if they left with Amjid and went to his house boat they will be left alone. They talked between themselves in German and seemed to come to some sort of agreement. I added that Amjads houseboat is

321

comfortable and they cook a good breakfast. Finishing their tea they picked up their large rucksacks which they appeared to struggle with, said thank you and went off with Amjad.

Having posted my letter I ambled back to the house boat, stopping at several shops on the way. Amjad was sitting outside and I asked if the Germans were staying, "no; they did not like having to catch a Shikara each time they wanted to go anywhere". This was a shame I was looking forward to having some company with so few Westerners in Srinagar.

Browsing through the books in my bedroom I found one that caught my eye. Lying back on the comfortable bed I read a few chapters then went ashore to browse around the shops and have something to eat. Taking my time looking in the shops I sat in a tea shop overlooking the lake, it felt idyllic watching the shikara's travelling across the lake whilst admiring the scenic view. After the sun had set and the air cooled I slowly walked back along the promenade and returned to the house boat. I tried to read some more of the book but soon found myself falling asleep and decided to call it a day, maybe the mountain air was making me feel drowsy.

The next morning was another bright day and whilst eating my breakfast of fried eggs and Kashmir bread Hajib suggested I should visit a small town in the mountains which at first I thought he called Belgium but turned out to be Pahalgam. Hajib explained it is in the Kashmir Valley and not far from Srinagar, and surrounded by snow capped mountains. Asking how to get there Hajib told me that I could catch a bus from the terminal. Pahalgam sounded like an exciting place to visit. Quickly finishing breakfast I caught a Shikara to the shore and rushed down to the bus terminal not wanting to miss the bus for Pahalgam. It was waiting at the terminal and was already half full with passengers that were either Kashmiri or Southern Indians.

Soon after boarding the bus it left the terminal and drove slowly through the Srinagar streets and out on to the open road. The country side was lush and green, in the distance trees clung to the mountains and rising above the tree line were snow caped peaks. Some people were working in the fields ploughing and tending their crops, occasionally the bus passed a cart drawn by a bullock. After about an hour the bus turned left off the main road on to a narrower one that was heading towards the mountains. I became transfixed by the rugged mountainous scenery and an urge to paint them.

The bus crossed a bridge over a fast flowing river then turned left on to a road that followed the river directly towards the mountains. The road headed towards a valley between two peaks draped in pine trees, soon they towered over us; the river was grey from the sediment washed down from high in the mountains which frothed and bubbled as it raced over the rocks. The mountains parted revealing wide open meadows and in the distance were some small buildings. Eventually reaching the hamlet the bus pulling up alongside one on a shingled parking area, the bus driver announced that we had arrived in Pahalgam and added that the bus would be

323

returning to Srinagar in two hours.

Once off the bus it felt cooler than Srinagar, but I was too excited to pay much attention to the weather as I gazed at the surrounding countryside in wonder. This may not be Nepal with its high peaks but this was part of the Himalayan range which was good enough for me. The mountains dropped down and met the meadows in the valley which was divided by the fast flowing river; it was the idyllic landscape for an artist to paint especially with the women in their bright vivid saris. I bought my self a tea and sat at a picnic bench admiring the Himalayan Mountains. Some Kashmiris joined me and asked where I was from, telling them Britain they had a quizzical expression on their faces, When I added "England" straight away their eyes lit up and exclaimed "England, a lovely place just like Kashmir"; smiling I jokingly said Kashmir looks much better than England. They asked me where I had been so far and explained I had travelled up from Rameswaram, to Hyderabad and to Agra then Amritsar. One of them told me that I had been on such a long journey.

I agreed, it had been a long journey and said I can now rest in Kashmir. They all laughed and said this was the best place to rest after travelling that far. One of the Kashmiris asked me if I wanted to drink some Kashmiri tea, pointing out I had one he enquired what was in it which seemed a strange thing to ask. When I said sugar he said no you want a proper Kashmiri tea and went off leaving me chatting to his friends and wondering what proper Kashmiri tea was.

324

He arrived back with a sort of reddish pink tea with milk and said this is proper Kashmiri tea. The tea smelt spicy, tasting it I cringed, "there was salt in it!" I exclaimed. They all laughed, "this is proper Kashmiri tea, that is how we Kashmiris like our tea". Not wanting to offend him and as he had bought it for me I drank it down. One of the Kashmiri's asked what I thought of the tea, being tactful replied I might get used to it one day which made every one laugh. The conversation was joyful and friendly with some banter, loosing track of time the driver called out that he was going to be leaving soon.

Saying good bye to my picnic bench companions and thanking the man for the tea I climbed on to the bus ready to travel back through the scenic countryside but disappointed I had not brought my rucksack, it would have been so good to stay overnight and thought that maybe next time I was in India I will stay for a few days in Pahalgam to paint the mountains and maybe even camp out. On the way back to Srinagar I pondered about the Kashmiri tea and decided it was best not to try it again and put it down to my Kashmiri experience.

By the time we arrived backing in Srinagar it was late afternoon and I felt hungry. Finding somewhere to eat with a view out on to the lake I watched the everyday Kashmiri life out side on the promenade and lake as I ate. Couples walking together, teenagers were being boisterous, people on Lambretta Scooters drove up and down, different types of Shikara's were being paddled across the lake, it looked so serene and relaxing in such a wonderful exotic place. I stayed in the tea shop until it was dark. Walking out in to the cool night air I could see the stars sparkling in the clear night sky, at the lakes edge the Kashmiri evening atmosphere almost intoxicating. People were intermittently silhouetted by the bright glowing shop lights as they walked past them and occasionally stopping to window shop. The cool evening air was feeling too cool for me in my shorts and T shirt and made my way to the small quay for a shikara to take me back to the house boat. Once in my room I got under the warm blankets and read for a while but found myself falling to sleep and eventually dozed off.

Waking early the next morning I lazed in bed looking out of the window. It was another sunny day and felt I should get up but I just wanted to laze where I was for the time being, looking out of the window. A knock at the door brought me back from my day dream; "breakfast is ready" Hajib called out. Once up and dressed I ate the fried eggs and Kashmir bread whilst talking with Hajib; he asked me what I was going to do.

"I had not really thought about doing any thing in particular, my money is getting low" I replied. I was down to £60 in traveller's cheques and about 100 Rupees which would be cutting it fine paying for the train back to Bombay, and maybe stopping in Delhi for a day or two and paying for a hotel or guest house in Bombay. More thinking aloud said "I'll spend the day in Srinagar exploring the parts of I had not seen yet".

Once at the promenade I made my way to the parade of shops that I saw from the hill top. The shop fronts looked similar to what you would find in most western shopping centres with large open windows, the pavement was wide but very few people were looking in the shops which sold items that could be bought in Southern India such as Saris, shirts and kitchen ware. Across the road was a group of smaller shops which looked more interesting. Crossing the road I found these were local craft shops. A man standing outside one of them asked me if I wanted to look inside his shop as he pointed to one of them. The shop was small but had a wide selection of crafts on display in the window which included shawls, jumpers, dressing gowns, wood work, jewellery, small rugs and stone work. I was spoilt for choice and was not sure what would be a good thing to buy except, I wanted something that was genuinely Kashmiri. When I told the shop owner this he told me that every thing in his shop was genuine Kashmiri craft work made by local families. The shop owner explained that in the winter when it is too cold to go outside families stay in their house boats and houses embroidering and weaving.

He held up a black shawl that had an exquisite floral border design of green foliage with red and yellow flowers. The embroidery was vibrant, it looked like silk but I was assured the thread was cotton. Holding up a plain mid blue shawl which had a silken sheen, I asked if it was made of silk. The shop owner explained it was Kashmiri cotton and invited me to feel it. Running my fingers over the material it felt soft and perfectly smooth, it definitely felt like silk but he explained that it was very finely woven to make a thin thread. He said the material was so fine the shawl could slide through the ring on his finger, it did not seem possible that it could pass through something so small. I must have had a sceptical expression on my face; he took off his ring then held one corner and slowly pulled the shawl through the ring, thinking it will get stuck half way, but it didn't the shawl passed right through. I could not help asking how much the two shawls were. When he told me I could not resist buying them thinking they would make marvellous presents for my mum.

The other thing that had caught my eye as soon as I walked in to the shop was the full length bright red dressing gown. It had white swirling floral embroidery around the cuffs and along the edges; the material felt soft and warm. The shop owner told me it was made of Kashmir wool; you will not get any finer wool in the world, he explained that the higher the goats or sheep go the colder it gets and the wool gets finer, the best wool is from Kashmir up in the mountains. Without thinking I asked how much the dressing gown was, again I could not believe the price; at first I hesitated thinking how much I needed to get back to Bombay but then impulsively said "I'll have it".

The shop owner asked if I wanted anything else, even though there were so many things I would like to buy I did not have enough money. The shop owner said it was okay, "you can have anything in the shop posted to your bank and you pay for it on collection". Being inquisitive I asked how this worked, he explained that the item would be posted to my bank who will hold it until it was collected; then all I had to do was tell the bank to pay the sender. This sounded so simple but first I had to get a job back home. I told the owner I would not have any thing sent now but if I had his address I could write and order something when I get home. The owner smiled and wrote down his address for me and said "no matter what you want I can send it to you".

Saying good bye and feeling happy that I had bought something that was genuinely Kashmiri headed back to the house boat, I did not want the presents damaged in any way. After dropping my purchases off I made my way to a tea shop, passing a shop selling rugs a middle aged man called out to me. Being curious I could not resist looking. As I approached the shop he said welcome and told me he had a good selection of Kashmiri rugs. Replying that I did not have any money he told me it was okay, "just look, would you like some tea?" Saying yes he called to a boy standing outside the shop, gave him some money and spoke to him in Kashmiri. In the shop there was a selection of rugs with intricate floral designs in rich colours. The man invited me to have a closer look and pulled back some of the rugs to show me those lower down in the pile. Running my hand over the woollen surface the inch thick pile felt smooth and luxurious. The shop owner said they were all made from wool except those made of wool and silk,

"I can give you a very good price" which made me smile, how many times had I heard that in India? I told the shop owner I did not have any money but he waved his hand "I could have the rug delivered to your bank then you can pay for it on collection" but found it hard to believe that my bank would have room to store a rug. The shop owner was determined to make a sale so in the end I played along with his sales pitch and asked the price of several rugs which were not too excessive.

The boy returned with my tea which I sipped as we talked rugs. Another man walked in to the shop; the two talked in Kashmiri then the shop owner turned to me and said he had more rugs that he wanted to show me. They were obviously not in this shop, "where are they?" I asked, "they are stored somewhere else".

I was now getting very curious, "where?"

With out hesitating he pointed at the fort on the hill above Dal Lake; "up there!" he exclaimed.

I felt a bit sceptical about these rugs being stored in a fort; but this was India and one thing I had found anything was possible, "how would we get there?",

the shop owner replied "in my car".

Having looked at the fort several times in the last few days and wondered what it looked like inside I was unable to resist the temptation and see it close up, "okay I'll look at your rugs".

With that I was told the car was waiting on the road and could not help thinking this was very slick salesmanship. I got in to the car with the shop owner and his assistant in the back, speaking to the driver in Kashmiri we sped off following the road around the edge of Dal Lake. Looking out of the windows I got to see a different view of the lake especially when the road started to rise up towards the hill fort. As the car climbed the road was lined with trees blocking the view of Dal Lake and Srinagar.

After some twenty minutes we drove through an arched entrance in to a gravelled court yard and stopped by a set of stone steps. The court yard had high sided walls constructed of grey stone, as we got out of the car the shop owner pointing at the steps and said "we have to go up here". In side it was chilly, Spartan without any decoration. Grey stone steps leading up to a landing, through an arched entrance we walked in to a large high ceilinged hall that would be ideal for banquets. All around the room were rugs of various sizes, colours and designs piled up on one another. There must have been hundreds from small prayer mats to large square ones measuring tens of feet. The shop owner told me I could sell it back in Britain for a profit; I knew Persian or Iranian rugs were very saleable, some backpackers had told me they had bought Persian rugs on the way to India to pay for their trip.

I spent about an hour looking at the rugs marvelling at the variety of intricate designs each one in a different colour. Most were wool or mixed wool and silk but a few were pure silk with a luminous sheen to them. Regardless of the sales pitch and even though all of the rugs looked and felt inviting I was unable to afford one but asked for the shops address details so I could order one. The shop owner thought this was a good idea and said he will give me the full details when we got back to the shop.

We left the fort and as we descended down towards Dal Lake I could see the evening light reflecting on the water. By the time we arrived back at the shop it was dusk and many shops had lit their lanterns giving a cosy homely feel along the water front. I was given the address details, said good bye and thanked the shop owner for showing me his rugs, an unforgettable experience.

Once I had something to eat I made my way back to the house boat; I wanted an early night because the next day could be a long one travelling back to Jammu and then to Dehli.

The next morning I was up early, whilst eating my last fried eggs and Kashmiri bread I took in the magnificent scenic view of the mountains and Dal Lake. Talking to Hajib I told him how much I enjoyed my time on his houseboat and said I would like to return again one day, "you are always welcome back" came his reply.

After saying goodbye I caught a shikara to the shore and made my way to the bus terminal and waited in the tea shop. When the bus arrived the Kashmiri teenagers descended on the tired back packers who looked perplexed as they tried persuading them to stay at the various house boats. Some of the back packers left the bus terminus with a guide but some looked distraught and retreated to the tea shop. Once the crowd faded away I made my way over to the bus and sat down on the back seat hoping to get the best fleeting views of my trip over the mountains. I reflected on how much I had enjoyed Srinagar and felt it was one of the highlights of my time in India, pleased I had met the Kashmiri stall holders in Bombay.

I had considered travelling up to Ladakh and visit Leh further up in the mountains but being over 10,000 feet I was convinced it would be a lot colder than Srinagar;

maybe next time. The driver boarded the bus, started the engine and pulled out of the bus terminal for the return journey through the Kashmir Valley past the fields, in to the mountains; through the tunnel then along the winding road to Jammu for the train south to Delhi.

Part Four
An unforgettable predicament in Bombay

Benevolent strangers

The bus arrived at Jammu train station late in the afternoon with the train waiting at the station. Every one hurried off the bus, collected their luggage and queued for their train tickets. I bought a second class ticket to Bombay, a journey that would take a few days with the intention of having a break at Delhi. Boarding the half full carriage I sat on the wooden bench, using my rucksack as a back rest stretched my legs out on the bench. The whistle sounded for the train driver and soon the train slowly pulled away from the platform to start its long journey south towards the hot open plains of central India. A sense of calm came over me thinking that I was heading back to Bombay to book my flight home. Not wanting to let my guard down and have my rucksacks stolen right at the end of my journey I decided to stay awake until I arrived at Delhi; maybe some time the next day. The train rhythmically rocked side to side which made the wooden bench feel more comfortable than it really was. As the sun set the nocturnal hues spread across the landscape until everything was shrouded in an inky black veil. The train clattered through the dark country side which was mixed with the chatter of the other passengers. Not wanting to fall asleep I stood up every so often to keep myself awake. I peered out of the barred window in to the darkness beyond hoping that I might catch a glimpse of life from any small hut or hamlet with its oil lamps burning but all I could see was the distinct line between the horizon and the sky. The train stopped briefly at several stations, passengers got on but even at these stations there were no buildings near by.

The night wore on, I spent more time standing for longer periods until at some point I did not sit back down. Eventually the sky on the horizon started to turn from indigo to navy blue and slowly to a lighter grey blue then a thin strip of yellow as the sun started to climb up from below the horizon casting long shadows across the dry landscape lighting up the low trees and buildings that dotted the countryside. Having stayed awake through the night I hoped that it would not be too long before we reached Delhi. As the sun rose higher in the sky the carriage became warmer with the dry heat. Having been spoilt by the cooler climate in Kashmir over the last few days I forgot how hot it could get on the dry plains of Northern India.

Sitting back on the wooden bench the sweat ran down my brow, back and arms. I decided to try and cool myself down with a shower, hoping the water had not warmed up yet. I left my large rucksack on the bench confident that no one would try to take it but kept my smaller one with me to ensure my passport, traveller's cheques, and camera with the roll of film I had used in Kashmir stayed safe.

335

Stripping off and standing under the shower I pulled the handle and released the rusty brown tepid water which gushed out of the spout; a welcome relief from the heat in the carriage. I spent some time under the shower and without drying myself put my clothes back on knowing the heat would dry me off very quickly.

I spent the next few hours watching the dry arid land roll by, occasionally spotting a building and people working in tilled fields. Now and then the train would stop at a platform without any sign of habitation near it and the engine was filled up with water. As we travelled further south there were more people going about their daily work and chores on the land, but there was no sign of us arriving at Delhi yet. A ticket inspector came in to the carriage, checking every ticket as he worked his way down past the seats, now and then taking longer to scrutinise the ticket and sternly frowning at the passenger, then spoke to them in Hindi as if he was interrogating them.

When it was my turn I handed over my ticket which brought on a very stern expression and without saying any thing gave me it back. I asked when the train would be arriving at Delhi and without a change in expression replied "soon!" I felt reassured because this comment came from someone with authoritative knowledge of the train times, also feeling hungry I wanted to have something to eat, soon.

Eventually the train pulled in to a station with several train tracks and broad platforms, looking through the iron grilled windows I caught sight of a large sign; New Delhi.

Quickly gathering up my rucksacks I hurried off the train, throwing them on to my back I walked out in to station foyer where I was greeted with a wide boulevard, some auto rickshaws and yellow cabs were parked on the road waiting for passengers. The prospect of having find some where to stay felt too daunting, I turned around and went back in to the station thinking I would have to book a seat on the next train, when ever that would be. To my surprise the train I had just got off was still standing at the platform, jumping back on I found an empty seat, relieved that I did not have to find some where to sleep. Even so I was in a quandary, not have any money to buy any food. Reassuring myself I had made the right decision and would be back in Bombay sooner than anticipated, then able to book in to a reasonable hotel, get cleaned up and book my flight ticket maybe on Friday or Saturday and fly out Sunday, perfect.

The train stood at the platform for several minutes then left New Delhi Station to carry on the journey through the dry Spartan landscape. When the train pulled in to a station I jumped off to fill up my water bottle with fresh water from a fountain. I had found drinking copious amounts of water kept the hunger at bay, as well as heat exhaustion. Sweat ran down my arms and my back soaking my T shirt. Other passengers fanned themselves and their younger children as the midday heat was being felt.

The day ran in to night as the train passed through various stations whilst I did my best to stay awake through another night. It was hard but the thought of having the rucksack stolen encouraged me to stay awake until the sun rose the next morning when the heat inhibited any thought of sleep, it was just too stifling now the carriage was almost packed full. The train was not stopping so often at the stations and I was starting to feel thirsty. Visualising my self suffering from heat exhaustion I felt this was an awkward situation. Trying to cool myself down with a shower was pointless, the rusty water was luke warm, even if it was a welcome relief to wash the dust and soot off. The thought of suffering from heat exhaustion played on my mind; I decided that drinking the rusty brown water would be better than nothing and guzzled down several mouthfuls which didn't taste good in the least.

After spending some considerable time under the shower I returned to my seat to find a middle aged man had sat down opposite. Saying hello he asked me the usual string of questions of where I was from and where was I going to. The conversation was a welcome relief and helped me to stay awake. But the journey seemed to drag on as the train was stopping more regularly, I just wanted to get back to Bombay, have some thing to eat and sleep somewhere comfortable.

The sun started to set and wondered how soon we would be arriving in Bombay. I asked the man if he knew when we would be arriving, he replied "some time this evening". This news was welcome and sounded more promising than the usual elasticated "soon". Buildings and people appeared intermittently beside the railways line, then buildings were constantly lining either side the railway track, a promising sign the train would arrive at Victoria station was exciting. The man I had been talking to must have read my mind and said it is not much further which put me at ease and I relaxed thinking about eating some food and being able to sleep in a bed, maybe even at the Taj Mahal Hotel. I had £40 in traveller's cheques which would be more than enough when converted in to Rupees which from my calculation was about R700, a small fortune.

I felt my leg being tapped and I sat bolt upright. Opening my eyes I saw a woman with a broom, she spoke abruptly to me in Hindi and waved her hand to signal for me to get off the train. I had fallen asleep, there was no lighting and the carriage was empty. Jumping up quickly I grabbed my large rucksack but could not see my small one with my passport, flight ticket, traveller's cheques and camera. Frantically I searched around where I had been sitting and further down the carriage, then asked the woman who did not understand what I was saying and most probably thought I was an absolutely crazy back packer as anxiety setting in.

The thought of having lost everything in the rucksack was too much to contemplate, feeling myself starting to hyperventilate and wondering how was I going to manage in Bombay was starting to make me lose any sense of rationality. Thinking that I needed to calm down told myself "stop, don't panic and take a few deep breaths". Standing still I gathered my thoughts and decide what to do next. Now a bit calmer I had another look around the carriage the woman swept up but kept glancing at me most probably ready to defend herself with the broom; the rucksack was definitely gone. Getting off the train I made my way along the platform and tried to put a plan together of what I had to do. Report the theft to the police, go to the British Consulate, talk to British Airways about the flight ticket but the one stumbling block was money. I did not have any money on me at all which was bit of a predicament; I could not buy any food or a tea. This was the one thing that was making me palpitate.

Trying to find the police office in the station made me concentrate, I asked somebody in a uniform where the police were and he pointed at an office similar to the rest. The office was the size of an average bedroom, well lit and had a light brown wooden desk. There were three men wearing beige uniforms standing in the room, they all looked at me, one of them with sergeant's stripes on his sleeve asked if he could help. I explained that I had just had my rucksack stolen whilst travelling on the train from Delhi which contained my passport, traveller's cheques, flight ticket and camera. He told me I had to make a statement and describe what happened and the missing items. He gave me a sheet of paper which had "Logging Sheet" printed on one side and said I should write on the blank side of the paper and start by addressing the statement to the Inspector of Police, Bombay Central Police Station and put the date at the top. Having to write the statement helped me gain some composure and think more clearly and wrote
"Sir
I have lost my two bags in a train between Palgha to

Bombay Central. I was personally travelling from Delhi to Bombay Central when I fell asleep on the train. I was woken up at Bombay Central on 2/5/80 at about 10:10pm. The two bags contained a towel, one book and 3 cups, these items were in a white bag. My other bag was a red and green rucksack containing a Pentax Camera with a zoom lens, I T shirt, my passport, £40 in traveller's cheques and my flight ticket. Please search if found inform me at my address below, thank you.
Yours faithfully PG Morffew"
I added my UK address at the bottom of the letter and handed the statement to the police sergeant. He read the letter and then told me it is unlikely we will find the bags but if you go to the Central Police Station in a few days and show them this letter they might have it there.
The Sergent then stamped the top of the letter; Police Inspector, Bombay Central Rly. P Stn.
He then used the same stamp at the bottom of the page, signed it and wrote "Rd on 2/5/80 at abt 22:30pm"
Having written out the statement I felt a lot calmer, or due to the tiredness, the thought of hunger had faded, I just wanted to sleep. I started to make my way out of the station then sat down on a step wondering what to do next. I did not get a chance to make a decision; a policeman came up behind me and indicated with his rattan for me to move on. Reluctantly standing up and throwing my rucksack on to my back I slowly walked off. At least I knew my way around Bombay but at 11pm with out being able to book in to any accommodation it seemed that I would have to sleep out on the street for the night,

but where?

I was surprised how quiet the streets were, hardly any noise and no body walking about. A stark contrast to what it was like during the day with the throng of commuters shoulder to shoulder. I decided to make my way to the British Consulate and be ready when it opened in the morning.

Along the pavement people huddled together sleeping in door ways, some were on reed mats or cardboard but most lay on the pavement. As they slept rats were scurrying around scavenging for food, there were so many, more than I had seen so far in India. Making it to the Commissariat and the British Consulate where about twenty people were sleeping on the ground. The entrance to the consulate was a large heavy wooden door some five feet wide and eight feet high with metal stud work on it. By the door was a notice with the opening times. 9am did not seem too bad, then I realised that this was during the week. Saturday and Sunday the consulate was closed. I froze in disbelief and re read it hoping I read it incorrectly due to being tired, but I had read it correctly; closed at weekends. A moment of despair swept over me, the prospect of having to spend a weekend out on the streets of Bombay with no money seemed absolutely dire. Cursing civil servants for not working at weekends I looked about for some where to sleep. The urge to sleep was getting hard to resist, I just wanted to lie down but even being extremely tired I could not bring myself to sleep on the ground with the rats running about.

A large wooden stand some four feet square and about

three feet high was on the street corner. I remembered it was used by a man who sold lottery tickets; he laid the tickets out on the box so customers could choose for themselves. Placing my large rucksack on the stand and climbing on to it I felt a safer. Laying my head on the rucksack I curled up so my feet did not hang over the edge. As I drifted off to sleep it occurred to me how ironic it was that I planned to stay at the Taj Mahal Hotel not too far away, the most expensive hotel in India and I end up sleeping out on the street.

Waking with a sudden jolt as commuters walked past. The sun was up and already it felt warm. I got off the wooden stand and stretched my legs and arms. My first thought was to make my way to the British Airways office which was not too far, having all weekend whilst I waited for the British Consulate to open on Monday morning I wasn't in a rush. There weren't that many commuters about which made is easy walk along the pavement and was soon at the British Airways office, it was closed at weekends. Despondently resigning my self to not achieving much over the weekend I deliberated over my predicament. The best place to go would be Chowpatty Beach, at least I could lay down on the sand and sleep. What I really needed was something to eat and drink but with out any money I was stuck. Crossing the road to the promenade that followed around Back Bay I made my way towards Chowpatty Beach. About half way along the promenade a group of young men standing on the central reservation waved at me, I waved back and carried on walking. They became more insistent with their waving, not being in a

343

rush I decided to cross the road to pass some time with them. They had a tea stall which would have been useful if I had a few paisa. They all said hello and we all shook hands.

One of them asked me where I was from and where I was going.

"I'm was going to Chowpatty Beach to have a rest".

"Why don't you book in to a hotel?" one of them asked.

"I don't have any money to pay for a room",

"What have you got to sell?" one of them asked,

"I don't have any thing interesting".

"Show us what you have got" he retorted.

Not having much too loose I took out the diving mask and straight away one of them asked how much I wanted for it, plucking a price out of the air I said twenty rupee's. The young man said this was too much and offered ten rupees. Realising that he wanted to haggle I said fifteen, he countered this with twelve. Smiling I said that was a good price and was handed twelve rupees, at last I had some money. Another asked if I had any thing else to sell. Excitedly I rummaged through my rucksack and found several items which they bought for five rupees. Now I could buy some rice and a tea, what a relief. They offered me a tea as they all asked about England, Britain and what I did for a living; the least I could do was talk to these generous men and spent the rest of the morning answering all of their questions. Urgently needing something to eat I said good bye unable to believe my good fortune.

At Chowpatty Beach the smell of cooked food from the kiosk was over whelming and intensified the hunger. I

344

wanted to eat every thing on the menu but had to be prudent with my few rupees if I was going to survive the weekend. In the end I opted for some rice with chopped fried vegetables and a poppa dom which I crunched up and sprinkled on top.

Sitting down on the sand I ate with my fingers, trying not to shovel the food in to my mouth in case I dropped some. Swallowing each mouthful with out chewing I felt the food settling in my stomach. Having finished I bought two large samosa's and a tea which I ate more slowly this time savouring the flavours as I chewed, at the same time taking in the scenery of the Bay with its high rise buildings. The soft Chowpatty Beach sand felt smooth as I rubbed my feet in it, the beach was quite busy with men in their trousers or sarongs and loose white shirts and the women in their vibrant coloured saris, it felt peaceful, an idyllic Saturday morning at the beach.

I spent some time on Chowpatty Beach reflecting on my situation and how I was going to get through the weekend. Having had some thing to eat and still had some money in my pocket the next problem was to find some where to sleep for the night; that was relatively safe. Having been lucky so far, I just needed to get through the next two nights, but was determined not to sleep on the ground with rats scurrying around me. Eventually deciding to walk back towards Churchgate Street Station, maybe I could find somewhere around there.

The walk around Back Bay promenade felt strenuous mostly from being tired and the lack of food. Arriving at Churchgate Station I felt hungry again and went in to the tea shop next to the station. This was an ideal place to eat. Large broad windows faced out to Back Bay letting the bright afternoon sun light shine in to the large airy room. I collected a palm leaf, ordered some rice and a tea which was served promptly. The rice was ladled on to the palm leaf, I wanted to get my money's worth and did not say stop until there was a large pile of rice, three small spice dishes were placed on the table, I ate to my hearts content. By the time I had finished my tummy absolutely full. Still not sure where I was going to sleep for the night, it was late in the afternoon and I needed to find somewhere soon before it got dark. There was the Water Front but doubted if I would be allowed to stay there too long and would be moved on. After several more teas I left the tea shop and crossed the road to sit on the sea wall to watch the sun set across Back Bay. The wall was low and wide, a tempting place to lie down and doze. The concrete wall felt hard and rough but the urge to sleep was too much, resting my head on the rucksack I felt my self drifting off. I woke with a jolt and found a man standing over me, pocking me with his finger, "you cannot sleep on the wall, somebody might stab you". I was annoyed about being woken up and then noticed it was night time. The man said he can show me where I could sleep safely; looking at him sceptically I asked where it was, not far he replied. As he walked off I decided to follow him and see where his safe place was. He crossed the road and walked towards the Commissariat which was silhouetted by the lights behind making it look sinister and menacing. Once we had walked past the large parks he turned right and crossed the road. After a short distance the man walked through an arch that led in to the commissariat grounds. It was dark and could just make out my guide; I began to feel this was not a good idea. He stopped and beckoned me with a wave of his hand then turned a corner, for some reason I followed. We climbed some stairs on to a dark balcony, at the top the man stopped turned around and said "you can sleep here it is perfectly safe" pointing at some wooden benches.

Replying it is not possible to sleep here, to which he remarked "I sleep here all of the time",

"I'm not going to".

The man looked offended and without another word he walked off along the balcony through an arch and vanished in to the dark shadows. Being left there by myself I decided to get out quickly while I can. Descending the dark stair case and turning the corner at the bottom I saw some body approaching across the dark court yard. My fears of somebody catching me had come true. I moved back round the corner quickly, but decided that the best thing to do would be to walk out and pretend I was lost; just in case he was armed I raised my hands. Stepping out we were almost face to face and instantly raised my hands, the man looked completely shocked, as any body would be but he quickly gained his composure and waved his hand to indicate I should lower my arms. He took hold of my arm and I silently complied as he led me towards a small flat roof building with a light on. He opened the door and inside were four other men dressed in the familiar beige uniforms. Their expressions showed they were all shocked to see me; a deathly silence hung in the room then one of the uniformed men asked why I was on the premises.

A man told me I could sleep here and he slept here all of the time".

There was an almost deathly silence, and then frantically they talked to each other in Hindi. I could see the anxiety in their faces, obviously something was wrong. They stopped talking; the man in charge looked at me and with a wave of his hand sternly said "go!"

Instantly the vision of me having to spend a night in a prison cell faded away, I thanked the man in charge and quickly walked out of the commissariat before they changed their minds. In the busy street I made my way across the busy junction to some benches by the water fountain which I had passed so many times but never stopped to look. Trees hung over the benches giving the feeling of some shelter, sitting down I was back where I started, nowhere to sleep but at least nothing had come of the incident in the commissariat. There was a tea stall near by and bought a tea, maybe it would help me think about what to do.

A man sitting on the bench said "hello my name is Nick", Nick looked middle aged with greyish hair and spoke with hardly a trace of an Indian accent.

Saying hello I told Nick my name was Peter. Nick smiled and said that Peter was a good biblical name and asked where I was from.

"Britain",

Nick replied "I thought so, what part of England?"

348

This was the first time since arriving in India that some one has asked what part of England I was from, "originally London but now live in Essex",

"What is Essex like?" asked Nick.

I described Essex talking about the towns, villages and countryside and its rivers.

"It sounds like a nice place to live". Nick asked where I had been in India, and described my journey through India at length from arriving in Bombay then travelling down to Cape Comorin, across to Rameswaram for the ferry to Sri Lanka. Arriving back from Sri Lanka and taking the long journey up through the centre of India to Rajasthan and on to Kashmir. Adding I was back in Bombay and planned to fly home to Britain.

Nick told me I had taken a great journey that many Indians don't experience in their life time. Surprisingly Nick asked me if I wanted a tea, I did not want to refuse in case of offending him.

As we drank our tea I asked about the fountain and mentioned that it was a strange place to have it. Nick explained that it was not a fountain but a well called the Bhikha Behram Well, it is under the custodian of local Parsi community, "any one can come and collect water or drink from the well which was the freshest water in Bombay". Nick explained the history of the Parsi community, having migrated to India many centuries ago from Persia and settled in Bombay.

Nick mentioned that he sleeps on the bench because he was unable to rent a place any where, it was far too expensive but every now and then he slept at a friend's

349

house. Nick asked where I was staying, "no where" and explained what happened. Out of the blue he suggested I could sleep on one of the benches, adding it would be a safe place. I was over whelmed with relief at the thought of having somewhere to sleep, even if it was on a wooden bench. Using my rucksack as a pillow I settled down and very soon I was having a relaxing sleep.

I was abruptly woken by metallic clanging and clanking sounds. Sunlight filtered through the over hanging branches and leaves creating a soft dappled shade. The pavement was already busy with pedestrians even though it was a Sunday. There were several manually drawn carts parked beside the pavement with the owners running backwards and forwards with stainless steel churns, these were making the clanging noise as they were carried over to the well, filled with water and the lids put back on. Then the heavy churns was taken back to the cart and a second man helped to lift the full churn on to the cart with a thud. Each cart had at least ten churns. Once the churns were full and loaded on to the cart the owners stood between the shafts, lifted them and walked slowly off along the edge of the road as the cars drove past. I could not help wondering how they might stop in an emergency if a car pulling out in front of them; as ever India, especially Bombay never ceased to amaze.

The tea stall was already set up, after ordering a tea Nick asked if I would like a banana; feeling hungry I said yes please. I watched the tea stall vender make my tea, he put tea leaves in to what looked like a toe of a stocking. This was dunked in to the boiling water and milk was added.

This was the first time I had seen any one make tea this way and was sure the UK hygiene standards would not approve; but this was Bombay and I had drunk worse since I had been in India.

Whilst drinking my tea there was a sudden chiming, banging of drums and chanting that gradually grew louder and closer. It sounded familiar but it was hard to place it until I saw a procession of white people with their heads shaved and wearing white sarongs. Now I could make out the repeated chanting; "Hari Krishna". As the procession made its way along the pavement with the constant loud cacophony and chanting I mentioned to Nick that I only thought they were part of the London scene and not actually here in India, Nick replied "we don't like them here",

Thinking aloud said "I wonder where they came from?". As the procession walked off in to the distance and faded away it appeared nobody really paid much attention to them but I did wonder why they were out walking along this time of day and where they were going. It occurred to me that maybe they were acting in a similar way as the pied piper and hoped to attract new followers.

Having eaten and had a tea I said good bye to Nick and set off for Chowpatty Beach to rest on the sand. The pavements were relatively peaceful compared to what they would normally be on working day. Not many people were walking along the promenade which I put down to being a Sunday morning.

At Chowpatty Beach I noticed several people appeared to be washing themselves at the far end of the beach. When

351

closer I could see they were by a drainage hole where a small stream lead down to the sea. I was mystified, these people seemed to be washing with sewage water. Leaning against a railing that over looked the beach a man asked me where I was from.

"Britain" I replied.

"What do you think of India?"

"it is a very interesting country.

"Do you like India?"

"Yes!".

As we talked he mentioned what India was like under the Empire, "we all had jobs".

I was surprised about his comment and enquired "didn't everyone want independence?"

"No not everyone" he said with a resigned expression on his face.

I changed the subject and asked why the people on the beach were washing in the sewage; he instantly looked offended and replied "they are not washing in sewage; it is clean water that filters through the rocks from the gardens above". Reiterating that it was clean water he told me to go and try it myself.

Smiling, I apologised for my comment and said I would. Once on the beach I scooped some water up in my hand, it looked clean; it smelt okay and tasted just like water from a tap. Having not had a wash or a shower for a few days I decided to take advantage of the clean water and have a wash. It felt so good to rinse myself down and feel clean using the cold filtered water. Whilst washing a audience had gathered; I would not have thought me washing would be so entertaining but maybe very few westerners washed in a public place on Chowpatty Beach. Having spent the last three months in India and Sri Lanka it did not feel out of place at all.

After finishing and packing my things away I let the sun dry me off. Buying a tea I sat on the sand, although hungry I decided to eat at the tea shop where the rice was cheaper and they served up more for your money. Slowly drinking my tea I reflected on the weekend and how it has gone from what seemed like an absolute dire nightmare to what has so far has been an unforgettable experience. I just hoped that the rest of the weekend and Monday was just as kind.

Of everything that had happened and what had been stolen it was loosing the camera film I used in Kashmir that made me angry. But tried not to dwell on this mishap and concentrated on getting through the weekend. Laying down on the sand and relaxing I felt my self dozing off, trying to resist and conscious of getting sunburnt it was impossible to resist and drifted off into a slumber.

Waking sometime later and unaware of the time, the position of the sun indicated that it was sometime in the afternoon, the beach was busier, everyone was enjoying themselves. I was distinctly thirsty and hungry and made my way along the promenade to Churchgate Station at a sedate pace.

The tea shop was virtually empty, one person sat at a table. Now I felt absolutely hungry, picking up a palm leaf I sat down and almost straight away the rice was served and I ravenously ate it. Whilst eating a young

353

Japanese woman came in, ordered a tea and sat down at my table, she smiled "hello my names Sumika, this is a nice place to drink tea".

"I'm Peter, its a lovely view from here of the bay.

"How well do you know Bombay?" Sumika enquired

"I can get around reasonably well, why do you ask?"

Sumika pointed across Back Bay to the large structure on top of the hill "how can I get there?"

"If you walk around the bay there is a path that leads up to the top of the hill but you cannot go in side the tower". Sumika seemed disappointed. She asked where I was staying and explained my predicament. She listened intently then when she had finished her tea Sumika gave me five rupees saying it should help until tomorrow. I was speechless at first then thanked her; I could not believe her generosity.

Sumika said good bye and went off for her walk around Back Bay. I sat for some time in the tea shop just staring out of the window watching the people walking past. Having done this many times at train stations, it was like taking a snap shot in the day to day life of Indian's as they pass by.

After my second tea and contemplating where to sleep for the night, there was no obvious place I could think of except the wooden bench at the Bhikha Behram Well. It felt like an oasis amongst the swirling Bombay City street life; it was just for one more night then I would be able to get some help from the British Consulate.

Walking back towards the well I stopped to watch a cricket match on the large parched playing field next to the well. A large number of spectators sat at the edge of the field; some sat on picnic blankets. Every time the ball was hit everyone applauded, nobody seemed to be supporting any particular side in the cricket match. When a four or a six was hit spectators had to move out of the way of the cricket ball when it came in their direction. The bowlers and batters put so much gusto and determination into their bowling and batting as if to outdo each other with their performance. As the afternoon ebbed in to evening the cricketers finished their game with the spectators applauding and the cricketers shaking hands in the traditional gentlemanly way. Watching the Cricket was very therapeutic and for a while distracted me from my dilemma.

I made my way over to the Bhikha Behram Well and saw Nick sitting on one of the benches, we said hello then Nick told me I could not sleep on the bench because it would be taking advantage of the benevolence of the well custodians. I explained that having looked around for somewhere suitable to sleep there weren't many places and they did not seem to be too safe. Suggesting it was just until the morning when I will see the British Consulate.

Nick gave me a doubtful look, paused briefly then said "you can stay for one more night"; I promised that this would be the last night. Sitting down on the bench we talk for some time about India and how people struggle across the country and also the magnificence of India with its architecture, some of it dating back to some 3000 BC. We drank tea from the nearby tea stool. Eventually Nick said

355

he had to get some sleep, he had to be up early for work the next morning.

Welcoming the idea of an early night, I wanted to be ready for when the British Consulate opened. Lying down on the bench in the crook of the seat I felt strangely comfortable, so much better than being on the ground but looked forward to sleeping in a bed.

Waking the next morning, Nick had already gone and the street was very busy around the well. Pedestrians were making their way to and from Churchgate Train Station, there were a large number of carts filling up their churns with water from the well. Also some people collected water for themselves, maybe to take to work. I got some water from the well for a wash to freshen myself up and look reasonably clean and not look a vagrant. I had a few hours before the consulate opened which gave me time to have something to eat from the tea shop which was very busy.

Having been away from Bombay for so long I had forgotten how busy it was during the week. Making my way through the packed pedestrian traffic to the consulate was relieved to find the imposing metal studded wooden doors open. Climbing the flight of marbled stairs that lead to the British Consulate door, I noticed directly opposite was the French consulate. The doors were made of a heavy wood with polished brass fittings and a glass panel. I entered a spacious air conditioned room with a marble floor and a highly polished wooden desk on the right, some Indians were sitting on the seats waiting to be interviewed.

356

A white woman at the desk speaking with a fake posh accent asked if I needed any help, I smiled at the irony of the question; do I need any help? Explaining that on the Friday I had travelled down from Delhi and had my rucksack stolen which contained my passport, flight ticket and travellers cheques and I did not have any money on me; I produced my police report that I had made out on Friday evening which she gave a cursory glance.

"Where have you been staying over the weekend".

"I slept on a bench by the well".

She explained that she would have to take my details and consult someone. She then suggested I could telephone home to have some money sent out to me. Repeating that I did not have any money to make a telephone call.

"You can reverse the phone call".

This sounded okay, then asked "would I have to pay for the reversed phone call?"

"Of course, but it is only a small charge".

I stared at the woman in disbelief, paused then said slowly hoping she would under stand "I don't have any money".

With a terse tone in her voice she told me to come back in about an hour's time. Leaving the consulate I was unsure if anything would be sorted out. Before I had got too far I heard somebody calling then my arm was grabbed.

Turning around there was a white young woman of about 22, "I heard you in the consulate, they did not seem to be listening".

I was glad someone thought the same, she then held out her hand, "there's some money, it's not much but it might help".

357

Smiling I managed a garbled "thank you", not knowing how much she had given me but any amount was better than nothing.

"I hope you get things sorted out", she then walked off waving. I waved back and stared at her as she vanished in to the Bombay crowd. I stood motionless for a while in disbelief and realising I did not even ask for her name or address so I could pay her back. Suddenly snapping out of my trance looked at the money in my hand. 18 rupee's, my heart leapt with excitement. I could not believe my luck. After the weekend 18 rupees (about 95 pence) felt like a small fortune; I did not want to lose any of it and making sure it was safe I split the notes up and put some in each pocket.

With an hour to kill I made my way to a tea stall and treated myself to a biscuit which I took a long time eating. Trying not to think about what decision the consulate was going make wrote a letter letting my mum and dad know what had happened over the weekend. It was difficult putting it all together and describing the different events but this helped me focus on the positive things over the weekend as I glossed over some of the detail. By the time I had finished the letter it was time to go back and face the music at the consulate. When I returned there was a young slim white man who looked a bit dishevelled sitting in one of the chairs. The woman behind the desk told me to sit down in an officious tone. Complying with her direction and wondered how long I would have to wait. The way things were I felt the longer they took the better, they would have to find somewhere for me to stay plus the air conditioning felt so good.

The dishevelled man was called in to an office behind the desk. I looked around the room, there were some Indians waiting to see the Consulate officials. The people interviewing were also Indian which made sense for those applying to visit Britain who did not speak much English. The dishevelled man had been in the office for some time. He looked disgruntled when he came out, I was then invited in.

The office was small with a modest wooden desk, sitting at the desk was a slim well dressed man who's demeanour gave me the impression that he was a retired officer from the British armed forces. He spoke very directly as an officer would command. "Sit down", there was a pause "can you describe to me what happened". Repeating my story that I had told the woman earlier, this time in more detail. He then asked if I could remember the authorising signature on my passport. I looked at him with some bewilderment unsure who it would be. I remembered it was issued when I was in the Army whilst posted in Gibraltar, it was issued prior for an exercise in Kenya. He immediately replied "I need to know who authorised your passport" as if he was hunting for a culprit. Silently I thought about who it had been and suggested Colonel Tarver but then quickly mentioned that it could have been Major Thorpe. With out a change in expression he then asked if I had any money,

"no I don't.

The official behind the desk stared at me sternly. Responding as I would have when in the army and sat expressionless without showing any sign of concern for the outcome of the decision regardless of what ever it might be. "What we are going to do is book you in to the Salvation Army Hostel which you will have to pay for; we will contact your family to see if they can send you some funds and also get a flight ticket reissued. We will also issue a temporary passport which will be valid for just a month to get you back to Britain".

On being told all of this I felt relieved but kept the same expression and said "thank you".

"We need some details from you which you can give out side then come back in a week's time".

Once out side I was asked how much money I needed. Doing some mental arithmetic of the cost of the hostel and to buy some clothes I calculated £100 which was about 1800 rupees, this would leave me with some spare cash. "Where did you buy your flight ticket?"

"Carousel travel in Feltham".

"We need some photographs taken for your new passport, come back in a three days time to see how things are progressing".

The woman called the other man over to the desk. She told us we would both be staying at the Salvation Army Hostel and should not try to book out, then asked if we knew where it was.

"I stayed there when I first arrived in India",

"good, show this gentleman where it is; the staff have been informed that you will be arriving soon".

I was now feeling a lot more relaxed, out side I asked the man his name.

"Alan!" he exclaimed; Alan told me how anxious he was with his interrogation in the office, "I felt I was being inspected for needle marks. He was looking at my arms as he talked to me. What about you?"

"He just asked a few questions about what happened".

As we made our way to the Salvation Army Hostel Alan explained that he had been living in Pune, a hill town for the last few months. I asked if he had been any where else.

"I spent all of my time in Pune".

This sounded a bit tedious, why stay in one place when there was the whole of India to explore. Alan mentioned he was asked to get some funds together but the only person who could help him was his sister and he did not get on very well with her.

A familiar place; home from home

After booking in to the Salvation Army Hostel we were shown to a small dormitory with six beds which felt like an ideal size, not too crowded. Two other back packers were in the dormitory having a private conversation, saying hello; they both replied hello and carried on with their conversation, ignoring our intrusion Putting my rucksack down I fished out my washing things for a long overdue shower. Crisp, pristine clean bed sheets and a blanket were brought up for me and Alan. Making up my bed I could not resist running my hand over the clean bedding which must have looked strange, after the train journey from Kashmir and spending the weekend sleeping on a wooden bench the white material felt heavenly.

Not wanting to waste any more time I got into the shower, hot water gushed out as I turned the tap; it was absolute bliss as the grime from the last several days washed off. I could not help reflect on the contrast between the wash I had with the cold water running on to Chowpatty Beach or the rusty water on the train and this clean hot water; I could easily have stayed in the shower all day. Once dry and wearing clean clothes I told Alan I was going for a walk, Alan said he preferred to stay in the hostel.

"See you later" I replied and left the hostel for the Water Front. Turning the corner of the Taj Mahal Hotel it felt like I was back home seeing the familiar sight of the bay, the giant structure of the Gate Way to India with the boats

362

moored up close by and people promenading. Crossing
the road I leant against the wall and looked out on to the
bay where several tankers and cargo ships were moored
up waiting to be unloaded, small sailing craft gently
cruised along in the light breeze. Remembering the small
craft market I walked over towards it when a young
chubby boy wearing just an old pair of shorts came up to
me and asked for baksheesh, my reaction was to
dismissively say "jow!", the boys response without saying
a word was to go down on his hands and knees and kissed
my feet. I could not help feel embarrassed with so many
people about possibly watching. Reflecting on how lucky
I had been over the weekend with total strangers being so
benevolent I fished out a hand full of change from my
pocket and handed it to the boy, he bowed and walked
away.
Recovering from my embarrassment I went over to the
laden stalls displaying their soapstone crafts, woven lamp
shades, crystals and semi precious stones, wooden crafts
and metalwork. All of this craft work had not lost its
attraction and amazement even after my trip around India;
I just wished I had enough money to buy some of these
things. Suddenly it occurred to me that it was close to
lunch time at the Hostel, not wanting to miss out on a free
meal I made my way back. The meals were already being
served and I managed to sit on a table with three others.
One of the hostel assistants came over and asked what I
wanted. Surprisingly toad in the hole was on the menu
and asked for this. The others at the table looked bemused
and one of them said "toad in the hole, what is toad in the

hole?"

"Its sausages cooked in a batter and with gravy on top, my mum cooked this a lot when I was younger. But it might not be as good as what my mum made".

Very soon the Toad in the Hole arrived, it was not as good as what my mum made. The batter was hard and the sausages were cooked to a dark brown crisp, and no gravy but there was mashed potato.

"is this toad in the hole?" some one asked.

Unconvincingly replied "yes" and cut in to the crispy sausages and batter then ate the over cooked meal, regardless of what it looked like it was better than nothing, and it was not rice. After washing down the meal with a cup of tea I went and sat on the veranda where Alan was sitting with several other back packers. He was talking about his time at Pune and the book he was writing there but had to sell his type writer to pay a bill. The others talked about their experiences which all sounded interesting to listen to as they all compared notes, it occurred to me that these stories should be written down and published.

Someone asked about my time in India. Explaining about my journey south from Bombay to Cape Comorin, catching the ferry to Sri Lanka then travelled north to Kashmir they seemed surprised I had managed to travel so far. When asked if I had made it to Calcutta I explained that Kashmir seemed like the better place to go after some Kashmiri's persuaded me that I should visit Srinagar. This all seemed so long ago. Where I had kept travelling many found a place they liked and stayed there, some only got as far as Goa. When asked if I had been there I explained that somebody had suggested it is best to avoid Goa, so I did. Someone said I missed a fun place with lots of parties but on personal reflection was glad I had avoided Goa and seen the real India; it did not sound as if Goa could compare with Amritsar, Kashmir, Chittorgarh, or the Taj Mahal.

The conversations went on for some time until eventually deciding I would sooner be out walk around the streets than cooped up in the hostel. Letting everyone know I was going for a walk Alan asked where I was planning to go,

"nowhere in particular" I replied; "just a walk to look at the sights".

Alan said he wanted to come along; "I haven't seen much of Bombay". Out in the afternoon sun we walked to the Regal Round about. Strangely I felt more comfortable and relaxed out wandering about than stuck in doors, Alan looked a bit apprehensive as we made our way past the shops weaving between the crowds. I asked Alan about Pune and what it was like, I was curious about why one place could tie someone down.

"A friend had told me about Pune and made it sound like a pleasant place to stay in India; soon as I arrived in India I caught the bus to Pune and stayed there in an ashram".

I could not help asking if Alan wanted to go anywhere else in India;

"not really, I didn't have much money and wasn't sure where to go". I could not help wonder how many people arrived in India and just stay in one place and not see the

365

rest of the country. At the Floral Fountain we turned left towards Churchgate Station and Back Bay, I wanted to see if Nick was at the well and to say thanks for letting me sleep on the bench; also to tell him I had managed to get a place in the Salvation Army Hostel.

Unfortunately Nick wasn't there so we went on to Back Bay. Having some money left over from the 18 rupees I asked Alan if he wanted a tea at the corner tea shop. Whilst drinking our tea I pointed out a few land marks around Back Bay and Chow Patti beach and mentioned the mosque beyond the hill. Alan commented on how far it was to Chowpatty Beach,

"its not that far";

"when I travelled anywhere in Pune I hired a motor bike" Alan replied.

It was obvious Alan wasn't interested in walking any further, once we had finished our teas he suggested going back to the hostel which was disappointing but I walked back with him.

At the Hostel we went up to our dormitory, another guest had arrived who sounded American and seemed to enjoy talking about his self, regardless if anyone was listening and didn't stop for anyone to reply to his chatter. As he talked the rest of us gave the occasional nod or occasional uninterested "yeh".

The American wore a blue check shirt and pressed trousers and had a small beige leather suitcase that had seen better days. He did not seem to be a regular backpacker and appeared to have just arrived in India. Rummaging through his suitcase he pulled out a syringe, a small bottle and a strip of rubber. None of us said any thing; this was the first person I had come across who blatantly used drugs. With his equipment he shut his self in the toilet; there was a silence as we all looked at each other and it was obvious we all thought the same, idiot!. Just at that moment one of the hostel wardens came in to the dormitory and asked if everything was okay. In unison we all said it was when the American let out a brief yelp. The warden called out "are you okay"? There was a brief silence then the American announced he was okay but had a slight change in the tone of his voice. The warden left and a few minutes later the American appeared from the toilet looking very relaxed and not so chatty. Putting his things away in his suitcase he announced that he needed to find an opium den, without a comment from any of us in the room the American left to find his utopia. The meal time gong resonated through the building. Walking down the stairs Alan asked what I thought of the American; "he doesn't seem to be very sensible" I replied. The evening meal was salad; it was not my favourite choice but thought beggars cannot be choosers, it was just one meal and maybe we would get a choice. How wrong I was, the salad consisted of cucumber, lettuce, tomatoes, boiled egg and the two things I dreaded, beetroot and salad cream. The two things I had always had trouble eating and avoided at all costs. What made it worse the beetroot and salad cream was laid on top of everything else; I just shivered at the thought of eating the salad crcam. Thinking to myself that it won't kill me and I had eaten worse in the past, if I ate it quickly without chewing it might not taste so bad. Taking the first fork full I forced it in to my mouth and swallowed.

Even though I thought it tasted disgusting I quickly shoved the next mouth full in, then the next. I finished before anyone else had eaten half of their meal, and then gulped down several cups of tea to take the sickly taste of the salad cream away. One of the others at the table remarked how quick I had eaten the meal; putting on a brave face I replied how hungry I was and really enjoyed the meal.

Before the other's had finished eating I decided to go out for a walk and left the table. Once out in the sun lit street I walked to the Regal Roundabout and crossed over to the cigarette stall and bought two cigarettes. After lighting one with the slow burning cord attached to the wooden frame I decided to visit the jewellery bazaar down the small alley. Making my way along the pavement I went to cross the road when a uniformed policeman came running from behind me and stood in the middle of the road waving his arms indicating for everyone to stop and not enter, another man ran past him in plain clothes brandishing gun and dashed down the alley towards the small shops. The uniformed policeman was joined by several others, one stopped with him whilst the others ran down the alley. The policemen were now waving their hands indicating to everyone to move away. At first I ignored this and tried to look over the policeman's shoulder. Shouting at me in Hindi with a stern expression he made it obvious I should move away. Slowly walking down the pavement I watched as a police cordon was formed to stop any one getting too close and anticipated hearing gun shots but there was no sound of gun fire which was reassuring. This showed how quickly things can change on the Bombay streets even if it looks quite calm at the time.

I made my way to the well by the park hoping to see Nick and give him some money for his kindness and maybe he could find somewhere to sleep for the night. Again he wasn't there.

A crowd had gathered on the pavement near the Churchgate Station, something had attracted numerous commuters who were about to catch their train home. I just had to find out what was so interesting; drawing closer I could see that someone was doing some sort of acrobatics. Finding a suitable place in the crowd I could see what looked like a family performing a sort of circus act. The mother and father were doing some juggling, somersaults and catching the children on their shoulders as they bounced off a spring board. The three children were of various ages, the oldest being about ten then seven or eight and the youngest looked about four; all had bare feet and wore faded threadbare clothes. They climbed up on to their parent's shoulders and balanced and formed pyramids. The show was extremely entertaining and ended with a finale where the children were propelled in to the air by the mother jumping on to the opposite end of an improvised seesaw; they landed on the fathers and siblings shoulders with the adept skill of any Olympian gymnast. All three children stood upright balancing with the youngest at the top without any

369

wobbling. Everyone applauded with some money being thrown on to the ground. The children jumped down, the family bowed to the appreciative crowd then scurried about collecting the money. I gave two Rupees to one of the children as the small wicker basket was held out. Who wouldn't reward such fearless entertaining feats.

Having made it to The Churchgate Station I crossed the road on to Back Bay. Even though I had spent a lot of time here over the last few days I wanted to catch the sunset whilst gently strolling down to Chowpatty Beach. A cool breeze came off the sea, a perfect end to quite a weary day. Others had the same idea and many were gathering at Chowpatty Beach.

About half way along to Chowpatty Beach I sat on the sea wall listening to the sea lapping against the break water and waited for the sun to dip below the horizon. Smoking the other cigarette it had a calming effect. I was glad I didn't have to find some where to sleep for the night. Once the sun had set with a golden glow I took my time walking back to the Water Front as the last few workers made their way to Churchgate Station, some bought food and tea from the stall set up by the station entrance.

The Waterfront had the usual mixed crowd of Westerners, men in Arab dress Indians in various styles of dress, along with the peanut seller; craft stall vendors, beggars and couples promenading. Tankers and cargo ships were still moored up in the bay; I wondered where they might be destined for once unloaded. It suddenly occurred to me if for some reason things did not work out and I could not get a flight home I could always try and stow away on one of the ships by swimming out and climbing up the anchor chain. Then hide until the ship set sail, surrender myself then offer to work my passage. The one snag might be the next destination, would it really matter? Now having a plan B as a backup I felt not all was lost. If things got really desperate I could try and walk home but this would be a last resort; it would mean walking from India, across Pakistan, Afghanistan, the Middle East to the Mediterranean and across Europe; then some how get across the English Channel, all without a passport.

Back at the Guest House I sat with the others out on the veranda. It felt so good to be able to sit out in the warm evening air, unlike the chilly evenings in Kashmir. We sat up talking until the guest house attendants advised us to go to our dormitories. I did not need to be asked twice remembering I had a clean bed to sleep in. The light was already out, once in bed I fell asleep almost immediately. The next morning I woke to the sound of the traffic and pedestrians outside. Not wanting to miss breakfast I got up, showered and dressed before any one else was awake. The American was conspicuous by his absence, his bedding still pilled on his mattress; maybe he had found his opium den and stayed over night.

Breakfast was toast with jam, cereal, a pot of tea and orange juice; absolute heaven. Alan joined me at the table but did not look too good.

"Are you okay" I enquired

"I don't feel too good"

I had this vision of Alan projectile vomiting at the table, "are you going to be sick?".

"No!" Alan exclaimed, then asked, "do you have any plans for the day",

"not really I was just going for a walk";

"I don't think I'm up to any thing today" he replied. Alan ate some dry toast then sat in one of the large sofas on the veranda. Having eaten I said bye to Alan and left the cool interior of the guest house for the hot morning air.

Making my way to the Regal Round About I crossed over to the cigarette stall; the stall owner was making up a betel nut for a woman. Wrapping a nut in a leaf he added some lime paste. I still could not understand the attraction for chewing this even if it did give you a buzz as many put it, especially when it results in bright blood red saliva that the chewer spits out on to the pavement.

Having bought three cigarettes and lit one from the dangling smouldering string I carried on towards the Floral Fountain along the crowded pavement. Out of the blue an elderly man approached me with a broad smile and asked if I could help him; "I have been trying to find the Quakers in Bombay but I don't know where they are". As he held up his piece of paper I stared at him in disbelief unable to say a word;

"I have a letter of introduction".

Without looking at his piece of paper I tersely rebuked "I saw you three months ago and you told me the same thing".

The man's expression changed from a smile to one of anxiety and panic, he looked around "no I have not seen you before, you must have mistaken me for someone else".

I snapped at him "you told me the same story three months ago".

The man quickly replied "no, no" and walked off in to the crowd looking over his should as if to check he was not being followed. I stood there watching until he vanished in to the crowd. Once the man was out of sight I smiled to myself thinking that shock might deter him from using the same story again.

I turned left at the Floral Fountain, past the large fields where the cricketers were already setting them selves up. My arms were covered in tiny beads of sweat; it was hot and also felt very humid even though it was quite early. Realising if the sweat was not evaporating the humidity must be close to 100% and not a time for any sort of exertion. Remembering when posted out in Belize we were stopped from any exertion over the midday period after somebody had died of a heart attack.

Making it to Back Bay I walked around the bay to Chowpatty Beach and sat on the sand where a number of Indians had gathered, some were even swimming. Sitting on the warm sand I took in the view of the horse shoe bay with the high rise buildings on either side leading off to the distant head lands. I wanted a tea but was now totally out of money and opted to have a cigarette after asking an Indian for a light who smiled as he let me use his cigarette to light mine.

Pondering what or where to go next I decided to climb up to the top of Malabar Hill for the panoramic view from the top and wander around the Rose Garden which should be out in full bloom; also there would be the shade from the overhanging branches. The climb seemed more strenuous than when I first arrived in Bombay which I put down to the heat, even under the shade of the trees it felt hot. The gardens at the top of Malabar Hill were in full bloom; roses of every colour, hue and shade were out contrasting with the green lawn. The flower heads looked vivid in the bright Indian sun. Breathing in the air it felt fresher than down below in the streets. Having spent a few hours up on Malabar Hill and unsure of the time I thought it would make my way back for lunch.

Winding my way back through the now crowded streets I arrived back just in time. Lunch had already started and after my walk I was ready to eat any thing that was served up which happened to be salad again. The others on the table were talking about how hot it was in Bombay and they would like to leave. I was asked if there was anywhere to go that would be cooler than Bombay and suggested going south in to the Kerala Hills or to Kashmir.

Having finished eating I sat on the veranda, Alan was there and not looking any better. "I need to visit the hospital and see a doctor" then asked me to go along with him. I was amused by this request, it was only a visit to the hospital but if he felt like I did when I was ill maybe it was best Alan had someone with him. Alan had been given directions to the Saint Georges Hospital in the Fort area which was near the Victoria Station, once he mentioned Victoria Station I had a good idea where it was. We made our way past the Prince of Wales Museum and followed the road to Victoria Station where we looked for a sign pointing to the hospital. Not seeing one we asked a passer-by who pointed down a road by the side of the Station Terminal. Behind the terminal was a large building that looked similar to the old Victorian Hospitals of London. A large number of people were coming and going and felt we might have problems finding the right department. Patients lined the pastel green corridors as they waited to see a doctor. Navigating the warren of corridors was relatively easy after asked a nurse for directions; she pointed along a corridor where patients were sitting on benches at the far end. Alan was relieved to find a space on the packed bench whilst I stood. It seemed that it would be a long wait which Alan despaired at. The doctor worked quickly and before long Alan was seen, diagnosed and given some medicine for his ailment.

Outside it felt cooler than the hospital, even if it was warm; also it was a lot quieter. Alan wanted to go back and rest and said the walk to the hospital had knackered him. The walk back to the hostel took some time, even I felt relieved to be back.

As we climbed the stairs we met two Australians on the way down, saying hello Alan asked about the stick topped with a white metal knob one of them was carrying.

"It's to ward off rabid dogs";

something that had not occurred to me, "I haven't seen any dogs that looked rabid whilst travelling around India".

"They were around and should not take any chances".

I shrugged my shoulders and thought that it was a bit late

now; I will be going home in the next few days. Once up stairs we sat out on the veranda with some other back packers. A few of them seemed to always be there, never going out which seemed a shame not to explore the streets where no hour was the same let alone any day. We sat talking when someone wondered what would be on the menu for the evening meal. Everyone suggested a meal that was obviously their favourite; I could not help suggesting a large steak with roast potatoes, pea's and cabbage.

"Stop! That's too much, don't even think about it. Carrying on I added "with Black Forest Gateau for pudding",

"you are torturing us, shut up" someone quipped.

Not taking the hint I added "this should be followed by a large Brandy or a glass of wine"; one of the hostel rules was no alcohol which was a shame.

By the time we had finished fantasising about what we would like the gong sounded for the evening meal which turned out to be sausages, mashed potatoes and pea's; we all laughed and someone suggested we will have to use our imagination eating it.

Over our meal we exchanged antidotes of our travels in India and other parts of the world we had visited. Having finished our meal we returned to the veranda.

 Feeling a bit restless decided to go for a walk to the bazaar. It was turning dark and the small shops had their lights on. Nothing had been affected by the incident earlier, whatever it may have been, everyone was cheerful and friendly. I browsed the shops and the glass cabinets, feeling immersed in the humid atmosphere as I weaved through the crowded street. It almost felt like second nature walking along these crowded streets with the lively, compact hustle and bustle. Several vendors invited me in to their shops, I could not refuse especially when a tea was offered. Having spent a few hours looking at the shops and drinking tea with the vendors I made my way back to the hostel with the intention of joining the others but decided to go to bed. It was obvious that the American had still not come back, none of his possessions had been moved or the bed made up; I wondered where he might be now. Once in bed the American was forgotten as I drifted off to sleep.

Getting up early then next morning I decided to visit the Central Police Station to see if they had found my belongings. I was not holding my breath but I hoped that they might have been able to recover something, even if it was just the roll of camera film with the photographs of Kashmir. Alan gingerly made his way down to breakfast, he was not well enough to go any where. He struggled with the stairs let alone walk about Bombay. Having eaten I asked one of the hostel assistants where the Central Police Station was. All he did was wave his hand to indicate he was not sure, he asked another of the hostel staff who also did not know, the logical thing to do was to ask a Policeman but finding one could be quite difficult in the crowded streets of Bombay. As it so happened I found two by the Regal Round About, one of them pointed down the main road towards the bazaar and said it was on the right. I asked how far it was, the usual reply came back," not far, on the right".

As it turned out the Police Station was not far and was almost opposite the street leading to the bazaar, no wonder the police had turned up so quickly the day before. I climbed the steps and stood at the wooden desk which came up to my chest. The policeman behind appeared very tall but was obviously on a raised platform. Looking down at me he asked if he could help.

Taking out the letter I wrote on the Friday night at the train station and handed it to him. "I had a rucksack stolen and wondered if you might have found it".

He read the letter, "I do not recall any thing like this but I will check for you".

He went through a door and soon came back empty handed. "We do not have any of these items; it is very unlikely that we will be able to recover them for you".

My heart sank, I did not have any real expectations but just the thought of never being able to get the roll of film back was so disappointing, all of the Kashmir photographs gone. After having the letter handed back I left the police station and walked aimlessly through the Bombay streets; I did not want to be cooped up in the hostel but wanted to be outside making the most of what should be my last few days in India. Being out amongst the crowds seemed to be therapeutic, I felt at home seeing familiar faces each day and thought if I had the money I would like to stay a few more months.

I lost track of time and eventually noticed a clock which said 1pm. Not wanting to miss lunch I rushed back to Merryweather road where an elderly man had a small

378

crowd around him in the road. At first I thought he was a Sadu but found he was performing some magic tricks. They were the usual tricks that you might find on a TV show but these were being performed right there in front of me and I could not resist watching. I had always been sceptical of the magic on TV but this man was doing them with out any obvious props and just a few feet from me. One trick that had us all transfixed was the age old 'ball under the cups'. He shuffled the cups around on the tarmac and when some one was invited to choose a cup it was wrong each time. Having finished his act a young helper passed around a hat; I felt guilty not being able to give any money but was adamant once I had some from home, and if I saw him again would give him several rupees. Once sat in the dining hall and eating I talked to the others on my table about the magician down stairs which was dismissed as everyday party tricks. Some made a cynical remark about being able to see that sort of stuff on TV any time. Explaining that this was just inches away did not stir any excitement.

After lunch I went out again to make the most of my possible last day in Bombay. Aimlessly walking along the pavement through the throng of pedestrians I found my self at Back Bay after stopping at the Parsi Well to see Nick, but he was not about.

At Back Bay I sat on the wall and watched the waves lapping up on to the concrete breakwater; then receding away. It felt therapeutic watching the waves rippling on to the rocks and found the time had slipped away and was getting late; reluctantly I headed back to the hostel for the evening meal.

The evening meal was not ready and sat on the veranda with a small group, then noticed a news paper written in English with a photograph on the front of some men in black crouching outside a window on a balcony. The head line read "London Iranian Embassy siege ended", picking up the news paper that had just a few pages to it and read the rest of the story. The SAS had carried out the assault on the embassy and released the hostages; it showed how being in India you can be cut off from the rest of the world, it made me wonder if any thing else had happened whilst I was away. Reading the story made me feel proud that the British Army had managed to release all of the hostages with out any casualties. In side the slim news paper was a long column devoted to the professional beggars in Bombay and some of the tricks they employed. The editorial implored the public not to be taken in by their tactics and tricks and said that the police were cracking down on the beggars. Maybe that was why the man claiming to be looking for the Quakers became so anxious. I suggested going to the Water Front but no body else was interested.

The Water Front was busy with people promenading in the usual variety of garb filling the air with their chatter. After looking at the craft stalls I leant against the wall looking out in to the bay with the ships illuminated and reflected in the water which lapped against the tourist boats with the occasional thud. Having spent long enough on the Water Front I made my way back for an early night. Tomorrow Alan and I had to get to the British

Consulate for our flight tickets and money, at long last. Once I was awake the next morning the first thing I thought of was going to the British Consulate to pick up a new passport, my flight ticket and some money then flying home; maybe tomorrow. There was an element of excitement at going home but felt a reluctance to leave. The American had still not been back which was in some way concerning. A hostel assistant came up and asked if we had seen the American. Shaking our heads we all said no, to which the assistant said he would have to take his things down stairs.

Having showered and had breakfast the pair of us went to the British Consulate in anticipation of the good news. Alan was not sure if his sister would have sent any funds to help him get home, he had not seen her for several years. I just wanted a new passport and the flight ticket but some money would help out for the train fare home from Heathrow Airport.

Walking from the hot, humid and noisy street in to the quieter air conditioned room; the cool air was such a relief. The receptionist asked us to sit and wait, a few minutes later a tall portly well dress white man came out of the office smiling, spoke to the receptionist then left. The receptionist went in to the office and soon reappeared and asked Alan to go through. Alan seemed to take some time and I wondered if there were any problems but eventually he appeared smiling. I was beckoned through by the receptionist, The Consulate official invited me to sit down, looking stern he started "your parents have sent the £100 you requested" this was a big relief. He then told me I should get a passport photograph and bring it in to the consulate so they can issue me with a new passport. The official then said that the company I had told them did not issue me with a flight ticket. Leaning forward the official asked "what travel agent did you buy the flight ticket from". My mind raced trying to remember where I bought the flight ticket, then out of the blue I had a eureka moment "it was Bartholomew's in Harlow".

Still looking very serious he asked "are you sure, you need to have the right travel agent",

replying that I was sure it was Bartholomew's the official told me that they would follow this up and will have a reply in the next two days.

He explained that the £100 would be given to me in rupees,

I could not believe it; I had to have British currency when I returned to Britain to pay for the train and asked if I could have it in sterling. "No we can only issue you with rupees; you can exchange it at the airport; you cannot take the rupees out of the country". The consular official added "because you had lost your passport there was no proof that you had not been in India more than 90 days. You will need to get a tax clearance certificate from the tax office before leaving India".

Out side Alan explained that his sister had just sent enough money to pay for his flight but he was not sure if he could get a job when he got back or if his sister will put him up but he was leaving the next day.

I explained to Alan that some money had been sent and that I had to get a photograph for my new passport, but they had not traced the company that sold me the flight ticket; I will have to stay a few more days.

To cheer our selves up I suggested we go for a tea and something to eat which I offered to pay for with my new found wealth.

We found a crowded tea shop and ordered a rice meal and Naan bread; it some how felt like a proper meal after having eaten the meals in the Salvation Army Hostel. Alan seemed apprehensive about going back home partly because he will have to see his sister who he had not seen for a long time. I tried to reassure him it would be okay but he was not sure. I asked where his sister lived, "Hounslow"; I told Alan that I had worked in Feltham for a few months before coming out to India, "when I get back I hope to get my old job back and might see you around".

Having finished our meals we went back to the Hostel to find out what was for lunch which turned out to be curry, I could not help laugh at the irony but still ate the meal. Now Alan had his flight ticket he appeared impatient and wanted to catch the flight back to London, which was the next day and in the afternoon. Alan was unable to contain his excitement and told anyone he talked to that he was going home. Not wanting to listen to Alan's exuberance all afternoon I made an excuse that I had to go out and buy some clothes for the flight home. By the Regal Roundabout were some stalls that sold shirts and trousers which seemed like a good place to start. They had a wide variety colours and were cheap, I could not resist buying several so that I had a clean one for the next few days and for my next visit the British Consulate and of course for the flight home so that I looked semi smart on arriving at Heathrow airport and not like some long lost Wildman from the jungle. Thinking about Heathrow Airport reminded me that I had to get a photograph for my passport but was not sure where to get one taken. There were no photo booths but I remembered seeing a sign for a photographer somewhere near Victoria Station. I walked along the street but could not see it and wondered if it had closed down.

Eventually I was compelled to ask someone if they knew where it might be. Luckily I found someone who knew and described where it was, I had walked past the door. It was a tall wide dark brown wooden door with a sign written with large flowing filigree letters in faded gold, "Photographer for personal and official portraits and passports". I climbed the dingy wide stair case and knocked on the door at the top. A slim man of about forty answered and invited me in. Explaining that I needed a photograph for a new passport he asked me to sit in a chair in front of a rather old camera on a tripod, it had a concertina lens that looked like a relic of the British Empire and a cape draped over the back. I sat still thinking that I was going to have my photograph taken but the man went to a set of draws and took out what looked like a shaving brush and a small pot. As he approached me he said I need to just put some of this powder on your face to reduce the reflection and take away the shine. I went to say that he could just take my photograph but he must have second guessed what I was

384

going to say and interrupted and said "you need to look your best for the photograph and to lighten your suntan". He brushed the powder on to my face then stood back as an artist would when standing at the easel. Applied some more powder then went to his camera, loaded the film, stooped down under the cape; adjusted the lens then pressed the shutter button.

As the shutter clicked the man said "good, I have to develop and print the film now, it will take a short while". Having done a photographic course whilst in the army I had a good idea the problems he might have with the temperature and humidity when developing the film. I sat in an old large comfortable chair and waited whilst the photographer went in to his dark room. This gave me a chance to look around his dusty studio with all of its props and screens to help create the perfect portrait photograph. Eventually he appeared with the finished black and white photograph, he asked me what I thought; "it's a good likeness" which was an obvious statement and thanked him.

Rushing to the British Consulate hoping to be in time to give them the photograph and with any luck the passport would be ready for the next day and possibly catch the evening flight home. The consulate was still open and managed to hand the photograph to the receptionist. After taking my details said the passport would not be ready until Monday, my jaw dropped open; I had to stay in Bombay for another weekend. Thanking the receptionist I enquired about the flight tickets,

"We are still waiting to hear from the travel agents" came

the reply. It didn't seem to be going too well and wondered if I had to use my back up plan.

Opening the door to leave the British Consulate I stared directly at the door of the French Consulate and had a Eureka moment. If things did not work out I could go in to the French Consulate and say I was a deserter from the French Foreign Legion. Maybe they had an obligation to repatriate Legionnaires, it made sense. It could go two ways. They would not believe me because my French was not good enough to pass off as a Legionnaire; alternatively I might convince them and end up back in France serving in the Foreign Legion. Either way this was better than my other plan, swimming out to a tanker and stowing away.

Trying not to dwell on the thought of spending the weekend in Bombay I went back to the hostel for the evening meal. It was a bit early and joined the others on the veranda where Alan was still talking about going home the next day. He mentioned about what he was planning to do and that he needed to catch up with his friends and try and find a job, then hinted at returning to India again. Eventually the gong signalled the meal was ready which I felt was long over due; I felt so hungry. The conversation over the evening meal revolved around where we lived and what it was like. The American at the table described his home town in the mid west; it sounded like something from the Wild West with everyone owning guns and driving around in beat up old cars on the open roads. The Australian described his home outside Sydney in the bush which sounded inviting and exciting. Alan

386

talked about London and I explained I had lived in South London when I was younger then moved to Harlow where there was a lot a green areas and farm land with in walking distance.

Having finished the meal we sat on the veranda, after some time I found it hard to resist taking a walk to the Waterfront and left everyone with their stories.

By the Gateway to India I mixed with the Indians dress in clothes suitable for the warm evening sea air filled with the different accents and languages. I bought some peanuts from the vendor; filling the paper cup from his basket I walked about eating them as I browsed the craft stalls reflecting on the difference between these stalls and those in Jaipur. Talking to the owners now and then haggling over a price then saying "no, no too expensive". Small children came up holding out their hands asking for paisa or baksheesh which at times was hard to resist with their wide eyes, dirty faces, thread bare clothes and matted hair. With the thought of going home soon my resistance relented and occasionally put a rupee in to the small out stretched hand.

Losing track of time, it felt late and thought the hostel would be closed soon. Arriving back only to find it was early and the others were still chatting whilst some one played a guitar; joining them I sat and listened. It felt very cosmopolitan with the different accents in such a small space, everyone with their own story to tell of India and back home. Some body out of the blue asked if it was possible to get to Sri Lanka and I explained that they needed to go to Rameswaram and catch the ferry from

387

there. "You should be at the ferry terminal as early as possible which sails in the afternoon once everyone is aboard and arrives in Sri Lanka late at night".

As the evening wore on those on the veranda started to drift off to their dormitories, I hung around on the veranda listening to the night time noise reverberating down on the street below, it had a comfortable soothing tone. I listened for some time then when the lights were turned off I went up to bed.

The next morning Alan was up early and seemed to be making enough noise to wake any one from a deep drunken stupor. He hummed to his self as he packed his things; Alan's excitement was blatantly obvious. Somebody was asleep in Americans bed but it was not the American. I wondered what might have happened to him and where he ended up. Not dwelling on his plight I got showered and dressed and went down to breakfast.

Alan had been told that he needed to catch the train from for the airport from Churchgate Station. He asked if I knew where Churchgate Station was. I explained it was near Back Bay where we had walked during the week, "what all that way. I laugh and said it's not that far, "maybe half hour walk". Alan asked if I could walk there with him and help him find the right platform. Not having much else to do I said of course. Alan's flight was at 3 pm so he had a lot of time to kill. I did suggest that maybe it would be best to leave early in case there was a technical hitch. Alan was sure there wouldn't be any but it would best be safe than sorry than miss the flight. Collecting his rucksack which looked virtually empty Alan went down

388

to the dining hall and said good bye to everyone who was there. Having said fare well we set off for the station along the crowded pavement stopping at the cigarette stall and bought a packet and lit one on the smouldering cord. As we walked past the British Consulate Alan said he was glad he did not have to deal with them again. Alan complained about the heat, I agreed that it was hot and quite humid but wondered if it was because Alan had spent most of the time up in the hills at Pune where it was cooler and was not fully acclimatised to the now hot, humid atmosphere in Bombay. I told Alan that once he was at the station it would be a lot cooler in there. Once in the shade of the station the temperature dropped by several degrees.

Alan bought his train ticket and was told by the ticket office what station to get off. light heartedly complained about the inconvenience just to catch a plane. The station was busy making it difficult to find the correct platform, but was directed to the right commuter train by a platform attendant. Alan seemed to be getting quite aggravated at this point and decided to leave him now he knew which train to catch.

After saying good bye I headed over to Back Bay and walked around to Chowpatty Beach and up to Malabar Hills for some fresh air. There was a cool pleasant breeze coming off the sea in Back Bay, walking past Chowpatty Beach I climbed the path up to the hill top under the shade of the trees. Once at the top I sat down in the open air café with a tea and some biscuits. Looking out over Bombay, regardless of the problems of the last week I had come to

389

love the city. It was vibrant, colourful and exciting. No day was the same or predictable. If it was to become predictable there were plenty of places tucked out of the way that added excitement to the day.

After spending some hours on the Malabar Hill, walking around the garden and drinking tea in the open air café I made my way back down to Chowpatty Beach and around to the other side of Back Bay. The sun did not feeling so intense; it was obviously late afternoon and decided to make my way back to the hostel. The afternoon meal had started, sitting down at a table where there was an empty seat the others were talking in German; ignoring them I ate my meal then went back out for a walk around the streets. As I walked around the corner I saw a white man wearing a grubby cheque shirt and grey flannel trousers but had nothing on his feet. I stopped and watched in case he was having any problems but the Indians did not look as if they were acting aggressively; I realised the man was violently shaking, at first I could not under stand why, it wasn't cold then it occurred to me that he could possibly be shaking from withdrawal symptoms and was trying to buy drugs from these men. Watching from the other side of the road, the man was vigorously waving his arms around and shouting. In the end the Indians walked away as he raved at them. He went to follow them but the shaking was making it difficult for him to walk as quickly as them.

After rounding the corner by the Taj Mahal Hotel and on to the Waterfront I stood by the wall and for some reason remembered Bob who I met when I first arrived and

390

wondered how he was getting on. Having been out on the Waterfront so many times in the last week I was sure that I would have seen him. Then wondered how many other westerners were in a situation where they had no money and were stuck in Bombay or even Calcutta. I had been told several times that the French Consulate and Embassy tended not to help their nationals if they were suspected of having sold their passports or taking drugs. Before helping the French consular officials tended to err on the side of caution and were reluctant to help in any way regardless of the situation.

I spent some time on the Waterfront watching the people, took in the view and bought some peanuts from the vendor. The last few boats arrived back from Elephanta Island and were being moored up. Whilst standing by the Gateway to India I watched the palmist sat next to the huge arch reading various people hands. Telling them their future and how their life will change if they make a certain decision whether it was marriage, business or education. I had been told a number of times on my journey around India that many Indians consult a palmist before doing anything that could affect their future. I pondered whether to have my palm read to see how things would unfold for me over the next few days and the coming years, but concluded that it was most unlikely he could predict what was going to happen on Monday. I watched as his customers listened intently then smiled at what they were being told, everything seemed to be good news.

Another man was sitting by the arch used some sort of

prong and scooping something out of his customers ears. I had seen this in several places in India, when I enquired about this strange practice the reply each time was they were having stones removed from their ear. When querying this I was quite categorically told that I would have stones in my ears. Standing close to the man I watch him and sure enough he was somehow appeared to be scooping out small pebbles from his customers ears. It looked so strange that anyone would allow him to do this to their ears but they were quite happy with this strange practice.

Whilst watching the two men several children came up to me and asked for paisa or baksheesh, they all looked grubby and wearing old clothes. Not all of them appeared to be that needy but one young boy with his even younger sister in tow definitely looked as if they could do with a meal and gave them some money, with wide toothy smiles they ran off. Having browsed the craft stalls I went for a walk around the busy and noisy main street with the huge articulated buses and ambassador taxis and the busy pavements. It all felt so normal and common place now; far different to when I first arrived three months ago, apprehensive and unsure but excited.

I walked around to the well to see if Nick was about but he was not there, maybe he had managed to find someone to put him up for the night.

I had a tea from the stall near the well and sat on the bench watching people collecting water in various containers; maybe for the mornings wash. Finishing my tea I went back to the hostel where a number of back packers were still sitting on the veranda. Having had what felt like a long day I decide it was time for bed.

Dealing with Indian red tape

The next morning I was up early; showered and went
down stairs to the dining hall, it was too early for
breakfast. Sitting on the veranda, the cool morning air felt
refreshing, a welcome relief before the hot humid day
ahead. Several others came down and commented on how
cool it was and how good it would be to get out before it
got too hot. Breakfast was announced with the gong and
back packers drifted in to the dining hall. Whilst waiting
to be served someone mentioned how nice it would be to
have a cooked breakfast, we laughed when it was
suggested "ideally on Wedgewood plates". A tea pot was
brought out for our table along with a rack of toast. The
breakfast choice was either porridge or cornflakes a far
cry from an anticipated cooked breakfast.
Somebody mentioned what they had planned for the day
and then asked me. I hadn't thought about doing any
specifically but mentioned that I would most probably go
up to the Malabar Hill for some fresh air. They looked at
me quizzically and asked where Malabar Hill was,
"it's across Back Bay above Chowpatty Beach". Having
thought of it this seemed like a good idea to make a day
of it and eat in the café on top of the hill.
Having eaten I set off to the Regal Circle, stopped at the
cigarette stall and toyed with the idea of buying a packet
of bidi cigarettes to save some money but having seen the
thick gooey tar that comes out of the end I opted for

394

ordinary filtered cigarettes.

Weaving my way through the pedestrian traffic, past sadhu's with their snakes and the lottery man and his customers. The Parsi Well looked busier than usual but Nick was not about. The cricketers were on the large parched fields setting up the wickets whilst spectators were gathering around the edge ready for the match. The Back Bay looked calm and inviting but with so many high rise buildings lining the bay I was sure the water it self would not be hygienically safe to swim in. As I walked along the promenade to Chowpatty Beach it was warming up and becoming desperately humid, sweat was now running down my arms. Sitting in the shade on Malabar Hill would be the best place at midday. I stopped at Chowpatty for a tea and sat on the sand, a number of people were already on the beach, women's saris gently fluttered in the sea breeze, some playfully paddled in the sea. Others brave enough waded out to their waist and were dipping down under the water.

Having finished my tea I made my way up the path under the trees; the dappled shade felt pleasant. At the hill top I sat down in the open air café for a snack and tea. Taking in the view I thought this would be the idyllic place for a house with the scenic view across Bombay and above the pollution. But reflected that this would stop others from being able to appreciate the fantastic view, eat out and be able to breathe the fresh air high above the car fumes.

I spent most of the day under the trees and walking around the hanging gardens away from noise and bustle of the busy streets below. The women's saris added

395

colour to the already brightly colourful roses. Everyone talked quietly almost whispering and no traders hassled you to buy their goods. Instead of rushing back for the midday meal at the hostel I chose to eat in the open air café.

By late-afternoon it felt cool enough to walk back to the Waterfront. Coming out of the shade of the trees the afternoon's heat could be felt on my arms and legs as I walked around Back Bay past many of the pedestrians out for an afternoon stroll. The road at the Floral Fountain was as busy as ever.

The time on a clock said it was just four thirty; too early to go back to the hostel and decided to visit the gold and silver jewellery bazaar to kill some time. Just before the turning for the bazaar was a road that I had so far missed, at the far end a crowd of white people standing on the pavement and could not resist having a look to see what the attraction was. The crowd were outside a café called Bijous, which served iced fruit drinks. Inside it was packed and nowhere to sit, the reason for so many back packers standing outside. Bijous only sold freshly crushed fruit drinks of any flavour. Deliberating at what to have I eventually opted for a Mango juice. I watched as the mango was peeled and cut up then crushed in a metallic juicer by hand, then crushed ice was added. The bright yellow drink tasted as good as it looked, delicious, it was the best drink I had in India, and it was cold.

Whilst taking my time over the Mango juice I got talking to a few other backpackers and found they came to Bijous every day, how had I missed this oasis of cold refreshing drinks? But was glad to find it.

Bijous customers were a cosmopolitan bunch of every western nationality you could think of. Some looked like seasoned travellers. Several had managed to do the over land route through Turkey, Iran, Afghanistan and Pakistan. They were the centre of attention because the over land route was considered out of the question after the Russian invasion. Feeling slightly envious of these intrepid few I remembered that originally I intended to fly around the world with Pan Am and could not decide how long to stay in India, hence coming direct to Bombay.

After the drink I went back to the hostel for the evening meal which turned out to be salad again. Not wanting to put myself through the tortuous ordeal I ate out at a tea shop by the Regal Circle, opposite the Victoria Museum. This tea shop was always busy and had tables and chairs outside on the pavement, Parisian style. It looked as though only Indians ate here which felt comfortable and relaxing and did not have to worry about eating with my fingers. Having picked up my palm leaf I sat down, a large bowl of rice was brought over to the table and liberally served until I said stop. Two small dishes were put down to mix with the rice and a tea.

After the meal I walked to the Parsi Well hoping to catch Nick, not being anywhere I asked some of the other people looking after the well and the tea stall vendors if they had seen him but they shrugged their shoulders. Absent mindedly I found myself walking towards Back Bay, which seemed to have become my favourite haunt ideal for catching the setting sun and bask in the evening light. The sun sets were the same every evening with the bright blue cloudless sky gradually fading to yellow as the sun dipped down towards the horizon until vanishing and pulling the cloak of darker blue across the sky revealing the first stars; eventually the darker sky displayed the scattered distant galaxies.

The parade became busy with many pedestrians out walking by the sea, no different to what would happen by the coast in Britain. Having watched the stars for some length of time I walked back to the hostel which seemed to be relatively empty. I sat on the veranda with some other guests passing the time talking. A group who had just arrived in India asked about various places they intended visiting, I suggested going to Kashmir but they did not plan to stay long in India on their trip to Australia; the thought of going to Australia sounded attractive, with the beaches and the outback and wished I had enough money to fly to Perth or Sydney; maybe that would be another trip. Even though it was not too late I made an excuse that I wanted to be up early the next day and went to bed.

After breakfast the next morning I made my way to the busy Regal Circle, bought some cigarettes at the stall and again set off for the Malabar Hills to escape the vehicle fumes. It was already humid, the air felt sticky and the sweat run down my arms unable to evaporate. At Back Bay there was the welcome sea breeze, even if it was warm. The walk around Back Bay was pleasant with many people out for a Sunday Morning stroll. Tea stalls were dotted along the streets and parade. Buying a tea I sat down to admire the view of the wide bay then carried on to Chowpatty where I used the cold water running on to the beach to rinse my arms and cool down. It felt refreshing and was almost tempted to have wash but decided it would be best to get under the shade of the trees which turned out to be almost just as warm.

At the top of the hill I had a tea and something to eat at the open air café and looked out across the city scape with its sky scrapers and tall buildings lining Back Bay, away from the bay the smaller, older buildings fanned out.

After the tea I walked around the rose garden; as ever it was quiet and peaceful with the distant noise of the city below making the garden feel so detached from the rest of Bombay.

Having spent a few hours on Malabar Hill and having lunch I walked down the shady path to Chowpatty Beach and sat on the sand in the afternoon sun making the most of my last few days before flying home. It occurred to me that for the numerous times I had been on Chowpatty Beach I had surprisingly not seen any Westerners. Having watched the Indians enjoying their afternoon on the beach I took a slow walk around the promenade. At Churchgate Street Station a large crowd of at least fifty people had gathered in a circle. I had to find out what was so interesting and nudged my way through to the front. In the middle of the circle was a middle aged man dressed in a white shirt and trousers talking to his audience in Hindi. I some how managed to follow what he was saying because of his theatrical and animated performance.

As the man spoke he took out a ping pong ball from his

pocket, held it aloft to show everyone then tapped it to show it was a genuine ping pong ball. Next he took out a white handkerchief and waved this about to show everyone that this was a genuine handkerchief. He wrapped the ping pong ball in the handkerchief and tightly twisted it. To show everyone the ball was in the handkerchief he tapped the sphere which made a dull empty thud. He called out to the crowd and appeared to be looking for someone, he obviously wanted a volunteer but everyone appeared reluctant. Out of the blue he chose a man who was instructed to raise his hand above his head. The wrapped ping pong ball was placed in his hand and with a pointed finger instructed him to keep his hand where it was. This made the crowd laugh but the man did as he was told. The performer talked to the crowd went to walk away then turned abruptly, with a pointed finger spoke to his volunteer sternly which again made everyone laugh.

I was fascinated and wondered if the man was a magician. Realising he might take every ones attention away from this man with the ping pong ball I was determined to watch him to see if he changed the handkerchief at any time.

The magician held out his arms and looked around the gathered crowd and appeared to call for another volunteer, but none were forthcoming. Again he chose someone from the crowd and told this man to sit on a hessian sack which so far no one had paid any attention. Soon as the reluctant volunteer sat on the sack it started to move and instantly jumped up. The entertainer rebuffed his volunteer and instructed him to sit down again.

I continued watching the ping pong ball man with his hand raised. The magician held out his arms and spoke as if he was making an announcement, went over to his volunteer who leapt up again as the sack moved. Bending down the entertainer pulled out a large python which made the volunteer back away in to the crowd. This made everyone roar with laughter. Still the ping pong ball was being held up for all to see. At this point the magician went up to the man with the ping pong ball and spoke to him, he nodded but the magician looked at him with a doubtful expression and tapped the oval shape, the ball was still there.

The entertainer went over to a wicker basket similar to one used by the snake charmers. He bent down and took the lid off and straight away a large cobra raised its head and spread its hood. The entertainer pointed at it and appeared to tell it off, the crowd laughed. Still watching the man with the ping pong ball, he had not moved or changed hands.

Having told the cobra off he quickly picked it up by the tail and placed it on the ground, straight away it tried to escape and slide towards the crowd which made several people jump out of the way whilst the rest of us laughed. The magician caught the snake by the tail and whilst holding it again appeared to tell it off and placed it down on the ground; again the snake tried to escape and was caught. Whilst holding on to the cobra the man went over to another basket, taking the lid off a mongoose climbed. Instantly looking at the snake it crouched down ready to pounce. The magician then spoke to the mongoose which caused more laughter. Placing the snake on the ground it coiled its body and raising it head ready to strike. The mongoose quickly ran backwards and forwards then suddenly pounced biting the snake. Its body coiled around frantically as the mongoose bit it. After a few minutes the snake laid dead.

Still the man had the ping pong ball held up above his head with out any hint of the handkerchief being changed. The entertainer called to the man, he nodded. Again there was that doubtful expression, he walked over to the volunteer and tapped the ball it was still there. Turning to the crowd the entertainer raised his arms as if making an announcement, but there was no laughter, just spell bound silence. The magician reached for the handkerchief.

I wondered what he was going to do as he held it firmly ensuring it did not unravel. He took it away from his volunteer and tapped it again; there was a dull noise, it was still there. Taking hold of the handkerchiefs loose end with his other hand the magician turned around to show every one then letting go shook it. The handkerchief opened but the ping pong ball had gone. The whole crowd was aghast and applauded, it was such an amazing trick that was so simple but effective. I had watched the man with the ball virtually all of the time and had not seen him move, it was real magic, if ever there was such a thing. The entertainer took a basket around and everyone put money in to it, how could I not for such a well-deserved performance.

After being entertained I walk back to the hostel for the

evening meal. Whilst eating someone suggested going to a small bar on the front of the Taj Mahal Hotel. The amount of times I had been to the Waterfront I didn't know about this bar, it sounded like a fun idea to have a few beers, especially as a sort of celebration before flying home. After the meal it was mentioned to some of the other backpackers and before long there was a large crowd descending on the bar.

The smoke filled bar was absolutely crowded with other back packers. But we managed to squeeze in and ordered our beers. The atmosphere was exuberant, loud and full of lively conversation which almost drowned out the 60s music playing on a reel to reel tape deck. It was the ideal evening to finish my trip of India. Then to my surprise on the next crowded table was Bob. It was good to see him and to know that he was well. The evening flew by and soon we had to get back to the hostel before the 11pm curfew. It seemed a shame but having got carried away drinking several beers it was just as well. Back at the hostel the assistant told us to be quiet as we merrily went to our dormitories.

The next morning I woke with a mild hangover; it was a strange sensation, but I felt excited in anticipation of my visit to the British Consulate; will they have my flight ticket? At long last I was going to find out if I was going home or would have to resort to plan B. Having showered and got dressed I went down for breakfast for some toast and a quick cup of tea; even though the others at the table talked about their day and their plans all I could think about was getting my flight ticket and passport.

Out in the street it already felt hot and sticky, the roads seemed busier than usual; maybe because I was out earlier than usual. The pedestrian traffic was almost stifling as I weaved my way against the oncoming tide.

Arriving at the Consulate the large wooden doors were already open. The consulate office was empty, the cool air from the air conditioning was an instant relief. I optimistically explained to the receptionist that I had come to pick up my flight ticket and passport.

"Take a seat" she instructed then went in to the office behind the desk. I suddenly felt my stomach turning over with anxiety when she reappeared and asked me to come through; this did not seem to be very promising.

In the small office the stern looking official asked me to sit down, in his hand he had what looked like a passport and a flight ticket but I did not want to jump to conclusions.

"I have your new passport. It is a temporary one that is valid for just a month which will be long enough for you to get back to Britain. I also have your flight ticket that is booked for tomorrow afternoon at 1:40 pm. It is not transferable. You will have to settle up your bill at the Salvation Army Hostel before you leave. Do you understand?"

I nodded whilst containing my excitement. The official handed me the flight ticket and passport. "You need to get tax clearance before you leave India other wise you will not be allowed to leave the country", I was aghast; will I need to pay tax?

Outside at the reception I was given directions to the tax

office which was close by and made my way along the crowded pavement. Being curious how I looked in my new black and white passport photograph I opened it up; I appeared slimmer, almost scrawny and wondered if I would be recognised back to Britain.

The tax office was upstairs in a office block. It had a frosted glass panel door. Several dark fuzzy shapes moved inside making it look busy. The tax office itself was some forty feet by thirty feet, it had two rows of chairs down the middle for those registering their tax details and desks on either side where tax officials sat. All of the people waiting were Indians except for me and two women. One was smartly dressed as though she had just arrived in India and the other one was very distressed, had a wrinkled face and wore a loose cheese cloth top, a long red block print cotton skirt and numerous bangles around her wrist and had wild wavy fair hair.

They were talking to a tax inspector and what ever they were saying did not seem to be having any effect on the interviewer, the inspector was shaking his head as the woman seemed to be imploring with him.

A tax inspector pointed at me and bent his finger beckoning me to his desk. I sat down and was asked for my passport. The inspector then asked how long I had been in India. I gave him the date that I had returned to India from Sri Lanka. He asked if I had been in India for more than 90 days; I replied that I hadn't and showed him my Indrail ticket to prove when I had arrived in Madras. He asked if I had worked in India, replying I hadn't and had sufficient funds. He asked how I survived and explained that I went

405

hungry over the weekend and was then put up in the Salvation Army Hostel by the British Consulate. He asked if I had any money and again explained that I was sent £100 by my parents via the British Consulate. I wondered if he was going to ask me to pay tax on this money. He wrote down some notes on a sheet of A4 lined paper, paused then pulled out a Green sheet of A5 paper that had duplicate halves. Reading it up side down it was headed ITS Form No 35. Under that it had a serial number then Government of India. Below this it had clearance certificate under section 230 of the income tax act 1961. He wrote my name, the passport number then asked me for my father's name. He dated it from the days date to the following month. The sheet was then date stamped and signed; the information was duplicated on the other half and was stamped showing one half was for the airline or steam ship company and the other half was my own. The tax inspector handed me the green sheet and explained that I should hand this to the customs officers at the airport to show I had no tax liabilities in India, he then said good day and beckoned the next person over with the same gesture.

I was free to go and felt a great sense of relief. No more formalities, well not until I got to the airport but that would be straight forward; I did not need plan B, C or D. Having all of my documentation and not wanting to loose it decided the best thing to do was stay in the hostel. I made my way back to the Regal Circle and decided to occupy myself reading for the rest of the day and visited the small book shop by the cinema. After half an hour browsing through the packed shelves I found a book at the back of the narrow shop, it wasn't one that I would normally read but felt it would keep me occupied for the rest of the day.

The time I had spent at the consulate and in the tax office took longer than I had anticipated and missed lunch at the hostel. I deliberated over going for some thing to eat and maybe risk losing the passport and flight ticket or stay in the hostel, I opt to go hungry for the next few hours. Sitting on the large leather sofa on the veranda I read until the gong went for the evening meal. After the meal I sat back on the veranda again and read until late then went up to bed. Ensuring my passport and flight ticket were safe I slept with them under my pillow.

The luxury of air conditioned opulence

Waking the next morning I instantly checked under the pillow, the flight ticket and passport were still there. After showering I went down for a large breakfast, with the flight at 1:40pm I would miss lunch and might not be able to get anything to eat at the airport. Whilst eating breakfast someone asked what my plans were for the day, I smiled "I'm going home". This brought on a series of questions;

"do you really want to?"

"Will you be coming back?",

"how long have you been in India?",

"where's home?". Answering each question I was surprised how much interest there was in me leaving. I did not really want to leave but having little money it was time to leave and possibly come back again some time. On my journey around India several times I was told about Australia and New Zealand and really wanted to visit both of these countries.

After the long and chatty breakfast I paid my accommodation bill and collected my belongings then brought them down stairs so that the bed was empty for the next back packer.

I felt restless with an urge to leave; the flight ticket suggested arriving at the airport two and half hours before departure and decided it would be best to leave sooner rather than later in case there were any delays. Getting to

408

the airport involved catching the train from Churchgate Station for Santa Cruz station, catching a bus or taxi from there to Santa Cruz Airport. It sounded straight forward but this was Bombay and anything was possible, I did not want to take a chance.

Before leaving the Salvation Army Hostel for the last time I said good bye to some back packers I had got to know very well over the last week.

Making my way across the Regal Circle for the last time with my rucksack, it felt strange nonchalantly crossing the busy junctions and made me realise how acclimatised I had become to the Bombay hustle and bustle. Arriving at Churchgate Station was a relief coming out of the scorching sun. It did not take long to buy the train ticket for Santa Cruz and make my way through the packed station to the waiting crowded train. Squeezing in I found myself hemmed in on all sides. The train slowly pulled away and trundled along the track. I got a fleeting view of Back Bay from the raised railway line and thought about the many memories I had of Chowpatty Beach. Almost having just left the station the train started to slow down and stopped at a platform, passengers got off and on without any one waiting for each other, after about a minute the train pulled away. This was concerning, would I have enough time to get off the packed train. The train passed houses that backed directly on to the railway line, their white painted walls had greyed with the dirt from the trains.

I tried to ease myself over towards the open door with my rucksack on my back and grab a handle. The train stopped at eight other stations each time I was jostled by the other passengers as they got on and off whilst I frantically looked for the sign saying what station the train had pulled in to. By now I had attracted some attention; several passengers amused themselves with pulling at the rucksack straps at the back. As the train slowed down for another station I managed to catch a glimpse of the station sign, Santa Cruz, the platform was crowded and anticipated it being difficult getting off. Soon as the train stopped and before any one had a chance to get on I leapt at the crowd of commuters who jumped out of the way as I barged past them.

Needing to find the bus terminal or taxi rank I followed the passengers along the platform. Waiting outside were some auto rickshaws, regardless of past experiences the situation was desperate enough to throw caution to the wind and risk life and limb. Climbing in to the back seat of a rickshaw I shouted "Santa Cruz Airport".

A board in front of me had a list of fares for various destinations, Santa Cruz was just R2:75, soon the metre passed this amount and when we arrived at the airport the metre showed R5:5. I questioned the fare and was told that the board was old. I suggested that he should take the board out because passengers think that this was the real price.

The rickshaw driver raised his voice and pointed at his metre, "that is the correct price".

Our conversation had attracted the attention of four men who walked over to where we were standing. They looked quite menacing, two were holding meat hooks. Realising

410

the situation could get worse very soon as the rickshaw driver waved both hands saying "no, no". Taking the hint I felt it would be best to pay the five and half rupees, it was only twenty five pence more, it wasn't worth the hassle. They stood there as I paid the driver his R5:5 and as a good will gesture gave him a tip. They spoke to the driver in Hindi and he indicated that he was happy by shaking his head side to side and nervously smiling at them.

Saying good bye to the drive I waved then quickly made my way in to the airport terminal.

The terminal was hot, stifling and packed with queuing passengers having their luggage checked on trestle tables by customs officials. Being so busy I decided to wait for the queue to die down and tried exchanging my rupees for pounds. The Bureau de Change was a desk staffed by three men, surprisingly there was no screen or grill, it looked more like an information desk. When I asked to change up the 700 rupees they all looked shocked;

"no we cannot change that much, only three hundred rupees";

explaining that the British Consulate had given me the money in rupees and I needed to change it ready for when I got back to Britain.

They deliberated between themselves and said they will change five hundred rupees, resignedly I agreed just in case they changed their minds, it was a lot better than three hundred rupees.

They checked each bank note for any tear or signs of forgery. Satisfied the bank notes were genuine they gave me the equivalent in sterling; £27.

The queue was shorter and those who had their luggage checked were sitting just the other side of the tables directly behind the customs officials. Placing my rucksack on one of the flimsy tables I handed over my passport, flight ticket and tax clearance form. With a cursory check a baggage label was put on the shoulder strap and taken away by a baggage handler to a large trolley ready to be taken out to the aircraft. I joined the other passengers in the improvised departure lounge in front of the large glass windows which intensified the suns heat. Most of the passengers were westerners who were struggling with the heat and fanned themselves frantically with magazines and hats, something I had found only exasperated the discomfort. They were all smartly dressed in pristine pressed clothes, many looked pale despite the bright sunny weather.

A number of passengers became impatient and voiced their disapproval about the lack of air conditioning which they had come to expect whilst in India and accustomed to in the coaches and hotels.

The wait to board the plane was becoming drawn out when a well-dressed Indian gentleman walked in to the waiting area and called for every body's attention, the passengers fell silent. Just the sound of magazines and hats fanning could be heard as he announced that the British Airways flight from Bombay to London Heathrow had been cancelled. A murmuring of exasperation from some of the passengers reverberated around the departure area, the man raised his hand for every ones attention again; once silent he told us that we will be taken to by coach to a hotel and were to wait there until later that evening when a flight to London will be arranged. Many of the of the passengers made it obvious they were not happy, personally I was quite happy being able to spend some more time in Bombay, especially if it stretched to a few days in a hotel.

Our luggage was transferred from the trollies to the waiting air conditioned coach with its tinted glass windows, it felt luxurious compared to the hot and at times dusty buses I had travelled in. Some of passengers complained all of the several miles to the hotel which changed to sounds of approval when they saw the tall white fronted ten storey hotel. A large metallic sign above the entrance read 'The SeaRock Hotel'.

Everyone got off, collected their luggage and walked in to the large flamboyantly sumptuous, carpeted foyer with its air conditioning. Behind a large highly polished wooden reception desk stood a man waiting to book everyone in. The other passengers appeared nonchalant to their surroundings which they were most probably accustomed to, for me it was beyond my wildest dreams to be able to stay in a hotel with such opulence whilst travelling around India. I could not help noticing that I was the only one with a rucksack, the others had large heavy suit cases which were carried by the porters.

A porter offered to carry my rucksack, smiling and shaking my head said I could carry it myself. Booking in at the desk I was given two meal vouchers and the key to my room.

The hotel room had a double bed with pristine white sheets and large towels lay on the pillow. Large cupboards lined one side of the room. The large shower room had piping hot water and there was air conditioning. All this made me reflect on the day to day struggle of many who sleep out on the streets, especially those with leprosy whilst some of the passengers seemed to take the luxuries for granted and still had some thing to moan about.

Having showered and wearing clean clothes; a T shirt and loose trousers I went down for a meal. The dining area was just as luxurious with the other guests dressed as if they were going to a ball. Sitting at a dining table the menu read just like that of any five star restaurant with steak, lobster, Waldorf Salad and sea food with a variety of vegetables; but no Indian meals. The atmosphere was so different to the Salvation Army Hostel where everyone, whether you knew the people or not sat at the small round tables and shared the water jug and tea pot. Here everyone sat in their own small groups.

With so many different choices the one that I could not resist was a medium steak with vegetables which arrived quickly and perfectly cooked.

Taking my time I relished each mouthful that was washed down with a cold beer. This was followed by ice cream and mango, heaven. The sun had set which was a shame, I was hoping to see my last Indian sunset. Not knowing when the flight was I enquired at the reception desk and was told that I would be given a call when the coach arrived. Assured I went up to my room to try and get some sleep; the bed was so comfortable and very soon I fell asleep.

I could hear a strange noise, some sort of whirring sound and in my drowsy slumber I realised it was a telephone, quickly opening my eyes and lifting the receiver a voice at the other end told me the coach had arrived for the airport. Quickly getting dressed and making sure I had my passport, flight ticket picked up my rucksack and went down to the foyer where I was instructed to put my rucksack in the coaches luggage hold. Walking from the air conditioned hotel in to the warm tropical night was such a contrast which felt more comfortable to the cooled air of the hotel. Once full the coach left for the airport, it was obvious that several of the passengers had spent their evening at the bar and were quite rowdy. Bombay looked pitch black except for the odd lit window in the high rise blocks.

Stepping out in to the warm night air from the bus felt reassuring and glad I did not have to experience air conditioning on my journey. In the airport terminal we traded in the cancelled flight ticket for one with Bombay to London via Zurich on it, which was to leave at 1:40 am. The luggage was taken and put in the large trolleys for loading on to the waiting plane.

Soon we boarded the buses which took us across the tar mac to the parked Swiss Airline Boeing 737. At the top of the steps we were met by an air hostess who directed us to our seats. In front of me were some drunk passengers who I hoped would soon fall asleep from their excesses.

Once everyone was on the plane the door was closed with

a reassuring thud. The standard emergency instructions were given as the plane taxied to the run way. The planes engines revved up, it raced along the runway then there was the familiar sensation of being airborne and climbing in to the air, I was homeward bound.

Relaxing back in my seat I reflected on my journey over the last three and half months. The places I visited, the friendly people I met on the way, especially over the last few weeks; it was definitely a memorable journey.

Part Five
End Note

Since my trip to India and Sri Lanka in 1980 there have been many changes and events. One such change is some place names in India. They have changed from the old colonial name back to the Hindi name.

The most well known one is Bombay which has changed to Mumbai. Others include Madras which is now called Chennai, Calcutta is Kolkata and Cochin is called Cochi. As well as towns and cities changing their names well known land marks have changed such as Victoria Station in Mumbai is Chhatrapati Shivaji Maharaj Terminus , affectionately called CSMT for short. Also the Prince of Wales Museum has been renamed the Chhatrapati Shivaji Maharaj Vastu Sangrahalaya Museum

The population has increased considerably. In 1980 the Indian Population was about 750,000,000, now it stands at some 1,356,563,420. Towns and cities have expanded to accommodate this increase encroaching on land that was fields and sand dunes, such as the far south at Cape Comorin where I stayed in the palm hut. These sand dunes are now covered in buildings.

The ferry from Ramaweram to Sri Lanka stopped running during the troubles in Sri Lanka, and at present there does not seem to be an alternative ferry even though there have been some rumours of one running from other Indian ports.

There have been improvements on the trains. Passengers have more choices for sleeping in different classes of carriage rather than just the first class. There are also air conditioned carriages for the not so long journeys. When I travelled around India there was an effort to stop passengers sitting on top of the carriages but this habit seems to have crept back in, some trains even have passengers sitting on the front of the train or hanging off the side. India is also in the process of introducing a network for bullet trains

The Indian government has built a new road in to Kashmir. It is a dual carriage way that leads over the mountains through a new tunnel avoiding the vehicles precariously edging past each other on a cliff edge. Also a railway line has been built taking trains beyond Jammu which was meant to go all the way to Srinagar. But the troubles in Kashmir have put this on hold.

The Periyar Animal Sanctuary, now officially called 'The Periyar Tiger Reserve'. It is fenced off and tourists have to pay to enter. Camping is organised and for a considerable fee it is possible to camp for four nights. Since my return I have found that the Western Ghats is the natural habitat of the King Cobra. Reflecting on an encounter with a King Cobra whilst camping at the Periyar Animal Sanctuary would have been a very exciting moment

Since my trip to India the tourist industry has boomed and there are many companies that do package tours of India and Sri Lanka. Goa is a popular tourist destination which makes me smile at the irony of the advice I got about not going there. High end hotels have sprung up around the two countries such as Kuchchaveli with a luxurious hotel tucked away in amongst the trees lining the beach with small huts for the tourists, a far cry from the quiet fishing village I experienced.

Backpacking still seems to be as popular as ever with many would be intrepid explorers following in the footsteps of those before them.

There are many media postings on the internet especially Youtube. You can now search for information on the move with your smart phone making the journey that much easier and less hit and miss.

After the war in Sri Lanka the troubles in Kashmir and attack on Mumbai I wonder how the people I met have faired and hope they are all well

Regardless of these considerable changes India and Sri Lanka still remain amazing, exciting and mysterious countries to visit with their diverse cultures, history and endless places to explore.

At times I feel like returning for a second trip. This time travelling by train from Delhi to Kolkata. Visiting Varanasi and Nepal along the way. Having done this I could definitely say I have been to India.

Printed in Great Britain
by Amazon

85871476R00244